D0593632

# *SEASON OF DREAMS*

The Minnesota Twins'
Drive to the 1991
World Championship

Tom Kelly
and Ted Robinson
Foreword by Kent Hrbek

VOYAGEUR PRESS

Edited by Rosemary Wallner
Cover designed by Gordon Maltby, M Design
Book designed by Helene Jones, Kathy Mallien, and Gordon Maltby
Printed in the United States of America by Edwards Brothers
92 93 94 95 96 5 4 3 2

Library of Congress Cataloging-in-Publication Data available

ISBN 0-89658-209-4

Published by
VOYAGEUR PRESS, INC.
P.O. Box 338, 123 North Second Street
Stillwater, MN 55082 U.S.A.
From Minnesota and Canada 612-430-2210
Toll-free 800-888-9653



Partial royalties from the sale of *Season of Dreams* are being donated to the Minnesota Twins Community Fund

# Contents

# Acknowledgments

This book is the story of a season of dreams for the Minnesota Twins. It is told from one viewpoint, that of the manager. Other stories are left for other books.

The season of dreams applies to broadcasters as well. For those of us who express our love of baseball through microphones instead of bats and gloves, broadcasting the games of a World Championship team is a gift we cherish.

Writing about the season was the second installment of my dream. There are many who deserve thanks:

My broadcast partners: Jim Kaat (who has taught me more baseball that I ever could have hoped), John Gordon, Herb Carneal, and Dick Bremer, with our production team of Tim Scanlan and Dave Higgins, and our strength coach, Remzi Kiratli;

Those responsible for bringing me to the Twins: Jerry Bell, Stu Swartz, Joe Carney, Steve Goldstein, Jon Quick, Dave Jarzyna, Dave Mona, and the Pohlad family;

The media relations department of the Twins for their assistance every day and night of the season: Rob Antony, Steve Rausch, Wendie Erickson, and Gordy Gutowsky;

John Feinstein and John Heisler, for their counsel on the risks and rewards of this venture;

The entire Twins organization, from players to part-time employees, who all have helped at some time to make my job easier;

My parents, for my foundation, their love, and a comfortable haven in Naples, Florida, where much of this book was written.

And finally, thanks to those who dismissed the doubts and skepticism to make this dream a reality:

Voyageur Press, for their leap of faith with an unknown writer;

Tom Kelly, who helped break in a naive rookie broadcaster eight years ago, and whose belief and trust from the embryonic days of this project will be forever appreciated;

Annie and Patrick, for their patience and tolerance of a distracted father, and to Mary, my love and strength.

TED ROBINSON

# Foreword

I have finally learned something about Tom Kelly. He knows me better than I thought he did. It's no secret that I like to have fun at the ballpark, and I have had to learn just how far I can go without blowing his top. In a sense, Tom has been like my mom, except he's at the park. Now I know how far I can take him, but if I do wrong, I'll get a spanking.

Tom has a great way of communicating with his eyes. When he wants to tell you something, he can do it simply by looking at you in a certain way. You can read his eyeballs, especially when he flashes the "Don't do that anymore" look.

We go back to the instructional league in the late '70s. One of the first real talks I ever had with Tom was in 1981, when he had to tell me I wasn't going to start the year with him in Orlando. At the time, I didn't know that it wasn't his decision, but it turned out to be the best demotion I ever had. I hit .379 at Visalia and was called up to the Twins late in the season.

Those days are so far back that it's hard to realize what was happening. I see now, though, how much Tom has taught me about the game. When I'm playing, I feel like I'm in direct contact with him. At home, I sit by him on the bench, and now I feel like I know what he's going to do at critical points of the game. Tom knows that I like to get involved with decisions on how we're going to play things in the field, and he lets me.

When it comes to playing the game, I know what Tom wants out of me and I give it to him. For example, my weight has never been an issue with Tom, so it's not a problem with me. If it was a problem for Tom, then I might look at it differently. But Tom knows I give him 110 percent when I'm on the field.

Tom is a hard guy to get to know. I called him recently to tell him that one of the racing dogs we own in Florida had won a race. Now, there are not too many players who call their manager to shoot the breeze. Tom wanted to make more conversation than I did, and he told me about the things he had been doing recently. It would probably be difficult for some media people to believe, but Tom is a very friendly guy.

We have won two World Championships, but I don't think Tom was any different as a manager in 1991. In fact, the only time that I think he changed at all was in 1990, when Gary Gaetti was having some problems. Gary was a good friend to both of us, and I think it hurt Tom to see Gary struggle.

I enjoy the way Tom handles his relationship with the players. If he likes one person more than another, he doesn't show it. He'll give grief to anybody, veteran or rookie. He can chop down an ego in a big-time way, and guys who have come here with egos haven't lasted long. We operate with an attitude that says "the better we get along, the better we're going to do on the field."

We're very much alike, even though Tom may not enjoy activities like hunting or fishing. He doesn't try to come off as a Rhodes Scholar, or dress stylishly, or walk around like King Kong. He knows baseball is a lot smarter than he is and he knows he's a good manager when he gets good players. Tom never blows his own horn, but I'll blow his horn all day long because he's the type of manager I want to play for.

KENT HRBEK, January, 1992

# 1990: A YEAR OF REBUILDING

*"You can't get too giddy about this game or too down. You have to stay off the roller coaster, but that's personally where I ended up in '90. I got too low and had trouble getting back up."*

***Tom Kelly***

## A SEASON OF LETDOWNS

The end of a successful major league baseball season often resembles the last day of a grade school term. Similar thoughts fill clubhouses and classrooms. Players dream of days without batting practice just as schoolchildren dream of days without classes. The boys of summer boast of exotic winter vacations, while schoolchildren dream of the summer game. Both celebrate freedom from systems whose rules are designed to promote group harmony but which can often seem suffocating. There are rarely good-byes, for the assembled know well that the end of one year quickly becomes the beginning of the next.

The 1990 season was not a successful one for the Minnesota Twins. On a Wednesday afternoon in October, the Twins filed into their Metrodome clubhouse after the season finale knowing this would not be like the end of third grade. A 74–88 record meant there would be good-byes. This team was just three years removed from a World Championship, just two years removed from a season of 91 victories. The spring training lockout of players by owners had wreaked havoc with baseball's schedule, forcing the Twins and the Seattle Mariners to play three games of no consequence to complete a 162-game season. This appendix, played before sparse crowds and with little passion, provided an appropriate end to a season crying for the finish line. Now, as the Twins stumbled to the end, the overwhelming emotion in their clubhouse was one of relief.

There had been no grandiose hopes for 1990, but a last-place finish was unfathomable. More disturbing to Twins management was the road taken to the basement. The decision makers in baseball, while paying homage to the bottom line of wins and losses, lean heavily on style. The Twins' primary decision makers, general manager Andy MacPhail and manager Tom Kelly, could not like the style of the 1990 Twins.

A team feared for its hitting finished 12th in the American League in runs scored. A pitching staff, young but expected to show improvement, finished 11th in the American League in earned run average. The result was a team that, in Kelly's mind, had lost the "edge you need to win." Thus, there would be good-byes. Rick Renick, the third base and de facto hitting coach for four years, was the first casualty. Kelly and MacPhail had told Renick prior to the final game that they would not offer him a 1991 contract.

That meeting was not an easy one for Kelly, who had hired Renick in 1987. The security of his coaches was a primary concern to Kelly. When the Twins delayed in hiring a manager for the 1987 season, Kelly voiced concern for the coaches who would be left jobless if he were not chosen. Kelly required loyalty from his coaches, but he made it reciprocal. (Witness Kelly's delight in instructing fans to watch first base coach Wayne Terwilliger leaping and spinning after Kent Hrbek's 1987 World Series grand slam when the viewer's natural inclination was to watch Hrbek.)

Whenever Kelly had his contract status settled, he immediately campaigned for his coaches. This tactic worked in rehiring Renick for 1990. A season ending 74–88, however, left Kelly unable to fight many battles.

Renick's skills in the coaching box were not in question, but a series of business disputes with the front office left him vulnerable. MacPhail had more than enough work dealing with the demands of players and their agents. He would not tolerate a similar situation from a coach. The Renick announcement reached the majority of players in the initial moments following Wednesday's season finale. Stunned but not thoroughly surprised well-wishers filed by Renick's locker. A genuinely likeable coach had been removed and most knew he would soon have company.

Several lockers away from Renick sat right-handed pitcher Roy Smith whose bizarre season mirrored his team's fortunes. Smith had started the season's second game in Oakland, yet finished the year as a seldom-used reliever. This did not shock Smith, a wisened veteran and a rare player who understood baseball's cyclical nature. Possessing a repertoire of breaking balls and off-speed pitches that rendered the scouts' beloved radar guns irrelevant, Smith had won 10 games in 1989. As a reward, he had spent September in the bullpen while prospects auditioned for his job.

In 1990 Smith had halved his victory total, and the pitching prospects were no longer suspects, so this October afternoon left him in a particularly reflective mood, sensing the inevitable change.

Kelly and Smith had talked about Smith during the latter part of the season, communication made easier by a shared respect for the game of baseball. Kelly often said, "Managers change, players change, coaches change, but the game survives. It's bigger than all of us."

While Smith dealt with his fate philosophically and even planned a party for his fellow pitchers that night, John Moses dressed across the locker room quietly and quickly. Very quickly.

Moses was leaving for his winter home in Scottsdale, Arizona, immediately. A switch-hitting reserve outfielder whose assets were speed and defensive ability, Moses had completed his third year with the Twins. The first two years were successful, with batting averages of .316 and .281. But the 1990 malaise affected Moses whose average slumped to .221. This was bad timing for Moses as he had just achieved the requisite six years of major league service needed to file for free agency. The final month of the 1990 season left Moses certain the Twins were not in his future, a fair assumption given his age, 33, and batting average. Moses was a middle-class major leaguer, an endangered species in an era of exorbitant superstar salaries, who could be easily replaced by a minimum salaried player.

Leaving the Twins' clubhouse for the airport, Moses knew that change would claim him as a victim. He carried the disappointment that can only be understood by a player who had already been released by two teams.

Renick, Smith, and Moses would all be Twins for the last time on October 3, 1990. However, these were changes that would not substantially alter the Twins' future. One man, quite unknowingly, held that power. Gary Gaetti dressed at the locker he had occupied for nine years. Gaetti's decision to forego a 10th year enabled the Twins to design a second World Championship team.

## A LIFE OF BASEBALL

The 1990 season took a severe toll on Tom Kelly. A manager who lived by the creed of the even keel, refusing to bend to the emotional swings so prevalent over the 162-game season, finally felt his insides torn by a last-place finish. Kelly recalls days when he looked in the mirror and saw the dark circles under his eyes that he had often noticed in other managers who endured troubling times. Kelly had stored that "washed out" look away in his memory; seeing it on his own face was very disturbing.

Soon after the last out of 1990, an even more disturbing

emotion overcame the Twins' manager. "There were about three days there where I thought I didn't need this anymore," Kelly recalled. "It was the first time in my life I believed this, and it was a bad thought. But, there have been other managers who felt this way before. Whitey [Herzog] walked away. Now, if you're in a situation where you're financially set and your kids are grown, then you can take a vacation. I can't do that. So I got over it, but at the time it was scary to have those thoughts run through your head."

Indeed, the depression was temporary. Kelly does not recall specifics, only that after leaving the park early one day and heading to Canterbury Downs, the thoroughbred racetrack that provided his preferred escape from baseball, the feeling disappeared. This admission would not seem startling coming from most managers. But, in many ways, Tom Kelly was unlike most managers.

The antithesis of the style embodied by Tom Lasorda and Bobby Valentine, Kelly shunned the spotlight. His office guests were more likely to be clubhouse attendants than celebrities. On the field, Kelly preferred throwing batting practice and hitting countless fungoes to holding court en masse with the press, a maneuver he admitted learning from Sparky Anderson.

Since the age of 17, when he left New Jersey to sign with the Seattle Pilots, Kelly's whole life had been baseball. The memory of the five years he managed in the Twins' minor league system never left him and their impact would often be felt. Spring training spectators were often surprised to see Kelly raking the infield, not realizing that his day as a California League manager included player laundry detail before filling out the lineup card, and manicuring the field before handing the lineup card to the umpires.

Kelly loved baseball and the camaraderie within the clubhouse, where he exhibited a sense of humor and liveliness rarely seen by the public. Although the manner in which he dealt with the media, both print and electronic, improved greatly in 1991, Kelly saved his most personable moments for banter with his players. Kelly shared a trait with Bill Walsh, the highly successful professional football coach. Many times, both seemed more buoyant after a loss, particularly in dealings with the media. In Kelly's case, this was an effective disguise because he disliked defeat as strongly as any manager. But Kelly believed in the even keel, and he went to great lengths to insure that no one on his team would take a loss into the next game.

The 1990 season sent Kelly onto an agonizing emotional ride, the very thing he took great pains to avoid for his players. "You can't get too giddy about this game or too down," Kelly painfully remembered. "You have to stay off the roller coaster but that's personally where I ended up in '90. I got too low and had trouble getting back up." Rebounding would not be easy as the forecast for immediate improvement to the team was grim.

Before the end of December, Kelly was called into Andy MacPhail's office. With the door closed, the message was delivered to the manager: There would be no further pursuits of free agents. The Twins had negotiated with Mike Boddicker, Dave Righetti, Franklin Stubbs, and Kirk Gibson. They had finished a disappointing second to Kansas City in the Gibson derby. Now, the economic reality of a "small market" franchise being unable to keep spending with the New Yorks and Chicagos had collided with the competitive reality of a manager heading into the final year of his contract. Kelly understood this, but to him reality was looking at "getting your brains beat out again."

## LOSING THE "ULTIMATE TWIN"

As the calendar turned to 1991, Tom Kelly worked on his mental approach to the upcoming season. With the Frank Viola trade in July of 1989, the Twins had committed themselves to rebuilding with young pitching. The mandate from the organization had been to develop players, win your share of games, and be competitive and reasonably entertaining.

After a season and a half of this formula, the competitive side of Kelly was beginning to stew. "Nobody likes to lose, if you do, this is the wrong area," Kelly believes. "This job is four to six weeks of preparation for a six-month season. It's too long to accept much losing and maintain your health."

The Twins made one move in December, sending minor league pitchers Johnny Ard and Jimmy Williams to San Francisco for Steve Bedrosian. A former Cy Young Award winner in the National League, 33-year-old right-hander was insurance against the possible loss of reliever Juan Berenguer to new-look free agency.

This acquisition, while welcomed by Kelly, was not viewed as the major dose of medicine needed to cure the team's ills. That was put on hold as the new-look free agents, players judged to have been harmed by collusion among the owners in the '80s, tested their unexpected freedom. The Twins had two possible defectors, Berenguer and Gary Gaetti.

It was nearly impossible to perceive a scenario that did not include Gary Gaetti finishing his career as the Twins' third baseman. Gaetti and the Twins had grown up together in the major leagues. When the 1982 season opened, Gaetti was a rookie third baseman for a team that would lose 102 games. That Twins team was no better than an expansion team, and was fielded by Calvin Griffith in order to maintain the lowest possible payroll. To Griffith's everlasting credit, he maintained a fine player-development program throughout an ownership that ended with the realization that he could not prevent wealthier clubs from devouring his home-grown players.

Following the 1981 player strike, Griffith unloaded many veterans with higher salaries. The two survivors of the first purge, Roy Smalley and Butch Wynegar, were traded in the early months of the following year.

Thus, the 1982 Twins were centered around some of baseball's best prospects: Gaetti, Kent Hrbek, Tom Brunansky, Jim Eisenreich, Tim Laudner, Randy Bush, and Frank Viola. They were young, talented, and inexpensive, but they were major leaguers. This helped soften the sentence they knew was attached to this opportunity, an indefinite period of losing.

The young Twins could not commute this sentence, aside from a 1984 challenge in a weakened division. For five years there was more losing than winning. But the core of players, with added regulars Kirby Puckett, Greg Gagne, and Steve Lombardozzi, grew closer through the lean times.

When success was finally achieved in 1987, a memorable torrent of emotion was unleashed by this particular group of Twins. They had endured so much defeat together that the celebration was boundless. While wearing a major league uniform brings with it an understanding of the lack of permanence in the game, the young Twins assumed their bonds could not be broken, that their destiny was assured as a group.

As the Twins rose in the American League standings, so too did Gary Gaetti ascend among American League third basemen. For the three-year span of 1986–88, he was the league's very best at his position, averaging 31 home runs, 102 runs batted in, winning three Gold Gloves (he would be voted a fourth in 1989) and was named the Most Valuable Player of the 1987 American League Championship Series.

No player was more respected by his teammates. In June of 1988, the Twins traveled to Oakland for their first meeting with the Athletics, whose scorching start had opened up a comfortable six-game lead. The Twins were playing well, but Oakland had hammered home a message. The Twins had to win in head-to-head competition to have any hope of repeating their division championship.

The series began on a Friday night. Oakland led 5–0 after four innings, but Gaetti began a Twins' comeback with a solo home run in the fifth inning and continued with a run-scoring single in the sixth.

The Twins tied the game in the eighth, and gained the lead on a Dan Gladden double in the ninth. Eric Plunk, a tall, hard throwing right-hander with erratic control, was brought in by Oakland manager Tony LaRussa to end the inning. With two out and a runner on base, Gaetti came to bat. Plunk fired a 90-mile-per-hour fastball in the general vicinity of Gaetti's head, sending the Twin sprawling in the dirt of the batter's box.

Oakland's signal was clear. They had been steamrolled by the Twins in critical games the previous year, but that was history. LaRussa's team would not yield as easily in 1988. Neither would Gaetti. Two pitches later, a towering two-run home run left Gaetti's bat punctuating a six-run ninth inning. The moment was vintage Gaetti, answering Oakland's blatant attempt to intimidate with a knockout punch.

Less than two months after that night in Oakland, Gaetti's career and the fate of the Twins, so closely intertwined for years, took a different direction.

On August 15, 1988, the Twins began a series at Tiger Stadium. In the sixth inning, with the score at 1–1, Gaetti singled and stole second. On the slide into second base, Gaetti suffered a knee injury that was apparent to all in the park. Yet he finished the inning on the base paths and insisted on taking his position for the Tigers' at bat. Alan Trammell was the second Detroit batter and, aware of Gaetti's knee, laid down a rare bunt. Gaetti charged the bunt and threw Trammell out, a fine play for a healthy fielder, and a remarkable one for a player who had torn knee cartilage only moments earlier.

Gaetti left the game after that inning, and seven days later had arthroscopic surgery performed on his left knee. By the time he rejoined the Twins on September 9 in Chicago, his life had changed. During the first disablement of his baseball career, Gaetti had become a Christian, what is commonly referred to as a "born again."

A poll of Twins' players would have likely seen Gaetti voted the least likely to undergo a drastic lifestyle change. Throughout Gaetti's Twins career, the adjectives brusque, gruff, and crude had readily been applied to him with varying degrees of accuracy. There was no denying that Gaetti had lived as hard as he played, the very trait that made his conversion so much more difficult for his teammates to comprehend.

Gaetti's presence in the Twins' clubhouse would never again be the same. Some differences were noticeable right away. Traditionally one of the earliest to arrive at the ballpark on a game day, Gaetti began allowing just enough time to dress for the pregame workouts. An occasional instigator and frequent participant in the often raucous clubhouse life, Gaetti began spending much of his time at his locker, reading the Bible and answering mail. Kelly and his coaches always provided extra work opportunities for players struggling either in performance or for playing time. In his final two years as a Twin, Gaetti rarely took early batting practice, even though his batting average plummeted. This was difficult for Kelly to understand. Kelly remembered the routine he and Gaetti had established in the Southern League nearly a decade earlier. The manager would fungo the player hundreds of ground balls a day in the broiling sun and stifling humidity of a Florida summer. Kelly had firsthand knowledge of Gaetti's hard work through the formative years of his career, and the manager was proud of his own contributions to Gaetti's success. To see a player abandon such a work ethic, while his team was in decline, was painful for Kelly.

Yet there was no criticism or condemnation of Gaetti within the clubhouse. Gary was still a friend to all, and his change had left him a pleasant, sincere, and thoughtful person who was still a comrade in arms. Gaetti became closer to the teammates sharing his religious beliefs, changing what had become the team's most heralded and prominent friendship. Kent Hrbek and Gaetti had been best friends throughout their entire careers in Minnesota. While single hotel rooms had become a rule for most major league players, these two high-profile Twins shared accommodations on road trips. It was common to see the pair board a team plane each wearing headphones plugged in to the same portable cassette player. Those days were now over, and the two would not spend nearly as much free time together. In spite of these subtle changes, Hrbek was determined to keep Gaetti involved in the clubhouse banter that was a unique component of the Twins' success.

His teammates initially hoped Gaetti would remain the same player on the field. That hope disappeared early in the 1989 season, and by mid-season, Tom Kelly knew he had to act.

"We were in Boston and the players were in disarray," Kelly remembered. "They were trying so hard to get Gary to participate in what they were doing, but Gary didn't seem interested. It was noticeable to everybody. Some players were telling me 'I give up. I've tried to help him and I can't.'"

What Kelly saw in jeopardy were the bonds that form among those who wear a baseball uniform. On this subject, Kelly is passionate in his belief that no outsider can truly understand "the allegiance that develops between players and is so magnified within our own little family." The baseball way of life demands greater devotion to one's career than one's family for a seven-month period. Born from this is a "camaraderie and friendship that you can only imagine," and Kelly saw that threatened in Boston.

"The bonds we had with Gary were actually even stronger at that time, because we wanted him to be part of the team and it wasn't working out," continued Kelly in painful remembrance. "The players cared, but they were hurting. The only solution I could come up with was to get Gary to see what he was missing in the team structure. I told the players to keep going, play the game the right way, and if Gaetti wants to join in, great. My job was to convince the players that we had exhausted all our avenues in trying to get Gary to join in with the team."

Kelly and Gaetti met privately, and for the next week, Kelly saw an improvement in the clubhouse. But he remembers how hard it seemed for Gaetti to participate given the drastic change in his personal life. The situation soon reverted.

In 1989, Gaetti lost 50 points from his previous year's batting average and produced his lowest single-season number of extra-base hits. Nagging back and stomach injuries were a hindrance, but in good health the following year, his production worsened. A team-leading 85 runs batted in were offset by a career low .229 batting average and a meager 16 home runs.

Both Gaetti and the Twins pondered their dilemmas in January 1991. New-look free agency gave Gaetti his second taste of freedom. In the winter of 1988, he had spurned a more lucrative offer from Los Angeles in order to stay with the Twins. The club could not count on a repeat of that, given the upheaval of the past two years. Nor could the club count on Gaetti to reverse a dramatic two-year slide in productivity. Yet, any objective analysis of American League third basemen left Gaetti in good standing.

Gaetti's dilemma was more personal. His place in the Twins' lineup seemed so secure that the organization had no prospect even remotely prepared to fill his spot. Gaetti had to decide if his life would be better served and could withstand another change.

Andy MacPhail devised an offer addressing the concerns of both Gaetti and the Twins. Gaetti could sign a multi-year contract filled with incentives and a unique twist in which he could declare himself a free agent at the end of any season. The Twins were protected financially since Gaetti needed to perform for the incentive clauses to pay off. But Gary was protected on both sides. If he compiled good statistics in 1991, he could opt for free agency and seek a better contract, but he still would have a guarantee against subpar performance or injury. An innovative offer by the

Twins left Gaetti faced with a very difficult decision.

Meanwhile, the club prepared contingencies in the event of a Gaetti departure. Off-season personnel discussions were structured. Initial meetings were held at the Metrodome with MacPhail, Kelly, vice president of player personnel Bob Gebhard, minor league director Jim Rantz, scouting director Terry Ryan, and director of baseball administration Bill Smith. MacPhail encouraged dissenting opinions and relayed information and recommendations to the ownership. Major meetings were occasionally held at the Marquette Bank building in Minneapolis by team owner Carl Pohlad and his sons.

During the Metrodome meetings, the Twins targeted two replacements for Gaetti, Mike Pagliarulo, and Jim Presley. Kelly voiced his opinion firmly, saying it was "no contest." After four years in the Twins' third base coaching box, Kelly knew all the league's players. He had always liked Pagliarulo's work ethic as the Yankees' third baseman. Cable television reinforced that belief, as Kelly often unwound after home games by watching National League teams on superstations WTBS and WGN. For the last two seasons, when the Padres were featured, Kelly saw their third baseman Pagliarulo making all the necessary plays in the field. "His swing was different from his Yankee days," Kelly said. "It was more of a base hit swing. But, in all honesty, I felt [new batting coach] Terry Crowley could help him pull the ball again. Pags was the player I wanted. We liked the way he worked at the game. And we felt he was tougher to pitch to than Presley, who strikes out a bit more than we like."

For most of the winter, Kelly was a lone ranger in his belief. A more commonly held theory on Pagliarulo was voiced by Yankee executive George Bradley at the winter meetings, "He can't hit and he can't play third base." Those who knew Kelly understood that he rarely changed his mind about a player, and his mind was set on Pagliarulo if Gaetti left the Twins.

In January, two baseball meetings were held with the Pohlads in which Gaetti was the main topic of discussion. All attending these meetings were asked to voice an opinion. Kelly gave the Pohlads his recommendation on what would best serve the Twins on the field and in the clubhouse with regard to Gaetti. The contents of that recommendation remain private, but Kelly acknowledges the rewards he enjoyed in seeing Gaetti develop into an outstanding player. As troubling as the last two years had been for Kelly, this decision-making process made him confront the bonds built between manager and player on the bus rides in the Southern League and carried through to a World Championship. The manager knew Gaetti was torn by the same thoughts.

Andy MacPhail was open in his feelings about Gaetti. Admitting that his job should preclude him from personal feelings towards players, MacPhail still had a soft spot for Gaetti. At the winter meetings, MacPhail asked Gaetti's agents if a change of scenery would be in Gaetti's best interest. By January, still unsure of the answer, but with the California Angels offering a large sum of guaranteed money, MacPhail sculpted the creative contract offer that he hoped would keep Gaetti in Minnesota.

Kelly was besieged by phone calls during the negotiations. One came from a player Kelly believed was close to Gaetti with a message that Gary would take the best dollar offer. That call surprised Kelly at the time, but the information proved true when on January 25 Gaetti accepted a four-year guaranteed contract offer from the Angels. In the end, Gaetti walked away with everything—the money, the security, and the change of scenery.

Kelly knew how difficult the decision had been for Gaetti. He also knew "the door would be opened for the Twins to do other things" with the money that had been targeted for Gaetti. MacPhail remained optimistic. "We're going to finish above .500 this season. That's definite." Kent Hrbek reacted emotionally in learning of the departure of a close friend and another of the "young Twins," saying, "There ain't nobody left."

Hrbek's slight exaggeration notwithstanding, the public had a similar reaction. Patrick Reusse echoed the sentiments of much of the populace when he wrote in the January 26 *Star Tribune,* "There will still be a degree of credibility with the Twins, as long as the lineup includes [Kirby] Puckett."

While fans around Minnesota read those words, the Twins acted. Within 12 hours of Gaetti's decision, Pagliarulo was signed to a one-year contract. Kelly had convinced MacPhail to sign a player who had no other offers. Pagliarulo said, "I'm glad the Twins chose me," a stunning admission by any player in the free-agent era, but understandable since without Kelly's support, Pagliarulo might have been out of baseball.

The Pagliarulo signing likely made its strongest impact on Kelly's psyche. Heading into the last year of his contract, Kelly knew his job security hinged on improving the team's record. Although adding Bedrosian and Pagliarulo would help, they alone were not going to place the Twins in contention. Players were still available who could do that, but the Twins had to move. The Pagliarulo signing was a clear signal to Kelly that his opinion carried some weight with MacPhail.

## COMPLETING THE TEAM

Signing pitcher Jack Morris was still a possibility. The Tigers' veteran pitcher was, like Gaetti, a new-look free agent expected to return to his old team. Kelly had decided in January to ask management for Morris, the premier starting pitcher the Twins had been missing since the Frank Viola trade. Kelly's first move was to ask MacPhail if the Twins had the money available to pursue Morris. The answer could only come from Carl Pohlad. At the end of one meeting at the bank building to discuss the Gaetti negotiations, Kelly asked MacPhail if he could raise the Morris issue. MacPhail approved, and Kelly proceeded to deliver a short speech on Morris's ability to help the Twins. No decisions were made, but Kelly left the meeting pleased that his bosses would at least listen.

The Gaetti-Pagliarulo signings began a hectic week for the Twins. The day after Pagliarulo became a Twin, Kelly received a phone call from MacPhail asking for an opinion on free agent Chili Davis. This momentarily surprised the manager, as there had never been any discussions on Davis at the management meetings. Davis had always hit well against the Twins, especially in the Metrodome, and that was Kelly's first memory. The Twins had developed a useful video library and Kelly was able to watch Davis's at-bats for confirmation. Davis' personable approach had always impressed Kelly, from both the California League, where Kelly broke in as a manager while Davis was starting as a player, to the American League, where Davis always took the time to meet and kid around with former teammate Dan Gladden.

Chili Davis quickly entered the Twins' thinking; here was a player who could replace the power numbers of Gaetti. Kelly suspected Chili was a player who was not eager to change teams, so despite the Angels' lack of interest in retaining him, the manager embarked on a phone campaign to sell the Twins to Chili. "The toughest part was finding him," Kelly said. "We finally tracked him down and had Puckett and Gladden call. But this happened so quickly that my head was spinning. I called Chili and started to tell him about our lineup, all off the top of my head. Against righties, I told him he'd hit fifth with Puckett and Hrbek ahead and Harper behind. I think those names caught his attention. Then, against lefties, I told him he'd hit fourth. He really liked knowing where he would hit. That was the best I could do, then Andy did a great job working out the contract."

Kelly's next call was to Jack Morris. "I told Jack he would be the number-one shooter over here, helping younger pitchers and giving us innings. Then I told him not to repeat this but that our hitting was going to be better because we were adding Chili Davis.

Now this is all 'on the come' because we had discussed it, but I didn't know if we'd get it done. Jack liked it when I rattled off Puckett, Hrbek, Chili, and Harper as the middle of our lineup. I don't know if it influenced his decision, but I did what I thought was necessary for the sake of the team."

Davis was sold on the Twins, and on January 30 he signed a one-year guaranteed contract. The offense that was weakened by Gaetti's departure suddenly appeared strong. No one had seen Davis, but he offered words that would prove to be prophetic. "I'm healthy," he said, "I've been working out, and I'm ready to go." On the same day, Juan Berenguer accepted a two-year contract offer from the Atlanta Braves. The last pitcher left from the 1987 World Series team, Berenguer's departure was not considered critical by the Twins. Steve Bedrosian would fill his role as the set-up reliever, and Berenguer's salary could be used to make an offer to Morris.

That offer was on hold, awaiting the approval of team owner Carl Pohlad. A happier group of Twins, including Kelly, Hrbek, and team president Jerry Bell, accompanied Pohlad on a January 31 trip to Chamberlain, South Dakota, for a day of promotional appearances. Spirits were high after signing Davis. Kelly knew he had a much better ballclub, with one remaining hole that Morris could easily fill. Pohlad had never refused his baseball people when they wanted to add a player who could help the Twins win. There was no doubt in Kelly's mind that Morris fit that criteria. The last question was whether Morris could fit within the Twins' payroll. Signing Morris would require a strong statement of faith from Pohlad. Attendance at the Metrodome had dropped by 500,000 in 1990 and advance sales for 1991 were not strong. Toss in a collusion payment of $10 million and Pohlad's financial outlay was already significantly higher. When the group arrived home from the Chamberlain trip, Pohlad told his baseball executives he would deliver a decision on Morris the next morning.

In the February 1 issue of the *Star Tribune,* Patrick Reusse quoted Kelly as saying "I think there is a lot more enthusiasm the last few days. The boys have been saying 'Let's get to Florida and see what we've got.'" Although Andy MacPhail is quoted as characterizing the Twins' hope of signing Morris as a "long shot," that morning, MacPhail received the long-awaited call from Pohlad with approval to pursue Morris.

Morris was offered a contract similar to the one Gary Gaetti rejected. Loaded with attainable incentives, Morris also had the option of declaring himself a free agent after any season. Detroit had offered Morris a three-year guaranteed contract for $9.3 million. If Morris was willing to "roll the dice" as Kelly phrased it, he could earn far more money with one good year for the Twins. Kelly was confident that would happen; he and pitching coach Dick Such had been very impressed by Morris in a start against the Twins during the last week of 1990. Just as with Pagliarulo, Kelly was countering the conventional wisdom around major league baseball that had Morris's career on the decline.

On February 5, Morris decided to come home. He would gamble on the belief that "if I pitch like I have all along, then I've made the right decision." The *Star Tribune* broke the story and ran it on their front page. Kelly remembers that suddenly everyone around the Twins had "a little extra bounce in their steps."

The year was only five weeks old, but already a remarkable metamorphosis in the Twins had occurred. Tom Kelly had watched the New Year's Day bowl games convinced there would be no free agents added to his team this year. Now, the Twins had gone into the free agent pool three times. Pohlad and MacPhail had given Kelly a designated hitter, a third baseman, and most significantly a starting pitcher capable of exceeding 200 innings. Kelly knew the Twins had a chance of competing, and as he prepared for spring training, he realized that 1990 had quickly become a distant memory.

# A SUCCESSFUL SPRING TRAINING

*"We told the players 1987 is over, 1990 is over, we don't live in the past. Now all that matters is 1991."*
***Tom Kelly***

## NEW FACILITIES IN FORT MYERS

Jim Wiesner, the Twins' veteran equipment and clubhouse manager, was preparing for a spring training most unlike any he had experienced. Instead of following tradition and living in the clubhouse at the Twins' new facility in Fort Myers, Florida, he and his wife Marge were rented an apartment for their two-month stay. After 30 years in the cramped clubhouse of Orlando's Tinker Field, Wiesner admitted that creature comforts now took a higher priority, and it was time for his younger assistants to inherit the ballpark's living quarters. While the Twins finished their on-field restructuring up north, the Wiesners arrived in Fort Myers in early February of 1991 to open their apartment.

Wiesner and visiting clubhouse manager Jim Dunn were the advance team, the first wave of an armada that would number better than 225 at its peak. For the first time ever the Twins' minor league operation would join the major leaguers for spring training. The pair from Minnesota had the unenviable assignment of opening up the clubhouses and smoothing out the expected snags in time for the first player arrivals in two weeks.

From the apartment complex, Wiesner and Dunn drove down Six Mile Cypress Road to Daniels Road. Just south of this intersection, Lee County had taken 85 acres of undeveloped land and constructed the baseball complex that lured the Twins away from Orlando, their spring home for more than 60 years.

Like new homeowners, the Wiesners and Dunn pulled in to the new facility's parking lot for their initial walk-through. What they saw stunned them. A 7,500-seat stadium in the final stages of construction loomed before them. The ballpark was unparalleled in beauty, a structure whose exterior was reminiscent of a classic thoroughbred racetrack bordered by palm trees. In every direction were impeccably manicured baseball diamonds, fields that Gary Gaetti observed on a Christmas visit as the "best I've ever seen."

Walking toward the major league clubhouse, Wiesner was unsure what awaited him, but he knew it had to be an improvement over the undersized Tinker Field room. Two years before, Wiesner had been asked to contribute details of his "ideal" clubhouse for the architect's blueprints. He was savvy enough to realize that he would be fortunate to see 75 percent of what he had requested. Instead, Wiesner and Dunn opened the door on a clubhouse that, while lacking the finishing touches, far surpassed most current major league facilities. The room was large enough to hold infield practice with 60 full player lockers, more than ample office and storage space, and a training area that could double as a hospital emergency room. "I had tears in my eyes, which in all my years in baseball had only happened in 1987," Wiesner remembered. "Everything I had asked for was there. It was easy to see how great this would be for the Twins."

Wiesner's thoughts were the first of many accolades for the Lee County Sports Complex that would last throughout the spring of 1991. The Twins' new home became the envy of most other clubs. Carl Pohlad had Cleveland owner Richard Jacobs as a guest for a spring game, and Jacobs returned home to tell his executives that he wanted a "Fort Myers" facility for the Indians. The Cactus League teams were particularly jealous as Arizona communities had yet to match their Florida counterparts in developing modern quarters. There was no doubt in Wiesner's mind that if a spring training would ever directly impact a regular season, this would be the one.

The design of this complex would facilitate the best possible preparation of a baseball team. In Orlando, there had been only two fields with a parking lot between them. There had been no practice infields, just two covered batting tunnels and a cramped clubhouse that, like most of the facility, was in varying stages of disrepair. Lee County gave the Twins four full fields, two practice infields, 10 covered batting tunnels, each offering the option of pitching machines or mounds for live pitching, and the new stadium with superior clubhouse and office space. Every aspect necessary to ensure a successful spring had been covered. To employees like Wiesner and trainer Dick Martin who had endured the increasingly outdated conditions of Orlando, this was a new lease on their baseball life.

Twins' president Jerry Bell was equally proud of the end result of three years' work that symbolized a change in baseball's view of spring training. What had always been serious for the on-field staff was now serious financial business as well. Spring training was undergoing a period of explosive growth and popularity, and a number of Florida counties and communities were lining up to negotiate "sweetheart deals" for major league tenants, all in the name of tourism and commercial development. The Twins had watched several other teams, most notably the Mets, prosper from this change, so Carl Pohlad and Bell opted for spring training "free agency."

The timing was perfect for Lee County. Nestled in the relative anonymity of southwest Florida, the area had long been a favored retreat for retirees and vacationers from the Midwest and

Canada. There was an abundance of sun and palm trees, without the congestion that threatens to strangle Florida's east coast. The beaches of Lee County are clean, uncluttered, and offer the country's most dazzling array of seashells. Many of the area's residents preferred that Lee County remain status quo. County leaders, however, had decided it was time to bring back baseball.

Pittsburgh and Kansas City had previously trained in Fort Myers. The Royals left in the mid-'80s for Baseball City, an ambitious amalgam of baseball and amusement parks located 20 miles west of Orlando. Not long after the Royals' departure from a facility they deemed inadequate, Lee County realized that attracting a new spring tenant would require building them a new home.

The agreement bringing the Twins to Lee County was finalized in March of 1989. For the team, it was a springtime Christmas present. The county would build a state-of-the-art facility large enough to allow the Twins to liberate their minor league operations from Melbourne, an ocean coast town 55 miles from Orlando and considered the Siberia of spring training. The Twins would have a single spring training facility and it would be theirs to operate. Construction costs totaling $17 million dollars would be borne by Lee County, with the club eventually investing approximately $200 thousand in concession equipment. The Twins would pay rent but keep all ticket, concession, and parking revenues. Jerry Bell had piloted negotiations that turned spring training from a major expense into a profitable business venture.

Ground was broken for the project in October of 1989, and for the ensuing 18 months, Bill Smith served as project coordinator for the Twins. Meetings were held at a minimum of once a month, with Smith making 23 round-trips between the Twin Cities and Fort Myers. The Lee County Parks Department supervised construction of the playing fields and had them ready upon Wiesner's arrival. However, the contractors were still about three weeks from completing the stadium, so the Twins would begin spring training in the completed minor league clubhouse.

## KELLY AND THE MEDIA

The operative word for the Twins' spring would be "new," as in facility, city, season, designated hitter, third baseman, and starting pitcher. Tom Kelly was determined to keep the tag from being applied to the manager. He resisted the temptation to change his managerial approach in search of a better season. If there was one tendency Kelly abhorred in a player, it was inconsistency. The year was too long for many surprises, and inconsistent performances meant too many rides on the dreaded roller coaster. Kelly held himself to the same standard. "The players want the same guy as manager, they want consistency within the work structure," he said. "You change some formulas, like adding or deleting to your playbook in football, but the approach stays the same." That meant another spring of hard work, with particular focus on baseball's fundamental plays. Kelly's springs never included exceedingly long hours, but they were concentrated. They were a paraphrase of the Twins' regular season motto: If you worked hard, then you could play hard. Past history showed this method worked as the Twins ranked in the top four in the American League defensive standings during Kelly's tenure, something the manager attributes in part to habits started in the spring.

His protestations notwithstanding, there was one change in Kelly's approach immediately evident in Fort Myers. In an era dominated by the electronic media, the Twins had made a concession to the demands placed upon baseball personnel by hiring Andrea Kirby as a media consultant. A former network television sportscaster, Kirby had taken a different career path, helping professional athletes improve their performance and appearance in front of the camera. Andy MacPhail felt her expertise would be helpful for Kelly, Bob Gebhard, several players, and him in handling the expected questions on the 1990 last place finish. Often Kelly's manner with the local media was made more an issue by reporters than was his managing. This disservice to Kelly would be corrected in 1991.

Andrea Kirby and Kelly met several times over the winter and the results were seen immediately in Florida. Kelly seemed more comfortable and tolerant in the company of writers, particularly those with whom he had disagreed in past years. His behavior reminded longtime Twin observers of the Kelly who, as third base coach from 1983–86, showed a keen wit and a strong sense of humor and who developed relationships with several local writers and broadcasters.

The events of Ray Miller's managerial tenure in 1986 left their imprint on Kelly. He watched as Miller openly discussed personnel matters with the press and was often quoted in a way that appeared critical of management. Kelly learned a valuable lesson and when he succeeded Miller, decided personally to always err on the side of caution with the media. "I thought Ray's managing was fine," Kelly remembered. "But I thought his talking got him in trouble with the team. I took the direct opposite approach, some of which turned out to be wrong."

This method frustrated many national writers who, with their first contact with Kelly during the 1987 World Series, could not understand why the rookie manager was curt during what they felt should have been his moment of glory. For his part, Kelly could not understand why, at this most important time in his career, he had to answer questions that had easily obtainable or well-known answers. "Just look it up in the press guide," Kelly often said, startling the veteran scribes who were accustomed to managers that treated them with reverence. "I got the label short or smart with the media," Kelly recalled. "That was because I separated the media into groups. It was enjoyable to talk to people who knew something about the game. But if someone didn't have a clue about baseball, I would completely blow them off. I realize now that was wrong and I don't do that anymore."

Kirby helped Kelly with the mechanics of answering questions from a group of writers. She taught him how to divert attention from the inevitable questions that left him uncomfortable. She also gave Kelly a checklist "with seven or eight key points which I carried all year," he explained. "It was just like a scouting report: Keep your strong points, check your posture, don't get pinned in a corner, and look at the person you're answering. I kept it in my briefcase and checked it all season."

Kelly always had time for media members who respected the game. He found time for those who "made an effort" to understand the game. Sometimes there was intolerance of those who did not seem to care, like the broadcaster who approached Kelly before a game in Anaheim asking, "Who is Willie Banks?" Kelly wondered how someone making a living in baseball could not know Banks, who was to make his first major league start the next night and had been one of baseball's most publicized minor leaguers after the Twins made him their first round draft pick in 1987.

Kelly shared Andrea Kirby's media tactics with the players at the first team meeting in Fort Myers. The manager preached amnesia when it came to 1990. "The media won't let you forget it," Kelly said. "One point where Andrea helped was in giving us something to use to answer the question, 'How are you going to make up 30 games?' We told the players 1987 is over, 1990 is over, we don't live in the past. Now all that matters is 1991. We were also bombarded with the fact that so many people and publications picked us to finish last again. So we had to emphasize that we don't play on paper."

The players' attitudes pleased Kelly as the team assembled in Fort Myers. More players had lived in Minnesota during the winter, and there were several organized groups for winter workouts. Kelly had scheduled a February mini-camp at the Metrodome that had included the unveiling of Jack Morris. The workout had boosted the spirits of all in attendance.

## THE COACHING STAFF

Kelly's first day in Fort Myers with the team featured a speech that addressed the media issue, and the need for his team to regain their home field advantage. The Twins had posted seven consecutive winning seasons at the Metrodome, but the victory total had dropped from 56 in 1987 to 41 in 1990. Kelly's points of emphasis were clear in words, but he knew that Jack Morris was indeed the point of emphasis for the Twins in 1991.

"We lost in 1990 because we didn't pitch worth a darn," Kelly maintains. "The players hung in there for a while. But when you're in July, and falling behind 3–0 in the first inning nearly every night, they say that's enough. They lose their edge. Then, when the pitching improves towards the end of the season, the hitters have lost their edge. There was no slacking off in our work ethic last year. To me, it was a simple formula for 1991: If we pitch better, we'll hit."

On this point, Kelly and MacPhail were in fundamental disagreement. The general manager was not willing to absolve the offense for its role in the 74–88 season. "I kept preaching to Andy that if we pitched better at the beginning of the season, we would score more runs," Kelly admitted. "The hitting was terrible at the end of the year, but I saw them come off the field game after game in the first half with us behind 3–0 early, and they had that 'same old stuff' look in their eyes. By July, the hitters were gone. But Andy wanted to improve the offense and, that was fine with me."

In the final month of 1990, MacPhail and Kelly met to discuss a new hitting instructor. Kelly's first choice was Terry Crowley, a former Baltimore player and coach who was the minor league hitting instructor for Boston. "I asked around the league for names," Kelly said. "Sparky Anderson told me that Roger Craig had wanted to hire Terry in San Francisco. I had played with Terry in Rochester for one year and watched him for many others. His forte was pinch hitting, and a good pinch hitter is someone who takes pride in their job, and knows how to hit. Just think about someone who takes batting practice at four o'clock and hits at ten, usually against a big shooter from the bullpen. I always admired the way Crow did it."

In order to land the job, Crowley had to interview with MacPhail and Gebhard. Remarkably, it would be the first job interview of Crowley's life. He was nervous, but certainly impressed the Twins' management. During his four years as Orioles hitting coach, several players achieved career high home run totals. After seeing the Twins' power numbers suffer a dramatic decline in 1990, MacPhail was taken by Crowley's achievement in Baltimore, and the interview process sealed the position for Crowley.

The February mini-camp served as Crowley's introduction to his new team. Kelly helped Crowley learn and observe the hitters, watching tapes and discussing past history with the other coaches. "We gave Terry some hints," Kelly said. "I never tell my coaches how to do their jobs. I want them to make their own judgments. For example, we helped Terry with Hrbek, telling him that he changes stances all the time and his swing occasionally gets very long. And we explained that Greg Gagne hits one bad streak every year and we were all frustrated in trying to keep it from lasting for four to six weeks. We knew Crowley would adapt to each player and work with his strong points, instead of trying to get them to do something they can't."

Kelly never worried about Crowley insisting on one method for all to follow. Indeed, Kelly defends oft-maligned Chicago coach Walt Hriniak against the same charge. "Most coaches adjust to the style of the players they work with," observed Kelly. "Take Hriniak for example. He has one basic principle, keep the head down, but works with different players. I don't think Frank

Thomas has the same swing as Robin Ventura."

Some players certainly step easy when working with a new coach, and some Twins players were cautious with Crowley. Shane Mack and Chili Davis were two that blended immediately with Crowley in the spring, but Kelly remembers Randy Bush having trouble agreeing with the new theories at the start. By mid-season, however, Bush was among the first to visit "the Hole," where Crowley conducted his most strenuous drills. Instead of soft underhand tosses that players would hit into a small net, Crowley believed in flipping overhand pitches from 15 to 20 feet that players could attack with their regular swing. During batting practice, this drill was held in right field with batters driving the ball onto the oversized baggie that serves as the Metrodome's right-field wall. As the regular season progressed, and players felt more comfortable with Crowley, "the Hole" became a fixture for hitters in search of a tune-up on their swing. By the end of the season, Kelly referred to "the Hole" as a "monument" to the work ethic that was the Twins' pride.

In Fort Myers, Crowley and the new third base coach Ron Gardenhire worked on breaking in comfortably. Gardenhire had an advantage as he had managed for three years in the Twins' system and knew many of the prospects. In the Twins' continuing efforts to promote from within the system, Gardenhire had been rewarded for two successful years at Orlando.

The organizational aspect of the Twins' spring training was the responsibility of bullpen coach Rick Stelmaszek. The daily program was more complicated due to the additional space in the new facility, but this was certainly a welcome problem. Kelly's goal was to keep people busy and over many springs he learned to entrust Stelmaszek with the implementation of the daily schedule. Stelmaszek was in his 11th year as a Twins coach and working for his fourth manager, an amazing run of longevity that Kelly understood. "Stelly is one of the hardest workers in baseball," he praised. "That's why he has survived. He does a great job in the bullpen, having people prepared to pitch when we call their name. He does all of our extra catching, hits fungoes, and throws good batting practice."

Stelmaszek also served a role as the "talker" for the coaching staff. A native of Chicago's South Side, he used his bluntness to check and balance some of the clubhouse banter. Stelmaszek took special joy in his verbal battles with Dan Gladden, and the coach was often the first to challenge the outfielder when he adopted his defiant pose. It was often baseball's version of the "trash talking" that has become commonplace in basketball. During batting practice, Stelmaszek answered Gladden's challenge with pitches that jammed him on the fists. The pair often engaged in a pregame battle of "target," a game of catch that awards points for a throw that hits the other player in the head. The player that catches the ball judges its accuracy, and Stelmaszek knew just how far to go in igniting Gladden's competitive fire by questioning his calls and taunting his misses. More often than not, the game ended with a jubilant Stelmaszek listening to a still-defiant Gladden muttering over the injustice of the outcome, and their teammates thoroughly enjoying the amusement.

Stelmaszek's alterego on the coaching staff was Dick Such. In his sixth year as pitching coach, Such's low profile belied his influence on Kelly's handling of pitchers. Seated at Kelly's left during most games, he was the one voice in the manager's ear during tense moments. Kelly valued the "patience and subtlety" of Such's approach. "He's under control with good composure and he knows how to take a pitcher aside and explain things," said Kelly of Such. "If he has to give someone the 'A' speech, raising his voice twice a year, that's a lot." After five springs of occasionally rushing youngsters and hoping to squeeze the last vestiges of usefulness from ancient arms, Such deserved this spring when there was order rather than chaos within the pitching staff.

The sage of the coaching staff, Wayne Terwilliger, was beginning his 44th year in professional baseball. He was truly 65 years "young." Says Kelly, "It's amazing to see the work he does at his age. He really enjoys working with the young kids and he did a great job in the instructional league teaching infield play to Chuck Knoblauch and Scott Leius."

Kelly utilized Terwilliger as the "medicine man" of the Twins, leaning on his wisdom before making decisions. An example was the use of Gene Larkin as an occasional leadoff hitter during the 1991 season. Terwilliger had planted the idea in Kelly's head early in the year and Kelly "weighed it heavily," keeping it in reserve until the time was right.

## NEW AND IMPROVED PITCHING

Crowley's hiring and the arrival of Chili Davis allayed MacPhail's worries about the Twins' offense. Kelly was firm, however, in his belief that better pitching was the root of improved hitting.

Kelly had gotten his desired starter in Morris. One man had made Kelly, in his words, "a smarter manager." How smart Kelly really was would largely be determined by the development of a staff to surround Morris. This spring would feature legitimate competition for spots on the pitching staff, a first during Kelly's tenure with the Twins. The days of journeyman right-handers Les Straker or Fred Toliver as the team's number-three starter were gone. Allan Anderson, the 1990 Opening Day starter and former American League earned run average champion, was now in a battle for the number-three place in the rotation. No jobs would be handed to any pitchers, all would have to be earned.

Kevin Tapani won 12 games in an injury-shortened 1990 rookie year, but had impressed the Twins with impeccable control and unswerving poise. Given good health, Tapani was expected to improve on his first-year victory total.

Improvement was also expected from Scott Erickson, a 23-

year-old right-hander who provided perhaps the only highlight of the previous September with five wins. Kelly was often wary of September performances against inflated rosters and deflated teams, but Erickson's half-season earned run average of 2.87 secured him a starting spot for 1991.

Instead of searching for "breathing bodies" to fill out a rotation, the Twins had Mark Guthrie and David West, both regular starters in 1990, locked in a battle for the fifth spot. Guthrie entered the race as a favorite after pitching into the seventh inning in 14 of his last 15 starts in 1990. But West had pleased management by pitching winter ball in Puerto Rico, being chosen Most Valuable Player of that league's play-offs.

As Kelly assessed the starters, he had no concerns about Morris or Tapani. Morris brought an unwavering work ethic that eased his assimilation into the team. "Jack was the first player at the park every morning," Wiesner said. "He even beat the manager which is quite a feat. But you could see the example he set for the pitching staff by how hard he worked." Kelly loved the eagerness that Morris brought to the often-monotonous spring drills. "He was always the first one to jump on the mound for a drill because he wanted to do it right and get something out of it. I never had to worry about handling a 'big shot' because he worked his tail off."

The road was not quite so smooth for Scott Erickson, who provided Kelly his only real challenge of the spring. This was Erickson's first spring training in a major league camp, and he brought with him his own methods of preparation for the season. Erickson's successes at other levels had thus far sustained his independence, but this was the major leagues, and the Twins had not shared Erickson's success.

"Scott had his way of doing things, we had ours, and he was going to follow ours," Kelly said. "What Scott had done in 1990 was great for him, but we were last. Now people are watching the players and the players watch each other and if they see someone operate in his own carefree way saying 'I'll be OK,' that's not good enough, because we finished last and I can't play that game. Scott's way was probably good for him and it would probably work, but I couldn't be sure because I had never seen him in the spring. The decision became, 'You're going to do it my way because I'm the boss.'"

Erickson pitched well in his first spring outing, and to Kelly's mind, may have settled into a state of complacency. His next several starts were poor, so Kelly chose a pregame exercise session for a calculated explosion.

"Pat Mahomes, one of our prospects, came over from the minor league camp for a day and parked next to Scott during workouts," Kelly said. "Things got much too relaxed for both of them, so I told Mahomes, 'Son, this is no vacation day. You came here to work!' Sometimes, my job is to scream and I got a dual effect here with both Mahomes and Erickson. You can't be afraid to make somebody an example."

Kelly never felt any lasting ill-effects from the outburst with Erickson, and the pair kept a running dialogue open through the spring. What Kelly saw was a young pitcher with the capability of winning many games if he approached his job in the proper manner. Regardless, spring training ended well for Erickson who would start the season's third game in Oakland.

There was little concern over the bullpen, where Rick Aguilera prepared for his second season as the closer. The legitimate highlights of 1990 were few, but one was the respect Aguilera earned from his teammates for ably filling the role defined by Jeff Reardon. Aguilera had been a reluctant convert to the bullpen job, spurred on largely by the encouraging words of Kelly and his own teammates. Assuring Aguilera he was the best man to replace Reardon, their praise and confidence provided Aguilera's motivation.

Aguilera saved 32 games in 1990, but one question remained.

Admittedly "desperate for wins" at a time when the Twins were struggling, Kelly had pushed Aguilera into a heavy workload prior to the All-Star break. It was a rarity for a manager known for his cautious handling of pitchers. Reardon had badly wanted to stay with Minnesota because of his admiration for Kelly's use of the closer. With Aguilera, Kelly realized he had made a mistake when his pitching coach and confidant, Dick Such, became angry as Aguilera was summoned into yet another game. The pitcher's shoulder became tender and with the Twins out of the race, Kelly's concern became avoiding any work that risked injury to Aguilera. Only 11 saves and 25 innings were posted by Aguilera after the All-Star break. Kelly was confident that with proper handling Aguilera could provide the constant availability demanded of a closer for a successful team.

The Twins had prepared several contingencies. Steve Bedrosian arrived from the National League with a resume that glowed with a Cy Young Award winning 1987 season as Philadelphia's closer, and with the firm belief that he should play the same role for the Twins. Kelly told Bedrosian that he would replace Juan Berenguer as a set-up man, but the emotional thrills achieved as a closer were intoxicating, and Bedrosian wanted that chance again.

The Twins also had Richard Garces, christened the "closer of the future." Garces was the reason Kelly was quoted in February as saying, "Aguilera will be a starter for us one of these days." Armed with a 90-mph fastball, Garces was not an "if" prospect, but a "when." He had progressed rapidly, but was still 19 years old. There was time, and the master plan was to start him at Portland, the Twins' triple-A affiliate.

Kelly faced only two difficult pitching decisions in Fort Myers. A fifth starter, either Guthrie or West, and a left-handed reliever from a group that included holdovers Larry Casian, Gary Wayne, and veteran free agent Paul Mirabella would be chosen. By past standards, this was an easy spring for Kelly and Such to construct a pitching staff. The tougher decisions for Kelly and Twins' management involved the position players.

## FINE TUNING THE INFIELD

Kelly felt fortunate that his only spring concerns were on the field. The new additions were not only supposed to contribute with their talents, but were expected to easily mesh in the clubhouse. There were no oversized egos on a Kelly-managed team. Kelly was inflexible in that regard, and his prime examples were Kirby Puckett and Kent Hrbek. Both players of immense talent, Puckett and Hrbek were "just regular guys in the clubhouse," according to Kelly. To enter the Twins' clubhouse, you had to leave your status at the door. Once a player placed himself above the team, he was destined to be an ex-Twin, a lesson most painfully learned by Steve Lombardozzi whose locker room tantrum during Game Seven of the 1987 World Series Kelly never forgot.

For Jack Morris, Chili Davis, and Mike Pagliarulo, adapting to their new teammates was easy. Kelly saw quickly that each player was serious about hard work, an approach that promised few problems for the manager and quick acceptance from their peers.

Davis was something of a mystery as the spring began, as his signing was so late and so swift that no one with the Twins had seen him during the winter. Kelly had confidence in the abilities of the 31-year-old designated hitter, and knew that his years in Anaheim had turned Davis into a better run producer. Still, a back injury and added weight had curtailed his 1990 season, and dimmed the Angels' interest in retaining his services. Kelly loved the notion of adding a powerful switch-hitter to an already strong lineup, but anxiety over his physical condition lingered.

Kelly's remaining concerns vanished when Davis arrived in Fort Myers. Wiesner recalled seeing "A big, strong frame of a man," while Kelly relaxed at his first sight of Chili. "Once I saw the shape he was in, there was a lot taken off my mind," said Kelly.

Davis quickly became the talk of the Twins' camp because of his workout regimen, followed faithfully at the end of each day. "I went in to ride the bike after a workout one day," Kelly remembered. "Chili came in behind me and said he was going to ride the UBE bike for 30 minutes. I looked at him and said, 'No way!' He said, 'Watch me.' Now, I've done this for five minutes and died. He does the 30 minutes. I was shocked, but [trainer] Dick Martin told me later that Chili sometimes did this twice a day. I have never seen anyone do the things Chili did in spring training." Davis was lean and strong, and his play, including six home runs, was one of spring training's highlights.

Mike Pagliarulo's spring was a stark contrast to Davis's success. Pagliarulo brought his Yankee-bred work ethic and steady defense, but, after a decent start, very few hits. He worked endlessly with Crowley, but the baseball wasn't jumping off his bat with the liveliness generated by Puckett, Davis, or Hrbek. As March progressed, Kelly found himself having to again don the armor and fight for his player. Management heard the campaign promises in December, but saw the struggling player in March. MacPhail often said he had never seen such conflicting scouting reports on a player. George Bradley's opinion on Pagliarulo ("He can't hit and he can't play third base") still had a life.

"I heard that line as late as one week before the end of spring training," Kelly said. "We had a staff meeting and that opinion was voiced. I was irate, probably the angriest I've ever been in a meeting with our own people. But give credit to Andy. He likes a difference of opinion at our meetings and he encourages us to lay it on the table." Pagliarulo's play was still an uncertainty and Kelly knew he needed an alternate plan. Enter Scott Leius.

If anyone could challenge Davis for the honor of best physique among Twins players, it was Leius. For three hours a day, five days a week, he worked with weights during his winter in suburban New York City, and brought to Florida a chiseled look rarely seen in shortstops. Leius had impressed the Twins with an outstanding 1989, winning the Southern League batting title and being voted the league's outstanding defensive shortstop. Kelly had long maintained admiration for any player that can succeed in a double-A league renowned for its debilitating combination of marathon bus rides and sweltering heat. Leius came to Fort Myers with a chance to win a roster spot if starting shortstop Greg Gagne's hitting faltered.

On March 26, Leius stood by a batting tunnel outside the major league clubhouse, as the Twins prepared for a game with the Mets. The countdown to the season opener was 14 days, but to Leius this had been a lost spring. He strained a hamstring on March 9 and was just now prepared to resume playing. He worried that 13 games would not be enough to win a job in the majors.

Leius could not know that events were conspiring to give his career its biggest lift. Kelly had to make a decision on third base. There was no doubting Pagliarulo's glove, but his weak hitting forced Kelly to consider finding a right-handed hitter and to create a platoon system at third. Leius seemed a perfect fit, with one very small exception. He had never played third base. There had been one inning the previous September when he relieved Gaetti, but beyond that, Leius had never fielded the demanding position.

Kelly felt Leius, an exceptional athlete whose boyhood dream had been to play football at Notre Dame, had a chance. Leius also had little choice. With Gagne having a good spring, the prospect of playing shortstop was dim.

"We gave Scott a crash course," Kelly said. "We started hitting him balls at nine in the morning, continued through lunch, then again after the game. We beat him up pretty good the first three days, but he kept working and improving each day. Now we only had 10 days to accomplish this and Scott could see what this special attention was about. When a player gets his manager and coaches showing him interest, it should motivate him to say, 'Let's go. Hit me the ball. I'll do whatever it takes.'"

In the final week of spring, Kelly practiced some more salesmanship on MacPhail. "After three days, I knew Leius could handle it in the field, and he was swinging the bat so well I couldn't see sending him out. But he had to bust his butt to convince Andy. And that's what Scott did."

The platoon at third base was set, and the infield was beginning to take shape for Kelly, with great thanks to Chuck Knoblauch. This year speculation was rampant that a good start was imperative for the manager's job security. Management had spent big money on veterans in the hope that this team could contend. Now, here was a 22-year-old with one and a half seasons of professional experience being anointed the second baseman and number-two hitter.

"I was sure he could do it," Kelly said. "It was just a matter of convincing Andy. I understood Andy's apprehensions because it was a tall order, jumping a kid from double-A to the majors. And every time Andy had seen Knoblauch play at Orlando [in 1990], he played terribly. But I knew he had the ability and the spring training games proved that. Chuck had to get the point across himself, and he did that by the way he played."

Much of Kelly's confidence in Knoblauch had been bolstered by Wayne Terwilliger. In the October instructional league, the coach spent hours tutoring the converted shortstop on the fine points of second base play. Terwilliger's primary concern had been Knoblauch's adjustment to the double play pivot, but that one autumn week in Fort Myers convinced Terwilliger that the Twins had their second baseman.

Knoblauch carried himself with an air of confidence, the kind often labeled cockiness. The short hair, square jaw, erect posture, and the ability to look one in the eye during conversation were signs of his three years of military training at Texas A&M. The rookie learned early in the spring that his All-American honors and top draft pick status meant little in the Twins' clubhouse. Puckett was relentless in tagging Knoblauch with the nickname "Skippy," a term coined by Dan Gladden and Al Newman after they spotted the rookie seated next to Kelly at a Minnesota Timberwolves game. The players were sharp and immediately recognized the ability of their new second baseman, but they were also determined to make him understand their clubhouse structure.

The Twins roared through March with one of the Grapefruit League's best records. April arrived, and Kelly had to make his final decisions. Mark Guthrie was named the fifth starter, a role that guaranteed him only two April starts. David West arrived in Florida riding a wave of optimism following his winter ball success and an impressive February mini-camp. West experienced elbow soreness in March, but made the team as a long reliever. The left-handed short reliever was Larry Casian, who joined West, Bedrosian, Aguilera, and Terry Leach in the bullpen.

Quality position players abounded, and they proved Kelly's most difficult calls. Leius and Knoblauch were on the team. Both outfielder Pedro Munoz and first baseman Paul Sorrento had big league experience and had nothing to accomplish by returning to triple-A. With simply no room for either on the Opening Day roster, they would have to start the year in Portland.

Lenny Webster, the young catcher who impressed Kelly during stints with the Twins the prior two seasons, fell victim as well. A 21st-round draft choice in 1985, he had bypassed 1986 first round pick Derek Parks in the organization's thinking. Webster had been labeled a "future big-league catcher," and he came to Fort Myers hoping that a good spring would earn him a roster spot. He was 26 years old and had done all the organization asked. Webster excelled during a difficult assignment to Orlando in 1990 when Parks was sent to Portland, a move based on draft status and potential. Having overcome all these hurdles, Webster felt his time had arrived. Unfortunately, that made April 4 a very painful day for

Webster and his manager.

For Tom Kelly, the decision was clear, but the meeting hurt the most. Brian Harper was entrenched as the starting catcher and Junior Ortiz, a good defensive catcher who had magically compiled a .335 batting average in his first year with the Twins, would be the backup. Just as for Munoz and Sorrento, there was no room for Webster.

"For his sake and for the organization, he had to go back," Kelly maintained. "He was probably ready to play in the majors, but not as a number-two catcher. He could not improve sitting on the bench. What was best for him was a year at triple-A working with our good young pitchers. Now, trying to convince him is the most difficult thing. He's going to be mad, you want him to be mad, and you can only hope that in a day or two, he understands this was the right thing to do."

Tom Kelly had been a good triple-A player for seven years, but only received 127 major league at-bats. He had often heard the same speech he now delivered. "I know it's unpleasant because I've been there too many times," Kelly said. "You think you're ready to play in the big leagues, this is your dream, and somebody says you can't. That hurts a lot. Most words are useless, because guys are so hacked off, they're not hearing what you say. All you can hope is that the player is strong willed enough to accept it, go down and play well. If he doesn't, then he's probably not the right guy."

After hearing the news, Webster was consoled near his locker by Chili Davis, and Kelly sat in his office reflecting on the most unpleasant day of what had been a very positive spring. He flashed back to 1975, a year of both accomplishment and disappointment for Kelly, the player. There was the dejection of being sent out to triple-A for the fourth straight year, after hitting .308 the previous season. There was the elation of a May call-up, quickly followed by 10 days on the Twins' bench before he was ever put into a game. There was the greatest anger he felt as a player when he was sent back to the minor leagues by manager Frank Quilici. His managing would forever be influenced by his playing experiences. When a rookie was called up, Kelly did everything possible to get the player into a game immediately. He would never do as a manager what had been done to him as a player. After Kelly left in 1975, he would never come back to the majors as a player. Not so for Lenny Webster, who would most assuredly return, sooner than he expected.

## A CONFIDENT ENDING

The Twins were 21–10 in spring training, and calmed many concerns about the offense by hitting .297. The team's success on the field was matched by the financial success of their first spring in Lee County. The Twins played before 112,355 fans as only 200 seats went unsold during the entire spring schedule. As the team prepared to leave for the season opener in Oakland, there was a lighthearted joke that it might be better to simply extend the spring by four months.

The Twins team that boarded a plane for Oakland on April 6 bore more of Tom Kelly's influence than any prior edition. The veteran core of Puckett, Hrbek, Gladden, Larkin, Gagne, Bush, Harper, and Newman was intact. This was to be the year Shane Mack blossomed into an everyday player, while rookies Leius and Knoblauch established themselves at the major league level. There seemed to be that ideal mix of young and old, with a perfect blend of veterans in Pagliarulo and Davis.

The pitching staff was fortified by the presence of Morris, who was expected to win his share of games and lead his fellow starters by example. In 1990 Kelly's first two starters had been Allan Anderson and Roy Smith. Now the manager had the luxury of holding back Kevin Tapani, the team's "winningest" starter in 1990, to start the home opener, the season's fourth game. Kelly had high hopes that the pitching would be strong in April, giving the team a chance to avoid a fourth consecutive losing record in the opening month.

On the six-hour flight to the West Coast, Kelly felt confident this was not a last place team. Very few outside the team shared that conviction, but then they had not seen the hours of hard work in the spring, and the strong blend of new personalities that produced a harmonious clubhouse. There was nothing more Kelly or anyone else could have done to prepare the team. The work had been done and hope was strong; it had been a productive stay in Fort Myers. Baseball people knew this spring had been different than most others and Kelly felt what Jim Wiesner voiced, "If ever a spring training would have an impact on a season, this was the one."

# 2 AND 9

*"A lot of people are going to get off to a bad start when you fly like we did and face the pitchers we did."*
***Tom Kelly***

## A DIZZYING FIRST WEEK

Andy MacPhail roamed the aisles in the forward part of the cabin whiling away the Twins' six-hour charter flight to Oakland for the start of the 1991 season. An avid reader, MacPhail could usually be found on team flights buried in a favorite novel. On this flight, however, MacPhail had a pre-season ritual to complete. Each year, he canvassed the baseball staff and traveling party asking their predictions for the number of games the Twins would win in the upcoming season. MacPhail has an openness in his approach that is rare among general managers. While engaging others in conversation, he never places himself on a pedestal, but rather leaves others feeling he truly weighs their opinions.

On this flight, MacPhail learned that even the optimism generated by a wildly successful spring was tempered by the cold reality of competing in baseball's toughest division, the American League West. The predictions MacPhail heard ranged anywhere from 83 to 90 wins. No one close to the Twins could foresee a losing season, but all knew that a winning record might still leave them no better than sixth in their division.

One glance at the 1991 schedule was sobering for MacPhail. The American League's original schedule for the Twins had them opening with nine consecutive games on the West Coast. The thought of this triggered flashbacks to 1990 when the lockout forced the Twins to open with a 10-game trip to Oakland, California, and Seattle, Washington. Posting a 4–6 record, they were four games out of first place before playing their home opener. MacPhail did not want a repeat of the 1991 start. After consulting with the business department, he petitioned the American League for one home series during the first week. The League responded with an offer of a three-game weekend series at the Metrodome in the middle of the nine West Coast games.

Tom Kelly was not enamored with the revised schedule. Neither option looked appealing. Kelly would have chosen opening up in any city other than Oakland, but he preferred playing the road trip in its entirety. Now the Twins were faced with the prospect of flying to Oakland for three games, flying home for three games against California, and finally returning to the west coast for six games in Seattle and Anaheim. "Flying back and forth didn't sit well with me or with the players," Kelly said. "But it was not an excuse for our start." MacPhail accepted the revised schedule, a decision that was equal parts baseball and business. It was critical for the Twins to avoid being buried in the standings by a brutally difficult opening road trip. In addition, the club estimated it could earn an additional $125,000 in revenues by playing a home series during the first week of the season.

The Twins, after their spring filled with bus rides across Florida, began their regular season with a dizzying array of time zone crossings generally foreign to baseball travel. Furthermore, if the travel was a hurdle to the players, the starting pitchers they expected to face in the first two weeks would pose an even larger obstacle. From Oakland's Dave Stewart, Bob Welch, and Mike Moore to California's Chuck Finley, Mark Langston, Jim Abbott, and Kirk McCaskill, through Seattle's Erik Hanson, Randy Johnson, and Brian Holman, the Twins knew baseball's most intimidating group of starters awaited them. There was danger in each game, as every opposing pitcher was capable of pitching a shutout. The Twins faced a relentless stretch of baseball in which they knew wins would be a scarce and precious commodity.

Kelly flew west with a clear conscience. There was truly nothing more that could have been done in Florida to prepare this team. Every drill had been repeated endlessly. In fact, Morris commented that he covered first base in drills more times in one spring with the Twins than he had in 14 springs with Detroit. Kelly enjoyed that remark for it confirmed his determination to pound home the importance of fundamentals for his players. While the Opening Night roster showed fewer weaknesses, the games to follow would issue the final verdict on the decisions made in Fort Myers.

Before Opening Night, Kelly faced one more dilemma. He flashed back to August 16, 1990, at Cleveland's Municipal Stadium where his one simple, declarative statement, made with no warning, had shaken the senses of the Twins players and media alike. No person who saw the lineup card could believe it . . . on line number three was written "Puckett—9." The shift of the Twins' "signature player" to right field stunned everyone, and that suited Kelly just fine. He had timed this move with the hope of injecting some "spark" into a team that was "lifeless."

Kelly explained before that August night's game that Puckett had expressed a desire to move out of center field. Puckett demurred, but acknowledged he was in favor of the shift. A younger, swifter man, Shane Mack, would be the Twins' center fielder, and Kelly indicated the move could well be permanent. In the final six weeks of 1990, Puckett started 19 games in left or right field. Yet Minnesotans were generally oblivious to the critical change Kelly had wrought. This wasn't a case of just any player changing positions, but rather an institution being moved. Emblazoned forever in the minds of Twins' fans are images of Puckett leaping over the center-field fence to steal potential home runs from the opposition. To Minnesota, Kirby Puckett was not a center fielder, he was center field.

Tom Kelly looked beyond the highlight film plays of a four-time Gold Glove winner. He saw a player approaching 30 years of age, who was carrying more bulk than in his early years, and who just didn't catch as many balls as he once did. "We all get spoiled by a great player," Kelly said. "It's easy to say when a ball drops in that he's a good player, if he could have caught it, he would. But that's superficial and baseball is much deeper than that. You ask your pitchers to battle for you, and when they give up a hit that should be an out, then you have to make adjustments. Fans don't always understand, especially with Kirby's mystique in Minnesota. There is never a word written. If a ball falls in center field that should have been caught, it gets overlooked in the newspapers. I can't manage worrying about mystique. I have to do what is right for the team."

Kelly had made this move with the Twins headed toward a last place finish. Messing with Minnesota's most popular athlete can be described as anything but "safe." Kelly could never be accused of acting in the name of self-preservation. "I get paid to use my judgment to decide what's right for the Twins," Kelly said. "Kirby Puckett is a fabulous, talented player who should be the Twins' right fielder. To me, that's easy. Shane Mack is our best outfielder. He covers the most ground and throws well. If we are going to emphasize pitching and defense as the key parts of the game, then we have to put our players in their best positions."

Few people knew that Puckett had contributed to Kelly's decision. "Kirby dropped subtle hints for several years that he wanted out of center field," Kelly remembered. "He'd come in my office and say 'get me out of center field' in a half-joking, but half-serious way. I understood that. It's a lot of games over a lot of years for him."

Puckett got half of his wish in Fort Myers. Shane Mack was given the center field job, but Puckett was made the everyday right fielder. Kirby wanted to play left field, but Kelly felt that "left field at the Metrodome is at least as hard as center field. There's so much room to cover." Dan Gladden still had the speed to play left field at home. In Kelly's opinion, with Gladden in left, Mack in center, and Puckett in right, the Twins had their best defensive trio in the outfield. Kelly did wonder, though, if Mack could adjust to an everyday playing role.

Mack was eased in gently in 1990 with playing time increased in small doses. He hit .326 and improved as he played more in the second half of the year. He earned the opportunity to start, and came to Fort Myers determined to show the Twins he could live up to their expectations. Mack was the first batter to feel comfortable with Terry Crowley, and the pair spent hours improving Mack's ability to handle inside pitches. Since Mack had demonstrated a clear tendency to hit the ball to right field in 1990, Kelly expected the League to make the obvious adjustments.

One of Mack's spring missions was to learn how to pull pitches bearing in on his hands. "Shane was the only player I was concerned with," Kelly recalled about the beginning of the season. "It's important for the players to be comfortable in their positions, and I really felt Shane would be over the hump after his first year with us. I knew if he hit well early, he would be fine in center field."

## THE OPENING NIGHT LINEUP

"There was what I call cautious optimism about Chuck Knoblauch," said Kelly, describing the Twins' lineup. "He showed us so many good things in spring training, like handling Nolan Ryan, that we had confidence he could do the job." Kelly gave Knoblauch a double dose of responsibility by officially placing him in the second spot in the batting order for Opening Night. The Twins searched nearly a decade for a hitter possessing the patience, eye, and bat control needed to hit second. The disastrous trade of Tom Brunansky for Tommy Herr in 1988 was made partially in recognition of Herr's success in that role for St. Louis. In Knoblauch, Kelly saw the "prototype number-two hitter."

The manager hoped that Dan Gladden would increase his on-base percentage batting in the leadoff spot. Gladden hit .275 in 1990 but drew only 26 walks. Out of baseball's statistical frenzy, on-base percentage had emerged as a trendy means of evaluating leadoff hitters. After all, the logic went, the leadoff man's job is not necessarily to hit, but to reach base. That thinking forgets that the leadoff hitter is guaranteed to bat first in an inning just once per game. If Gladden could play his customary 130–140 games and Knoblauch developed as expected, Kelly felt good about the front part of his lineup.

The middle of the batting order was just as Kelly had "spontaneously predicted" to Chili Davis in their January telephone call. Against right-handed pitchers, Puckett would hit third, followed by Hrbek, Davis, and Harper. Mack would start the season batting eighth behind Mike Pagliarulo, allowing Mack to ease into his new role. When the Twins faced a left-handed starting pitcher, Davis would bat cleanup, with Harper, Mack, and Hrbek to follow. Kelly liked Greg Gagne in the ninth spot with his combination of power (in 1989 his total of 45 extra-base hits was third on the team) and speed. It was important for Kelly to keep his faster players bunched together, and his Opening Night lineup had Mack, Gagne, Gladden, and Knoblauch, the team's swiftest foursome, batting in order.

In Kelly's tenure with the Twins, he never had a stronger bench than at the start of 1991. Junior Ortiz returned as Harper's backup while Leius would platoon at third with Pagliarulo. Al Newman was established as one of the American League's best at the unheralded role of utility player. He had proven more than capable of fielding three major league positions and, as a switch-hitter, provided Kelly the freedom to get adequate rest for his infielders. Veterans Randy Bush, Gene Larkin, and Carmen Castillo were expected to be the pinch hitters and spot starters. For Bush and Larkin, this season brought the promise of a drastic reduction in playing time. Larkin had exceeded 400 at-bats for three consecutive seasons, while from 1983 through 1989 Bush had played on a platoon basis. The addition of Chili Davis changed life for both players. With Davis' arrival as the designated hitter and Mack slotted in the outfield on an everyday basis, Bush and Larkin had to accept a diminished number of at-bats. If the players were unhappy with their status, that was fine with Kelly. He would be more concerned with an air of indifference from a player. Kelly knew his reserves cared about playing time, and in the cases of Newman, Bush, and Larkin, they had been proven regulars for him.

The pitching staff had eight very solid members in Kelly's thinking. Larry Casian was a rookie and Kelly would not immediately thrust him into crucial game situations, and David West's elbow problem had yet to be addressed.

Choosing Jack Morris as the Opening Night starter was stage one of Kelly's evolution into a "smarter manager." "These were the games we signed Morris to pitch," was a refrain heard often in 1991. Morris seemed to revel in the attention and celebrity status he attained in his homecoming. As the Twins worked out at the Oakland Coliseum the day before the opener, most of the media attention focused on Morris.

Kelly spent much of the two-hour session throwing batting practice and chomping on a cigar stub. (The manager was ringing in the new baseball season by swearing off chewing tobacco.) If he picked up any feelings from the workout, the players seemed "too anxious" to begin playing, and they still had 24 hours and some pageantry to endure before the first pitch. Kelly could not have known what the first 12 games of the Twins' 1991 season would bring, but he was certainly ready for it to begin.

## THE 1991 SEASON BEGINS

Thirty minutes before the season's first pitch, Tom Kelly and many of the players were in the Twins' clubhouse at the Oakland Coliseum. Andy MacPhail was still at the team hotel, two miles from the stadium. There were no Opening Night festivities for the Twins. Starting the season on the road, the Twins were subjected to yet another Oakland celebration, as the Athletics received rings commemorating their three consecutive American League Championships. Kelly wouldn't watch. "Maybe it's some jealousy, but I don't enjoy seeing it," he said at the time. "The A's put on a great production for their fans, but it can get a little intimidating for us. They try to intimidate you the first day, and then we have to go out and face [Dave] Stewart." History had placed the Twins in this situation before. In 1988 the Twins were dethroned by the A's as the division champions with a loss in Oakland. Last year's lockout-delayed opener was played in Oakland and the Twins watched the 1989 World Championship rings distributed. The third time was too much for Kelly.

Tuesday's Opening Night matched two of the league's premier pitchers in Morris and Dave Stewart. The Twins had enjoyed mixed success against the four-time 20-game winner from Oakland, and they knew they had to hit Stewart early to have a good chance.

Stewart survived the first inning, allowing only a Puckett single, the second consecutive year in which Kirby recorded the team's first hit. As Rickey Henderson prepared to lead off for Oakland, Twins fans had two reasons to be caught staring at the field. It was hard not to be transfixed by the sight of Morris in Minnesota's gray road pinstripes. A man the Twins had done battle with for so many years while he wore the old English "D" of the Tigers was now on their side. Morris's presence almost overshadowed another oddity of this opener, the sight of Kirby Puckett in right field.

A Twins fan could not help but notice the striking contrast between the offensive catalysts of these teams. For 24 hours in December of 1989, Puckett was the game's highest paid player after signing a three-year contract for $9 million. Having finished an MVP season for a World Championship team, Rickey Henderson felt he should be paid accordingly. Oakland agreed, and later that winter signed him to a four-year contract with a salary that surpassed Puckett's. Before long both players had been surpassed in earnings by less accomplished players. Puckett never once complained about his salary and accepted his move to right field with the attitude Kelly admired. "He'll play where I put him," said Kelly. Henderson took the opposite road, as he harbored bitterness about his contract and became a disruption to manager Tony LaRussa's spring training. The Athletics couldn't justify revising a contract that was only one-fourth complete. Henderson began the season with his own form of protest, at one point wondering in the press if he could be expected to perform his best if this contract inequity was not resolved. To the Twins fan, the contrast with Henderson's approach heightened Puckett's mystique as a player to treasure both on and off the field.

Henderson did have some record breaking to deal with in this first series, and Opening Night provided an ideal baseball climate. In Morris, Henderson faced a pitcher who did not hold runners close at first base. The soon-to-be base stealing king had enjoyed free rein against Morris and Twins' catcher Brian Harper. It continued in the first inning when Henderson led off with a single. With Dave Henderson batting, Rickey stole the base that moved him within one of Lou Brock's career record. It was the 15th base Rickey had swiped while Morris was pitching and the 17th while

Harper was catching.

"We don't get too concerned about Rickey once he's on base," Kelly remembered. "The key is to get him out. If he reaches base, we have our pitchers hold the ball, step off the rubber, and throw over sometimes. But we won't let our pitcher lose his focus on the next hitter."

Morris walked Dave Henderson, but recovered to retire Jose Canseco and Harold Baines before Terry Steinbach lined a run-scoring single. The third inning was identical as the Hendersons were again ignitors, Rickey with a single and Dave with a walk while Steinbach contributed another two-out RBI single.

After three innings, the Twins trailed 2–0 and an unsettling pattern had developed. Morris was working too many deep counts, keeping the Twins in the field for much of the game. Harper was receiving a punishing workout as Morris' trademark forkball arrived at the plate on one bounce more often than not.

"Jack was just trying too hard," Kelly remembered. "He tried to be Superman, putting all the weight on his shoulders." Kelly had been worried about the emotions Morris would take to the mound for his first game as a Twin. The first three innings were dangerous, but the real test would come in the fourth inning.

With two outs and a runner on second, Rickey worked out a walk. Dave Henderson followed and lifted a fly ball towards the visiting bullpen in right field. Puckett had to range far to reach this ball as he was shading the batter towards right-center field. As Puckett crossed the foul line and approached the bullpen mounds, it appeared he would catch the ball. There was a moment of disbelief as the ball hit Puckett's glove and then fell to the ground. It was going to take time to adjust to watching right fielder Kirby Puckett, let alone ever accept the surest-handed outfielder to ever wear a Twins' uniform dropping a ball.

Kelly had dreaded this moment. His pitcher, the staff leader no less, was struggling to stay in the game. It was the season opener, and a ball fell in that should have been the third out of the inning. All eyes immediately shifted toward Morris, whose intolerance of misplays while he pitched was legendary. Many Twins players had grown to dislike Morris's demeanor on the mound as opponents, and now they watched their new teammate intently. Morris showed no visible emotion even as Dave Henderson sent his next pitch into the left-field bleachers for a three-run home run. It was an utterly deflating blow to the Twins who should have been batting in the fifth inning trailing only 2–0, but were still on the field in the fourth staring at a 5–0 deficit.

Kelly remembers Puckett offering no excuses. "He came in the dugout and said he screwed up the play." Nor was the manager surprised as Puckett "had dropped a couple of balls in center field early last year."

The nightmare for Morris had not ended. After a solo home run by Greg Gagne gave Minnesota their first run in the top of the fifth, Oakland went back on the attack. Two walks by Morris led to a run, and with two outs and the bases loaded, Rickey Henderson dug in for what seemed to the Twins his twelfth at bat of the game. Rickey had reached base in each of his first three at-bats, but Morris felt he had won this battle when he coaxed a ground ball from Henderson that required a routine force play at second base. But the fates conspired against Morris as Knoblauch, in his major league debut, dropped the throw. The seventh Oakland run scored and Kelly removed Morris from the game. He had allowed only three earned runs but contributed five walks. His 110 pitches ran completely against the gospel according to Kelly of "throw strikes, put the ball in play, and get the boys off the field."

With a 7–1 lead and Stewart pitching, Oakland was in a commanding position. The Twins had not hit Stewart early and totaled just three hits in his seven innings. Steve Chitren was LaRussa's choice to pitch the eighth, and the Twins mounted a small rally. With one out, Gagne blooped a double down the right field line, Gladden walked and so did Knoblauch to load the bases. Chitren made an impressive comeback by striking out Puckett. LaRussa did not want the Twins to make any inroads on his lead, so with Kent Hrbek due up to bat, left-handed Joe Klink was summoned from the bullpen. Kelly managed to deliver just one more shock on what was Oakland's night, and it arrived in the person of pinch-hitter Castillo.

"Herbie [Hrbek] wasn't swinging great. He had three chances in the game and had done nothing against Stewart," Kelly remembered. "I couldn't imagine him swinging any better against Klink. Castillo had hit a bunch of home runs late in the spring and we needed a long one."

There was more than managerial logic behind Kelly's move. Wanting to get each player into a regular season game as quickly as possible was a residual effect from his own 1975 experience playing for the Twins. Nothing, however, obscured the stark reality of this situation. The player who came closest in Kelly's estimation to wearing the mantle of a leader was being removed and replaced when his team was behind. The player of whom Kelly often said, "When he hits, we do well," had the bat taken from his hands when the Twins needed a critical hit. Having Castillo hit was "the right thing for the club at that time." But in a general sense, Kelly delivered a big message through this example. "It was time for me to get everyone's attention," he said. "The team knew that I would do what I felt was necessary to win a game." Hrbek said nothing for now, and Castillo grounded out harmlessly to end the inning.

Oakland won the game 7–2, and even Norman Vincent Peale would have had trouble extracting any positive signs from this game for the Twins. Morris' outing was a letdown, the hitters were quiet against Stewart, and the defense made two glaring and uncharacteristic errors. Knoblauch was admittedly very nervous, playing his first game with his father Ray, a former minor league pitcher, in the stands. Knoblauch had three fly ball outs, one to the left field warning track, a sure sign to Kelly and Crowley of the wrong approach at the plate. If Kelly was on the lookout for anything in Knoblauch's entry to the majors, it was that the rookie not fall prey to what Rick Stelmaszek called the "double deck syndrome." This tendency referred to players being truly tested by the expanse of major league stadiums, all of which have the second, and often third, deck not seen in the minors. Now that Knoblauch's first game and first error were behind him, Kelly would watch to see how he played the next night.

Tuesday evening had not been without some adversity for Oakland. During the game, Mike Pagliarulo had sent a foul line drive screaming into the home dugout along the third base line. This was a liner hit so hard that even professional athletes could barely react in self-defense. In some of the scariest moments at a ballpark, fans often unaware of their surroundings are injured by such balls. This shot targeted Oakland reliever Gene Nelson, who watched the early innings in the dugout, and hit him on his right hand. Later X-rays revealed a broken bone in his pitching hand, which would sideline a valuable member of baseball's best bullpen.

Kelly's immediate concern was to prevent the spring's good work and optimism to be dimmed by one bad game. "I think people are hard-pressed a month later to remember how you did on Opening Day," Kelly said. "You like to win the game, but there are 13 losers on Opening Day." He knew the Twins just needed to play and pitch one good game. In one night, he had seen Morris pitch poorly, Puckett drop a fly ball, Knoblauch drop a routine throw and, in a fitting ending to an eerie opener, Hrbek replaced by a pinch hitter. There was a serious need to regain some normalcy on Wednesday night.

Allan Anderson contributed to Wednesday night's success in a most unusual way. A left-hander who generally gave up many hits and few walks, Anderson held Oakland to two hits over seven-and-one-third innings. In his career, he had averaged only one-and-one-half walks per start. On this night, Anderson survived walking six Oakland batters. "Andy threw the ball well that night," Kelly remembered. "But we did notice that he was hell-bent on getting the ball inside." This tendency would haunt a major part of Anderson's season.

Bob Welch started for Oakland, and the Twins never had much success against him in the Coliseum. Brian Harper hit a two-run home run in the second inning, and Chili Davis, who hit his first Twins' home run in the ninth inning of Tuesday's opener, singled in two runs in the third. There was no more scoring against Welch, who completed nine innings, but Anderson's performance made that irrelevant.

Rick Aguilera made his season debut in the eighth by retiring the Hendersons with the bases loaded. Jose Canseco opened the ninth with a bloop single and advanced to third on a Steinbach double. But, Aguilera stiffened and struck out Harold Baines, retired Mark McGwire on a foul pop, and struck out Ernest Riles to complete the 4–1 win.

Within 24 hours, the Twins had totally reversed the mood. With two early important hits, strong starting pitching, the expected flawless defense, and strong finish by Aguilera, Tom Kelly's ideal Twins game had been played. To further the pleasure, Rickey Henderson was stalled in his pursuit of Brock's record. Anderson had picked Rickey off second base in the fourth inning, the only time Henderson reached base all night.

Thursday afternoon was the series finale and the first getaway day of the season. The Twins living in Minnesota had been away from home for two months. Their opponent was not just the Athletics, but also their own tendency to lose focus on the day's game in anticipation of a trip home. Oakland's scheduled starter had been Eric Show, but the veteran had left Arizona with an infected finger on his pitching hand. During Wednesday night's

A rare find . . . Tom Kelly eyeing a close pitch at Metropolitan Stadium in 1975.

Notice Kelly's sideburns (*above*) and his fluid swing.

Kelly rarely leaves the dugout without knowing that he will make a pitching change.

Gene Larkin delivered the hit that brought the Twins a World Championship.

Kevin Tapani won 16 games and provided the Twins with their most consistent starting pitching.

The hometown boy, Kent Hrbek, is now the senior Twin, having finished ten full seasons.

Shane Mack, greeted by Dan Gladden, was the Twins' leading hitter after the All-Star Break.

game, rookie Joe Slusarski was recalled from Tacoma to take Show's turn. Slusarski flew into Oakland Thursday morning, arriving at the ballpark just three hours before game time. Most teams would prefer facing a rookie pitcher who had little preparation for the assignment, but not the Twins. Tom Kelly was baffled by his team's inexplicable difficulties with unfamiliar pitchers. Slusarski shut out the Twins on five singles over seven innings. Dennis Eckersley finished with two perfect innings to save a 3–0 Oakland victory.

Scott Erickson's first start showed that the demands placed upon him by Kelly in Fort Myers had paid dividends. In seven innings, Oakland was fortunate to scrape together two runs, as Erickson registered fourteen outs on ground balls. On a quiet Thursday afternoon in Oakland, the first signs of a pitcher on the verge of dominance emerged with the devastating movement seen on Erickson's pitches. This was a game that on most days would have earned Erickson a win. On this occasion he took a loss, but Erickson's performance left an impact in Kelly's mind that would soon be evident to all in baseball.

There were other subtle signs in this game of things to come. Kelly started Bush, Larkin, Ortiz, and Newman in Thursday's game, fulfilling the manager's goal of playing all 15 position men in the first series. Ortiz threw out Rickey Henderson on an attempted steal of second in the third inning. Chuck Knoblauch hit in the leadoff spot as Kelly followed his pattern of resting Dan Gladden in day games that followed a night game. Hesitant to thrust too much too soon on the rookie, Kelly hoped that Knoblauch could capably replace Gladden on an occasional basis.

After a 1–2 start, the Twins flew home for a series with California played on a weekend so rainy that outdoor baseball would have been impossible. The safety of the Metrodome attracted 45,866 for the home opener and the return of Gary Gaetti.

Baseball players often adopt a callous attitude allowing them to sever emotional ties easily. The mercurial nature of a business that can uproot a life in five minutes and move it 3,000 miles away forces such callousness to develop. Gary Gaetti was different, and nothing Gaetti could say or do about his first trip back to Minnesota could keep his emotions in check.

Sadly, many Minnesota fans were in a similar predicament. Gaetti was greeted with a mixed chorus of boos and cheers. The boos increased with each at bat, and it bothered Kelly. "It was a shame to hear those boos," he said. "It seemed a little harsh after all the great memories he gave. He had so many great years, and people forget he did so much. You learn in this game, and I hear it every week on my radio show, that you can't please everybody, and that includes the fans." What fans did not see was Gaetti's press conference, held earlier that afternoon, where he patiently answered every question from Minnesota reporters. After that session, Gaetti visited with Hrbek, and even offered help with defensive positioning to Scott Leius, who was preparing for his first start at third base.

Tom Kelly hoped that Kevin Tapani could continue the quality pitching precedent set by Anderson and Erickson in Oakland. Starting the home opener was an honor for Tapani. It proved he had completed the long journey from his status as the third pitcher acquired in the Frank Viola trade. Scouting reports had labeled him a "fourth starter," and now he had the ball in his locker for a home opener. Tapani seized the moment as he pitched a seven-hit shutout with no walks and nine strikeouts, completing the game in two hours and 28 minutes. The second-year pitcher had an effect on veteran Morris who admitted he was impressed watching Tapani work fast, noting the positive impact it had on the team.

The Twins battered Jim Abbott for six runs in five innings. Leius tripled in his first at bat, and handled three chances cleanly on balls hit by Dave Winfield. A 2–2 record, with three solid starting pitching efforts in four games, pleased Kelly. The Twins, however, would not win again for nine days.

Winfield started the Twins' decline with a three-home-run, six-RBI game on Saturday. Mark Guthrie bore no resemblance to the pitcher whose consistency had earned him widespread respect in 1990. His first start lasted two-and-one-third innings and ended with Winfield's second home run. In a game too reminiscent of past years for Kelly, the bullpen was ineffective and the Twins lost 15–9.

Morris made his home debut Sunday and the results were no better than in Oakland. "We expected he'd be trying too hard," Kelly said. "We tried to convince him to throw like he knew how, but again he tried to do too much." Morris, who when he signed with the Twins acknowledged he would have to learn how to pitch in the Metrodome, was rocked for 13 hits and eight runs in five-and-two-thirds innings.

The anticipated consistency of starting pitching was totally missing in the first week, and the Twins knew the outlook could not improve until the starters did. Anderson provided little hope when the second half of the western swing began Monday in Seattle against a Mariners team that was 0–6. Edgar Martinez drilled a three-run home run in the first inning and Anderson was gone before the end of the third in an 8–4 Seattle win. The following night, Erickson was strong for his second consecutive start, but the Twins were shut out by Brian Holman and lost 3–0. The Mariners' sweep was completed with a 4–3, 11-inning win on Wednesday.

Suddenly, a five-game losing streak found the Twins in last place at 2–7, six games out of first place. A winter of worry and a spring of hard work had gone into preventing this repeat of one year ago. Kelly believed Morris would eventually settle into a more comfortable routine, as the pitcher's track record was too long to prove otherwise. The offense was sputtering with too many important bats remaining quiet, most notably Hrbek's. In the ninth inning of Monday's loss to Seattle, while trailing by four, Kelly pinch hit for Hrbek for the second time in seven games. In a move that surprised both players as much as anyone else, Al Newman was sent up to face Randy Johnson. If pinch hitting Castillo for Hrbek had been a shock, Kelly was now delivering a massive jolt to his first baseman's senses.

"Newman had a history of getting some big hits for us," Kelly recalled. "The way I manage is if someone had been struggling all night, he didn't warrant getting another at bat. Not only had Herbie been fighting the lefty that night, but his average against lefties had gone steadily down over several years. You can call it a shake-up designed to get his attention if you don't think he's doing well. But it worked. He resurrected himself." (Kelly made the same reference to Hrbek's improvement later in the season.)

First would come the anger Kelly hoped to see from Hrbek. After the Castillo move, Hrbek had said nothing. But in Seattle Hrbek and Kelly, friends and business partners away from baseball, had a manager-player session. "He was walking around in a funk," Kelly remembered. "It looked like it was going to be a game of who's going to say something first. The player doesn't really want to say anything. I recognize that and so I initiated a talk. I told him to get it out in the open. He said he was disappointed, and I explained why the move was made." Kelly had delivered phase two of his wake-up call and had demonstrated to the other players that he could separate his relationship with Hrbek from his responsibility for the welfare of the team.

As the Twins traveled to Anaheim, the inevitable consequences of facing superb starting pitching every night began to show. Chuck Finley threw a two-hitter in the series opener to outduel Jack Morris by a 2–0 score, marking the third time the Twins had been shut out in the first 10 games. The game surprised very few as Finley had been the toughest pitcher in the league against the Twins for the last two years. Kirk McCaskill followed Finley's outing with a three-hitter for eight innings in a 2–1 California victory, as Allan Anderson lost despite holding the Angels to four hits.

The Twins had lost seven consecutive games and had a 2–9 record, but Kelly tried to keep some semblance of a positive outlook. "A lot of people are going to get off to a bad start when you fly like we did and face the pitchers we did," he reasoned. He took stock of the starting pitching, which brightened considerably with Morris' strong outing in Anaheim, and realized that "the players had a good feeling about our staff." Eleven games were enough to draw more mixed conclusions. Dan Gladden had one hit in 31 at-bats. Kelly attributed this slump to Gladden's preoccupation with improving his on-base percentage. Kelly urged Gladden, always an aggressive hitter, to stop trying to work the count in his favor and draw more walks. Knoblauch was hovering at the .300 mark and had quickly erased any lingering doubts about his readiness.

Shane Mack, Kelly's biggest concern going into the season, was his biggest disappointment after 10 games. "Just like Morris, Shane was trying too hard to do well," Kelly said. "He got off to such a horrible start at the plate that I had to take him out of the lineup." Mack, with four hits in 28 at-bats, arrived at Anaheim Stadium for the second game of the weekend series to see Puckett starting in center field that night. After 10 games, the grand shift was over and Puckett was again the center fielder. Mack would not start for a week. "One thing I don't think is right is to move players around to different positions," Kelly explained. "Once we had to take Shane out and put Kirby back in center, that was the way it would stay. I didn't want to keep moving Puckett, so we just decided to work Shane back into right field with Bush and Larkin."

On Sunday, April 21, the Twins closed their western odyssey with an afternoon game against the Angels. The matchup of starters saw Scott Erickson take an 0–2 record, that with any justice should have been 2–0, to the mound. His opponent, left-hander Mark Langston, faced a "getaway day" lineup that was without Hrbek, Mack, Knoblauch, and Harper, a Kelly tradition. "We all look forward to going home, so it's easy to get sidetracked on getaway days," said Kelly. These are the times to throw in a gimmick or change the lineup. It keeps everyone involved and makes for a better attitude."

Nothing helped Erickson's attitude more than Puckett's first inning home run off Langston, the first run the Twins had scored for him in three starts. Davis added a home run with one runner on base in the third inning, his second of the series that marked his return to what had been his home stadium for three years.

California bunched four hits together in the fourth inning to produce three runs and tie the game. It remained tied until the eighth when good fortune intervened for the first time in 1991. Chili Davis started the inning with a single off right-handed relief pitcher Mark Eichhorn. Appearing as a pinch hitter, Hrbek grounded into a force play at second. With Junior Ortiz batting, Hrbek was able to steal second base on a failed hit-and-run play as the Twins capitalized on Eichhorn's elongated sidearm delivery. Ortiz then lined a single to right and Hrbek scored without a play as Max Venable failed to field the hit cleanly.

Venable provided one last dramatic moment in the bottom of the ninth. Facing Aguilera with his team trailing 4–3, two outs, and no runners on base, Venable attempted a drag bunt. The bunt appeared to be placed perfectly between the mound and first base, hit hard enough to force Hrbek to abandon the base in an attempt to field the ball. But Aguilera, an infielder until his sophomore year at Brigham Young, darted between Hrbek and the ball, gloved the bunt and in the same motion, dived for Venable with his glove extended. Aguilera tagged Venable just before the runner's head-first slide hit the bag. The endless hours of repetitive fielding drills for the Twins' pitchers paid their first dividend on Aguilera's spectacular play, and ended the seven-game losing streak.

The flight home was a bit happier, but the record was still 3–9. This team that everyone knew was better than a last-place team now occupied the cellar of the American League West. Ticket sales for the first three home stands were slow, and the North Stars' success in the Stanley Cup Playoffs was diverting attention away from the Twins. Kelly remained unconcerned about his own security. "That never entered my thinking," he explained. "I'd be the first to admit I should step aside if people aren't responding to my way of doing things. But that never happened here, and Andy had enough faith that things would turn around after a less than ideal situation to start the season."

On the first day of the Twins' home stand, Kelly made what perhaps was the smartest move he could have made. "I called in all the coaches, trainers, Jim Wiesner, even (traveling secretary) Remzi Kiratli, and told them that they were not to come into the clubhouse frowning," he said. "They had to keep smiling, work hard, and stay upbeat in the clubhouse. The message we all convey is critical, and if the players look at the manager and staff and see they're down, it will be contagious. It worked well during the home stand, and Terry Crowley said to me during the year how important it was that we had kept a good attitude early in the year."

What the Twins needed most at this point was a good home stand. They started in that direction by winning twice in a three-game series with Oakland, including Morris's first win. A four-game sweep of Seattle followed, featuring superb Minnesota pitching. Seattle scored just seven runs in the series, while Erickson pitched his first major league shutout and Morris and Tapani followed with wins.

Minnesota seemed to have purchased a ticket for a ride on that dreaded roller coaster. It was just April, and the Twins had already experienced a seven-game losing streak and a five-game winning streak. As quickly as last place had become a reality, the Twins rose to third place on April 28 with a 9–10 record. The four starters, with Guthrie still an irregular fifth man, were pitching well and the offense had definitely improved. Gladden was slowly rebounding. Davis was showing the necessary power, Gagne was off to a strong start, and Knoblauch, Puckett, and Harper were consistently contributing a daily dose of hits.

Hrbek and Mack were still not producing as was expected, but nevertheless, the Twins' fortunes seemed brighter on May 1 than they had on April 21. Ten days of baseball had shown Kelly that what he had seen and lived in the spring had not been an illusion. Not yet ready to discuss it openly, Kelly believed this team could contend. One major reason for this belief took the mound in the Metrodome to face the Boston Red Sox on May 1. As Tom Kelly watched Scott Erickson, he knew that no matter how illusory the pitching might seem, he was watching a rebirth of the Twins.

# SCOTT ERICKSON

*"We had a lot of spring training meetings about good starts. And Scott was the one pitcher who took tremendous stuff to the mound in the first inning."*
***Tom Kelly***

On a humid July afternoon in 1990, rookie Scott Erickson settled into the Twins' bullpen to watch a twi-night doubleheader unfold between his new team and the Baltimore Orioles. His major league career had begun just three weeks earlier, and Erickson was a spot starter and long reliever as play resumed following the All-Star break. Tom Kelly knew little about the tall right-hander who was just 12 months removed from the University of Arizona, other than his best weapon was a sinking fastball that moved so dramatically Erickson himself often had no idea where it would go.

Kevin Tapani was Minnesota's starter in the first game of the doubleheader. The second Baltimore batter, Joe Orsulak, hit a line drive that ricocheted off Tapani's right shin, forcing his removal from the game. Kelly called upon Erickson to enter with no warning, and the unusual circumstances affected his control. In four-and-two-thirds innings, he walked six Oriole batters allowing just one run. Toronto scout Gordon Lakey visited the press box and told the Minnesota media to watch "any pitcher with stuff good enough to survive six walks." It was a notable performance lost amidst a late-inning Oriole win, but Erickson showed the ability to make the one pitch necessary to retire a batter.

By September of 1990, Erickson's indoctrination to the big leagues, usually a cautious process for Twins pitchers, was accelerated. He won five games in the final month of the season, and impressed Kelly enough to earn a spot in the 1991 rotation. When spring arrived, however, a "meeting of the minds" was needed. Kelly felt Erickson needed to understand one point. This was the major leagues, and after finishing last in 1990 Kelly felt everyone had to follow the same program. Once Kelly communicated that point to his pitcher, the two established a good rapport. Erickson adopted a more serious approach to his preparation, and he showed he was ready for the season by pitching seven innings of three-hit baseball in his final spring start.

"He was fabulous in his first two regular season starts," Kelly said. "He pitched well enough to win if we had scored any runs." Kelly and pitching coach Dick Such saw a trend developing in those two losses that would render meaningless the issue of run-scoring while Erickson was pitching. The radar gun readings showed Erickson consistently breaking 90 mph with his fastball.

"Scott came to us as an 84 mile-per-hour pitcher," Kelly said. "That's where he was in 1990 and spring training this year. But on Opening Day, he started hitting 90–91 (mph) on the gun. Now a 17-year-old could mature physically and make that jump. But by 22 or 23 [Erickson's age], you are what you're going to be. More knowledge of pitching and added confidence doesn't get you from 84 to 91."

The movement of Erickson's pitches made him difficult to hit. Toss in an extra seven miles per hour and he became absolutely nasty. Rarely does a pitcher make major league hitters look helpless, but Erickson was on the verge of reaching that level of pitching. He shut out Seattle on five hits on April 26, then drew the Boston Red Sox in his next two starts.

Boston's lineup was regarded as the American League's best for pure hitters. Boston didn't beat you with speed or with power, but with one good major league hitter after another. Jack Clark's power had been added to a lineup that led the American League in runs in 1990. What Erickson did to Wade Boggs, Jody Reed, Mike Greenwell, Ellis Burks, Jack Clark, Tom Brunansky, and company in the space of one week was extraordinary.

On May 1, Erickson held Boston to a sixth-inning single by Jody Reed and a seventh-inning double by Tom Brunansky, but saw his teammates equally stymied by Red Sox right-hander Greg Harris. In his fifth start, Erickson faced the possibility of his team being shut out for the third time. The Twins finally scored when Dan Gladden homered in the eighth off reliever Jeff Gray. With the comfort of a one-run lead, Erickson calmly retired Reed, Greenwell, and Clark in the ninth. Only four Boston batters had reached base, and remarkably, just two fly balls had been hit, both by left-handed batters. For the Twins, it was a win of immediate importance, raising their record to within one game of .500, yet the long-term implications were even stronger. The Twins now had a pitcher fully capable of dominating a game

The Twins' second meeting with the Red Sox was May 7 at Fenway Park. Erickson received a run when Minnesota's first three batters, Gladden, Knoblauch, and Puckett, singled off Harris. Through eight innings that one run would have been sufficient, since Erickson held Boston scoreless. By the ninth inning, though, the Twins lead had grown to 9–0. The Red Sox looked as futile at the plate as they had 17th innings earlier, and the only suspense left was the safety of several Twins' club pitching records. No Twin had ever pitched three consecutive shutouts, and Erickson needed just two outs to surpass Frank Viola's record of 30.1 consecutive scoreless innings.

Ellis Burks started the ninth with a single and Clark followed with a chopped grounder to the left side of the infield. Scott Leius, who entered the game at third base in the eighth inning, had the only play and in his haste bobbled the ball for an error. Greenwell advanced the runners with an infield ground out, and Brunansky smashed a three-run home run into the netting atop the left-field wall to spoil the shutout.

As Brunansky circled the bases, there was a telling sight on the mound. The Twins still led 9–3 and Erickson had lost his shutout legitimately on a wickedly hit line drive. None of that provided any solace to Erickson, who stalked the area behind the mound in obvious anger. He later said the lost chance to set records was not the source of his displeasure, but rather just one very bad pitch to Brunansky. Erickson's performance that night demonstrated a personal drive that was equal to the intensity of his pitching.

In the space of six days, 23-year-old Scott Erickson had twice rendered a fine lineup helpless. "Any time you do that in back-to-back games, it's the best accomplishment a pitcher can have," Kelly said. "The same batters just saw you for three or four at-bats the last game, and to stop them again you must have awesome stuff."

It was very apparent to all that Erickson qualified on that count. He had won just four games, but his style left a trail of praise from opposing batters. "He had a sinker and a slider working that were devastating pitches," Kelly remembered. "Some guys have one pitch of that caliber, some pitch in the big leagues without any, but you just don't see guys with two pitches like that at the same time." The net effect left right-handed batters feeling inept. Left-handed batters hit Erickson for a decent average but little power, as his sinking action prevented most batters from lifting the ball. The incredible force of Erickson's pitches was felt most by right-handers who were prone to the deadly sinking fastball-slider combination. During Erickson's run, a right-hander felt lucky to make solid contact once in a game.

Erickson extended his winning streak to six with a pair of wins over Detroit, allowing just one run in 13.1 innings. The second

Tiger game was memorable, as it was the first game in which Erickson was judged to have pitched below his new "standard." In six-and-one-third innings, he walked five, hit a batter, and allowed six hits. Outstanding catches by center fielder Puckett and left fielder Gladden prevented big innings, while Erickson continued to show his ability to make a key pitch when he needed an out as Detroit left 11 runners on base against the Twins' starter.

Erickson faced Texas next, a team he defeated twice as a rookie. The Texas team that came to Minnesota in late May, though, was an offensive terror. The Rangers had won nine consecutive games, including the first two games against the Twins, scoring at least five runs in each game. As Kelly remembered, "It wasn't just their big guys hitting, but everyone in their lineup was smoking line drives." The contagious Texas hitting even overcame Erickson. He allowed two home runs in a game for just the second time in his career, and in seven innings gave up 10 hits and five runs. The Twins scored enough to send the game to extra innings, allowing Erickson to escape with a no-decision and his winning streak intact. Ironically, the authority with which Texas hit made the events of the next week even more astounding.

When the Twins arrived in Texas on Memorial Day, the Rangers' streak was at 13 wins. The state (whose sports interests were once prioritized by University of Texas sports information director Jones Ramsey as "football and spring football") was actually gripped by the early stages of baseball fever. Lines unseen in Arlington Stadium history formed all day for tickets to this series. The Twins were not the attraction. To the contrary, they were losing ground to .500 at 20–23 and were heading on a road trip to Texas and Kansas City, two places where they rarely played well.

The Rangers added to the festive atmosphere at their home park by winning their 14th straight in the series opener by a score of 11–4, the Twins' seventh loss in the last eight games. All the gains of the past month, recovering from a 2–9 start, were in jeopardy.

There had been two days at over .500 in mid-May, and with Erickson dominating teams and Morris recovered from his shaky beginnings, Kelly had hopes for a winning streak that could put the Twins in contention. Instead, the team needed desperately to break a free fall.

In the clubhouse after the first game in Texas, Erickson, who was due to start the next night, did his best Joe Namath impersonation. "He walked past me just after the game," Kelly remembered. "He came right up and said, 'Don't worry, their streak's over tomorrow night.'" Erickson was 11 months old when Namath made a similar boast at Super Bowl III. Although the events did not compare in magnitude, the Twins were learning that, like Namath, Erickson's self-confidence played a large part in his success. "It's a cocky thing to say," Kelly admitted. "But there's nothing wrong with some of that if it's under control. When it came time to put up or shut up, Scotty put up."

Erickson ended the Rangers' streak and returned to his May dominance. He pitched eight innings, allowed no runs, and gave up seven hits and three walks. All of Texas' hits were singles, and baseball's top scoring team had only one runner reach third base. Erickson silenced a lineup that had rolled over American League pitchers every day for two weeks. More importantly, he stopped the very same lineup that hit him only five days before.

"It was just like his win over Boston in proving how tremendous his stuff was," Kelly said. "To shut out a team that is hitting everybody and had just hit him in our own park is remarkable." An intriguing sidelight to the game involved Kelly's handling of a delicate first-inning situation. Dan Gladden started the game with a home run, and after the next two batters reached base, Kent Hrbek faced starter Jose Guzman. The count went to 3–1 when Guzman threw a pitch that appeared to clearly miss the outside corner of home plate. Umpire Jim McKean saw it differently, and his opinion mattered. The pitch was called a strike and

Hrbek, who had spent 10 years earning a reputation for a good eye, complained. Those who wonder why batters question umpires' calls were provided an answer. On the next pitch Guzman, seeing McKean expand the outside corner on 3–1, threw his full-count pitch to the same spot. Hrbek, armed with the knowledge that McKean had established a wide strike zone, knew he must swing at the pitch even if he felt it was outside. As a result, the left-handed batter hit a perfect double-play ground ball to the shortstop.

Hrbek was irate. As he returned to the dugout, he directed a string of comments at McKean. One struck McKean the wrong way, and he thrust out his right arm to eject Hrbek. Kelly came running to the plate, not to argue with McKean but to reason. "I told Jim that we had our best pitcher going tonight, he's been on a great streak, and I didn't want anything to screw up the game. Now the pitch to Hrbek was terrible, but after that Jim had a good game." The incident reveals much about Kelly's pragmatism. Nothing could bring Hrbek back to the game, so Kelly, who has been ejected only twice as a Twins' manager, insured that Erickson's night would not be ruined by lingering problems with the home plate umpire.

Not only was Erickson dominating teams (in four of his 10 starts he had not allowed a run), but he was able to maintain his newfound velocity from game to game. More importantly, said Kelly, "He was still throwing 90 with movement in the seventh and eighth innings." The Twins admired Bret Saberhagen for his ability to throw as hard in the ninth inning as he did in the first. It was a joy to speak about one of their own pitchers in the same way.

There was no question that the Twins took some extra pride in Erickson. He was a product of Terry Ryan's scouting system who had been drafted three times by major league teams and never signed. There were no college scholarship offers at the Erickson home in Sunnyvale, California, after Scott went 3–6 as a high school senior. Bypassing the Mets, who had drafted him in the 36th round, Erickson went to San Jose City College and on to the University of Arizona where he blossomed with a school record 18 wins. At six feet four inches and 225 pounds, many scouts expected a harder thrower, but Ryan and scout Clair Rierson loved the movement on his pitches, and the Twins drafted Scott in the fourth round of the 1989 draft.

Erickson won three games at Class A-Visalia in 1989, eight in Orlando in 1990, and suddenly became a major leaguer. He arrived quickly without fanfare, but that had changed by June of 1991. According to Erickson, his velocity jump in 1991 was the result of him abandoning his college routine of lifting weights between starts. Kelly had a different opinion. "We were worried that this great run just couldn't last," Kelly said. "He couldn't keep extending himself to the max every time. He was so jacked up to pitch, that's how he hit 90 on the gun. [Dick] Suchie kept saying 'I don't know how long this is going to last,' but he was in such good shape that we thought he could last the first half."

Conditioning was no problem for Erickson. Although Kelly did not appreciate Erickson's approach to team exercises in spring training, the pitcher did his work. He was in many ways a pitcher for the '90s, young and strapping with a body toned by weight lifting. He struck a fearless pose on the mound, holding his black glove over his nose and mouth, allowing only his eyes to show. After just the equivalent of one full season, he had the respect of the entire American League. "It happened very quickly," Kelly admitted. "People saw his ball moving all over the place and realized this was an awesome display. Our players were impressed by the way he kept pitching early when we didn't score any runs. Eventually, the players saw he was for real, and the day he pitches becomes 'score a couple of runs, win this, and get out of here.' Scott and [Kevin] Tapani both hung in when there were few runs. But, once Jack got squared away, the players had a good feeling about our staff."

Erickson's win in Texas started a flood of media attention. Suddenly, Erickson was being "labeled," as writers groped for new angles. His undeniable good looks and eligibility as one of the few single Twins players gained Erickson a spot in the gossip columns, leading to at least one unpleasant media experience. The label that most bothered Kelly was "maverick," which appeared in the headline of a *Star Tribune* feature on Erickson. He did like to wear black, and he did wear his stirrups low, and he did polish his shoes black before each start, but to Kelly, those were idiosyncrasies and superstitions that existed in varying forms for all players. There were no "mavericks" on the Twins, and Kelly was not going to let the media create one.

"We had put the spring incident far behind us," Kelly said. "But one writer kept bringing it up, well into June. Scott told me he was trying to get the writer off this track, but the writer wouldn't leave him alone. We helped Scott with things to say to divert the questions, and he did well."

Kelly and media relations manager Rob Antony devised a structure that served Erickson well over the ensuing month. Erickson gave as many interviews as possible the day after he pitched, freeing the remaining days between starts for his preparation. This was a delicate period for the Twins' balance in the clubhouse. There were no stars, and the acknowledged heavyweights of the team were always careful to deflect praise onto underpublicized teammates. Very few on this team had experienced the spotlight Erickson was under.

"We kept an eye on him," Kelly said. "You must remember, our players are not the types to be jealous of someone's success. And if I was playing behind someone winging it up to the plate like he was, I'd be ecstatic because it gives my team a better chance to win. Scotty handled the attention well. He gave credit to the other players, and I tipped him to little things like getting on the bus after a win and telling the guys 'way to pick me up.' The biggest thing was that he's a good guy and the players were happy for him."

Indeed, the Twins realized Erickson could be their fastest ticket out of last place. He had a tremendous impact on fellow starter Kevin Tapani, who could continue his consistent pitching in his quiet manner, and on the bullpen, which could rely on a nice break every fifth game. This sounded suspiciously similar to the help Jack Morris was to have provided the team, and most Twins felt it was not sheer coincidence that Morris followed Erickson's gem in Texas with a four-hit victory over Nolan Ryan the next night. The May 28–29 games were a pair that Kelly would look back on later in the season and recognize as crucial to the team's rise.

May ended with Erickson posting a 1.36 earned run average and capturing the league's Pitcher of the Month award. A new month changed nothing, as Erickson beat Kansas City 4–1 on June 2. The pitching line had become frighteningly routine: eight-and-one-third innings, five hits allowed, a career-high eight strikeouts, and just one walk. It was the third winning start in which Erickson had walked only one batter, remarkable given the way his pitches moved. One of Erickson's strengths was his "effective wildness," something Kelly hoped for in all starters. The concept was simple. The more fear in the hitter, the more effective the pitcher. "Scotty proved how important it is for hitters to move their feet once in a while," Kelly recalled. "A pitcher has a much better chance when he keeps the hitter from being able to look for a ball in a particular zone. Scotty was just wild enough to keep hitters from sitting on the outside part of the plate."

Erickson won his next two starts at home, his ninth and 10th consecutive wins, with Lenny Webster as his catcher. Junior Ortiz had developed a good working relationship with Erickson, and although Kelly dislikes the label, Ortiz had become Erickson's catcher. "We think Brian Harper is a five-days-a-week catcher, and since Junior had more experience at the position, we'd have him work with Scotty whose ball moves so much," Kelly said. "It's not that Harp couldn't catch him. It just seemed like this system worked well for everyone."

Ortiz turned an ankle running the bases in the win at Kansas City and landed on the disabled list. Webster returned, as Kelly knew he would, but he came back under less than ideal circumstances. "He hadn't hit well at Portland," Kelly said. "That's the one thing about Lenny that we can't understand." Yet Webster continued to perform well for Kelly and caught Erickson twice with no problems.

Erickson was creating the kind of streak that was reserved for only the game's greatest pitchers. At 23, he was catapulting himself into baseball's highest strata. With a winning streak at double figures and a microscopic earned run average, talk of the All-Star Game was natural. He was already halfway to 20 wins, a goal more difficult to attain in an era when pitchers make no more than 35 starts. Erickson made it look so easy.

"During the first half, he did some pitching, he threw breaking balls on 3–2 counts," Kelly recalled. "But think of it this way. [Boston's Roger] Clemens and [Texas's Nolan] Ryan throw consistently 90 to 91 and they can throw the ball just about anywhere and get away with it. Mix in Scott's movement and he's devastating. How could the hitter have any idea how his pitch will move?"

One at bat in June highlighted Kelly's point. The Twins were in Baltimore and the game was delayed by rain for two hours, after the starters had begun their warm-ups. This was a new experience for Erickson, and one of the most disliked by players. When the game finally began, Erickson received two runs from the offense in the top of the first. Mike Devereaux was the Orioles' leadoff batter and he doubled. Brady Anderson grounded to second with Devereaux advancing to third. Cal Ripken was up next, and he brought to the plate a league-leading .361 average. The Orioles' shortstop had been the league's best hitter in the first two months and, in addition, had always found a way to damage the Twins. Veteran Twins watchers fully expected Ripken to bring home the runner. Erickson knew little about baseball's past, though, and admitted he had not even been a true baseball fan in his youth. He did, however, attend San Francisco Giants games at Candlestick Park where he once met a young outfielder named Chili Davis. Half a continent away, Davis and Erickson now shared a rented house as teammates.

Erickson was facing Baltimore for the first time in 1991, and Ripken quickly received a firsthand look at the talk of the American League. A flurry of sinkers and nasty sliders sent Ripken away after three futile swings. Erickson faced over 800 batters in 1991 but this was one of the handful of at-bats with a meaning beyond one game. The new arrival to baseball's elite met a charter member of that club, and won the first battle. Despite the implications and impact of this at bat, Erickson had already set a standard so high that Kelly had some difficulty remembering it six months later.

The Baltimore game would be Erickson's 11th consecutive win, and Ripken's strikeout kept alive another amazing record. In 31 major league starts, he had not allowed a first-inning earned run. After the agony of watching repeated first-inning deficits for the past two years, Kelly finally saw a pitcher who would give his hitters a chance to score the first run. "We had a lot of spring training meetings about good starts," Kelly recollected. "And Scott was the one pitcher who took tremendous stuff to the mound in the first inning."

In the seemingly never-ending litany of Erickson's achievements before the All-Star break, his record on getaway day was one more. A two-hit shutout of the Yankees on June 24 at Yankee Stadium was his third win in the last game of a road trip. The Twins were on their way to becoming a winning road team and the masterful work of Erickson, particularly in the distracting atmosphere of getaway day, was a primary reason.

As Erickson's streak reached a club-record 12 consecutive wins, few saw the warning signs of its imminent end as clearly as Kelly and Such. It was natural to think all was well, as Erickson beat the Yankees and allowed just three men on base. There was no reason to suspect that the 12–2 pitching record and 1.50 earned run average would disintegrate. That is, nothing other than the knowledge gained only from years of experience that told the manager and pitching coach that the fantasy would indeed have to end.

It happened on June 29 at the Metrodome. The Twins took a 3–2 lead over Chicago into the seventh. Erickson was not dominant, but had pitched well. Two ground ball double plays had helped him, but there were no indications of a big inning. In the seventh inning Chicago exploded. Five of the first six batters reached base and the White Sox finished off against Steve Bedrosian for a five-run inning. "I sat there knowing this could be a big inning, and thinking that I should go get him out because he's done," Kelly admitted. "But I had to give him a chance because of the winning streak. I remember Suchie saying, 'We're going to have to ride this out and let it go!'" It went all right, to the White Sox by an 8–4 score.

Erickson's streak was over, and so was his arm. Kelly first noticed it when Erickson delayed his scheduled turn to throw in the bullpen before his next start in Toronto. "He kept saying, 'I'll go tomorrow' which is a warning sign that you have problems," said Kelly. The trainers and doctors thought he should be on the DL [disabled list] so the best thing to do was to shut him down."

Another easy decision for Kelly proved difficult for the pitcher to accept. Erickson said he wanted to continue pitching through the soreness in his forearm, so he could make his anticipated start in the All-Star Game. For selfish reasons, too, the Twins wanted to display their "homegrown" talent before the large media forum and television audience at the All-Star Game. Showing off Erickson, however, became secondary to his health and the team's welfare. Kelly also knew that if Scott was disabled for 15 days, he would miss just one regular season start. By July 1, Kelly knew the Twins had a chance at contending in the second half, so he could not afford to risk a long-term injury to Erickson. "Young players get their sights set on honors like the All-Star Game," Kelly explained. "But I was thinking about the World Series. It was the big picture that Scott needed to see, that the World Series far outweighs any All-Star Game."

Erickson was notified of the decision on July 2, before the Twins opened a series in Toronto. He told the media at the Skydome and several of his teammates that he wanted to pitch on, but "I don't think his teammates bought it," Kelly contends. "The manager would have to be a dummy to let him go out there. It would be a real disservice to the other players."

Tom Kelly knew he might never again experience the amazingly secure feeling he had watching Erickson pitch the past two months. This fearless pitcher had removed all doubt over the games' outcome, giving a series of performances that he may never duplicate. Erickson had won 12 consecutive games, and there wasn't a "cheap" win in the bunch. No 9–7 slugfests, or five-innings-and-fly performances polluted this streak. Only twice in the 12 wins did Erickson allow as many as three runs. In six of the wins, he held the opposition scoreless. He would come as close as any one player could to being credited with turning around a season. The Twins were 2–9 when his streak began, and in first place with a two-game lead when it ended. For two months, Erickson had been a virtuoso. As Andy MacPhail said in June, "If there was a league higher than the majors, he'd be pitching there now."

# THE STREAK

*"We didn't want to be like an NBA team that falls behind by 20 points but rallies to tie the game somewhere in the second half. . . . We couldn't be in that situation. We had to get to .500 and keep going."*
***Tom Kelly***

For 16 days in June, the Minnesota Twins achieved baseball perfection. Perfection is a term rarely applied in a game where success is a by-product of the acceptance of failure. Baseball's best hitters reach their goal only three times in every 10 at-bats, while the premier starters strive to win one-half of their assignments. (Jack Morris had 162 wins in the 1980s, more than any pitcher, but won only 48.8 percent of his starts.) Players learn to handle failure quickly, usually in the lowest levels of the minor leagues, so that upon their arrival in the majors a protective shell envelops their egos from hitless streaks and ineffective starts. Tom Kelly knew that players must shrug off the bad days in order to have good days. This explained his wariness towards Shane Mack, a player who cared so much and tried so hard that a couple of difficult at-bats could send him into a prolonged downward spiral. Baseball demands of its players an inner strength that can always turn one's focus to the next at bat, next inning, or next game.

What applied to individuals can also be employed by teams.

No degree of optimism can override the reality that every manager brings to Opening Day—that his team will lose at least 60 games. This guarantees at least 60 nights of fitful sleep and endless rehashing of plays and moves, the primary cause of the premature aging suffered by most managers. A 162-game season is so mentally fatiguing that all but the best teams use .500 as their goal, and take justifiable pride in anything that surpasses that mark. One of Kelly's lasting memories of 1989 was a base-running mistake by rookie Chip Hale in the season's last game. The blunder squelched a rally and the Twins proceeded to lose. A win would have given the Twins an 81–81 record and offered Kelly some solace during a tumultuous season in which MacPhail acknowledged he had done a superior job of managing.

The Twins began June with the primary goal of reaching .500. Kelly was not pleased because he had entered May with the very same objective, but the Twins rode a series of streaks to a 14–14 record for the month. Seven wins in nine games had lifted them to a 17–15 record on May 14, but they followed that stretch by losing seven out of eight to fall to 20–24 on May 27. Kelly was concerned that the effort exerted to rally from the 2–9 start was being wasted. "We didn't want to be like an NBA team that falls behind by 20 points but rallies to tie the game somewhere in the second half," he said. "You see this all the time in NBA games. By the time the trailing team has tied it, they are so exhausted from the comeback that they fall back and lose. We couldn't be in that situation. We had to get to .500 and keep going."

Kelly believed the Twins' pitching would have to carry the team over the hurdle of .500. What he saw in the final days of May gave him hope. Erickson's streak-breaking win over Texas on May 28 was followed the next night by a Morris gem. Nolan Ryan opposed Morris and his presence guaranteed extra fans and a unique feeling of electricity at Arlington Stadium. Ryan had been disabled just after pitching his seventh career no-hitter in late April, and this was to be his return. At 44 years of age, Ryan sparked emotions like no other player could. Many fans marvelled at Ryan's ability to simply walk to the mound and pitch, while sharper baseball observers were awed by his mastery of hitters 20 years his junior. Ryan's injury, though, cost him the sharp-breaking curveball that had bolstered his repertoire in recent years, and Greg Gagne was able to hit a rolling curve for a three-run home run in the second inning. From there Morris took charge. The man his teammates called "fossil" relished the matchup with the legendary Ryan, and on this night Morris pitched with the spunk of a teenager. He finished with a four-hitter and eight strikeouts.

With Erickson and Morris kicking their pitching into a higher gear, Kelly knew June could be a month to make a move. Mark Guthrie beat Kansas City on May 30 for his fourth win of the month, and despite a 2–6 record that was directly attributable to a lack of run support, Kevin Tapani had pitched well. As it had in early May, the starting staff commanded increasing respect from the players and manager. Straight ahead was a stretch of games against struggling Eastern Division teams.

This season had already brought its share of wild fluctuations in several teams' play. Texas had a 14-game winning streak, but followed with losses in 11 of their next 12 games. Oakland's five-game losing streak came immediately after seven consecutive wins. Seattle was affected the worst, with separate losing streaks of five, six and seven games. Kelly's team had already experienced too many rides on the roller coaster. He hoped the pitching would hit one good streak that would propel the Twins into contention and, more importantly, keep them there.

On June 1 the Twins stood in fifth place at 23–25, trailing Texas by five-and-one-half games. Over the next 16 days, the Twins won 15 games without a loss, only the 12th streak of that length in American League history. The team shot from fifth place to first, a position they would relinquish for only four days over the remainder of the season.

For a manager who thrives on involving everyone on his roster, and who glowed when reserves or rookies contributed to winning, these 15 games represented a state of euphoria. Tom Kelly saw seven different pitchers win during The Streak. Six different players amassed 15 home runs, an average of one per game, signaling a power resurgence credited largely to Terry Crowley. Five rookies, only one a starter, played significant roles in at least one win of the streak. Sixteen days in June legitimized everything that Kelly had worked for in the spring and what every person in a Twins' uniform believed could happen. As the events of early June unfolded, there were undeniable signs that the Twins could indeed contend for a division championship.

### JUNE 1 AT KANSAS CITY: TWINS 8 ROYALS 4

Allan Anderson had not won since the season's second game in Oakland. "In his first seven starts, Andy pitched well in five," Kelly remembered. "But then he hit a point where he couldn't make a pitch to get a hitter out." Anderson was failing where Scott Erickson was succeeding, in getting the out needed to stay in the lead or even just in the game. In fairness, Anderson went unrewarded for several strong starts during the time when runs were scarce.

Chili Davis changed Anderson's luck in Kansas City, with his first two-home-run game as a Twin. Victimizing right-hander Kevin Appier, Davis launched a towering fly ball blast to right in the sixth inning breaking a 3–3 tie. The two home runs gave Davis a season total of 11 in 49 games, just one shy of his 1990 total with California. Davis came to Florida with a new body honed through many winter hours of diligence, had been the spring's best hitter, and was proving when the games counted that none of it was a fluke. He was an anomaly to the Twins, batting with an extreme patience not seen in any other Twins' batter. Davis took pitches agonizingly close to the strike zone, and occasionally judged strikes, with the purpose of forcing the pitcher to work to Davis's strengths. Davis would strike out more often on called third strikes than any Twin, but this approach paid off with a team-leading number of walks and numerous hits on favorable pitches coaxed by his patience. The search for additional power had unearthed a gem in Davis. With one-third of the season yet to be completed, he had a .301 batting average with 11 home runs and 32 runs batted in.

Anderson lasted until one out into the seventh when he surrendered a home run to light-hitting second baseman Terry Shumpert. Although he won this game, Kelly's tolerance was waning towards Anderson's pattern of "being hell-bent on getting the ball inside."

JUNE 2 AT KANSAS CITY: TWINS 4 ROYALS 1

With Scott Erickson pitching, Kelly tried a "getaway day" special lineup. Greg Gagne was the leadoff hitter with Pedro Munoz in left field and Gene Larkin in right field. Gagne was enjoying one of the best stretches of his career at the plate, and his three hits in this game lifted his average to .319. "Crow [Terry Crowley] had him going great at the plate," Kelly remembered. "He was playing his great defense and doing something good with the bat. The key was keeping him from one of his bad streaks that seemed to happen every year."

Tom Gordon started for Kansas City and the Twins felt they had a reading on his pitching tendencies. "Once you get a man on base, he loses velocity on his fastball," Kelly said. "This helps the hitters plus it helps you steal bases when he throws more of his curve." Stolen bases did not lead to any runs, but the long ball did. Puckett in the third inning and Lenny Webster in the fourth inning hit solo home runs. Replacing the injured Junior Ortiz on the roster meant Webster would serve as the catcher for Erickson's starts. "Lenny did a great job catching, proving that it wasn't the catcher that made Erickson during his streak. We liked Junior working with Scott, but I know Harper could catch him as well," Kelly said. Webster walked twice in addition to his home run, and his first game of the year continued his personal history of hitting better at the major league level.

Erickson was so dominant that many runs were not required. Only six Royals reached base in eight-and-one-third innings, three hits coming from an original "young Twin," Jim Eisenreich. George Brett had been disabled but was hitting well since his return, until he met the man who had become the bane of American League batters. Brett's day at the plate consisted of two strikeouts and a pair of harmless infield rollers. Erickson's eighth consecutive win moved the Twins to .500 at 25–25.

JUNE 3 METRODOME: TWINS 3   ORIOLES 2

A 20-game stretch was beginning for the Twins against the teams with the three worst records in the American League, Baltimore, New York, and Cleveland. The 1991 schedule would present no better opportunity for the Twins to demonstrate their capacity to rise in their division.

This game belonged to Jack Morris. In his third strong start in succession, Morris pitched eight innings allowing just two runs. With Morris and Erickson pitching in tandem, one of Kelly's prerequisites for a streak was in place. "You need to have your starters pitch two good games in a row," he explained. "If that happens for each guy, then you have a chance to win eight or 10 in a row. Somewhere you'll have to win a 1–0 or 2–1 game, and one day your starter will struggle and the long reliever will have to pick him up. There are so many things that need to go right, but it begins with the starters backing up each other."

The nadir of Morris' season had occurred on May 19 with his return to Tiger Stadium. The outing was marred by boos from the fans, many of whom Morris reminded later had cheered his efforts for years, and seven first-inning runs by the Tigers. Since then, he had reeled off three consecutive winning efforts of at least eight innings, and the Twins had now won six of their last seven games.

Kent Hrbek was the offensive force with a solo home run and a run-scoring double. Fifty games had seen Hrbek drive in 20 runs, a number just three more than the team's ninth-place hitter, Gagne. His production in this game pleased Kelly, for the manager knew that Hrbek's golf tournament was to be held in three days. The annual affair raised funds to combat amyotrophic lateral sclerosis (ALS), the disease that took Hrbek's father prematurely. For Kent, this was a "hands-on" affair and he was involved in virtually every aspect of the event. "Herbie has a history of not doing much right before his tournament," Kelly recalled. "He worries about it, so this year, I talked to him and he admitted the golf gets to him. So he went out an did something about it." The night after his ejection in Texas, Hrbek started a hitting streak that lasted 13 games and produced a .408 average.

JUNE 4 METRODOME: TWINS 4 ORIOLES 3

This 10-inning win saw the Twins face a premier closer in Gregg Olson while their own finisher, Rick Aguilera, did not pitch. Aguilera had saved the previous two games and Kelly, remembering the lessons of 1990, would not use his closer on three successive days at any time in 1991. After Mark Guthrie was knocked out of the game in the sixth inning, three Twins relievers combined to shut out Baltimore for four-and-two-third innings. "This game pleased me because I need everybody to contribute for the team to succeed," Kelly maintained. "The bullpen is an example. If one guy falls, the others can get beat up and everybody suffers. Aguilera could come into this game, but what about tomorrow's game or his availability for the rest of the season? Everybody in the bullpen has to be able to pitch."

Terry Leach recorded five outs, Steve Bedrosian pitched two scoreless innings, but Cal Ripken opened the 10th inning with a double. After a walk to Randy Milligan, Kelly tested his theory by calling on Carl Willis to relieve Bedrosian. Kelly had begun to use Willis in important situations after 10 appearances. The 29-year-old journeyman, whose career had teetered on the brink of extinction six months earlier, responded to the challenge. He retired Dwight Evans on a fly ball to left field and coaxed a double play ground ball from pinch hitter Sam Horn.The outs were as important as any Willis had recorded in 73 major league appearances.

"Jim Rantz gets all the credit for finding Willis," Kelly acknowledged. "Over the winter, he tossed me a sheet and said we were inviting this guy to camp. All Rantz said about him was 'He'll take the ball.' I looked at the sheet, saw the numbers [6.39 earned run average at Colorado Springs in 1990], and realized that's all you could say."

Willis was among Kelly's final spring training cuts from the pitching staff. He left Kelly, though, with an impression of "throwing it over the plate," a key for any pitcher hoping to become a Twin. Three games in Portland and the decision to disable David West following his bout of elbow tenderness were all that Willis needed to return to the majors for the first time since 1988. At first striking an unassuming position in the clubhouse, Willis soon became a contributor to the banter between pitchers that formed a large part of their unique bond.

The relationship between hitters and pitchers on the Twins was no different than that of any other ballclub. Every team strives to minimize the separation, but like the offensive and defensive squads of a football team, the contrasting responsibilities and work schedules of the two groups create an atmosphere where pitchers tend to congregate together both on and off the field. They shared their own humor about the game, and Willis often chimed in on these conversations. So often, in fact, that he was soon nicknamed "Train" in reference to the amount of time he spent "tooting his own whistle" about his past. No player enjoyed needling Willis more than Kevin Tapani, another quiet character but the possessor of a rapierlike wit. With Willis in earshot, Tapani loved to announce that his own definition of a "quality start" was any game in which Willis did not pitch. In early June, Willis was still an unknown entity to most Twins fans. Before much longer, Kelly would give him the chance to make a contribution as important as any to the season.

Randy Bush moved into the on-deck circle with two outs in the bottom of the 10th, hoping Hrbek would keep the inning alive. Bush had just one at bat in the last 11 games, and for someone whose pride was in his hitting, entered this game with just nine hits for the season. Willis had kept the Twins alive and now the Twins faced Olson with a chance to win. Puckett and Davis were retired on infield outs to start the inning, then Harper singled to left field.

Now Hrbek dug in, hoping to continue his resurgence at the plate. In the unique world of baseball, Kelly judged Hrbek as having a "hell of an at bat" by drawing a walk from Olson. With Shane Mack scheduled to bat, Kelly called on Bush. "This move was made with a dual purpose," Kelly explained. "Shane wasn't swinging well enough [1 for 4 in the game, .247 for the season] to warrant the at bat and it was Bush's time to bat."

The last part of Kelly's statement spoke volumes about his managerial philosophy. Every player had a role and Kelly would often flount conventional wisdom to use a player when it is his planned turn to play. Mack was a starter who was fighting his way back into the lineup, and his removal meant the loss of the team's best outfielder in an extra-inning game. But Kelly saw a chance to win with one swing, and Bush was on the team to take those swings against right-handed pitchers. "If I don't put him in there, he wonders what's the deal here, and that's when problems start on a team," said Kelly. "The other players see that and they wonder what the manager is doing."

Despite Bush's low number of hits, Kelly felt comfortable sending Bush to face Olson. The manager who prides himself on never "putting someone in a situation where they can't succeed" had given Bush "enough at-bats for a foundation. I was taught by Joe Altobelli at Rochester in 1976 to give everyone a chance to play in the first 40 games without falling 20 games back. If everyone has a foundation, then you have a chance for them to help you later." Kelly had taken care to get Bush 52 at-bats in the first two months. But the impatience was growing from all fronts, including the manager's office, for production.

Olson threw a curveball that hung on the inside part of the plate and Bush, although he was jammed, dropped a soft line drive in front of right fielder Evans to score the winning run. The heroes were Bush, Willis, Bedrosian, and Leach, all veterans chafing for the opportunity to prove themselves capable. The Twins beat Olson without using Aguilera. As in no other game during The Streak, Kelly managed true to his beliefs, without panic. He enjoyed the kind of victory that he knew his team had not often captured in recent years.

## JUNE 5 METRODOME: TWINS 4 ORIOLES 3

Kevin Tapani lost all six of his starts in May. The pitcher that started the season with a shutout in the home opener had fallen prey to a blizzard of hits, too few of which came from his own teammates. Tapani had a 5.35 earned run average for the month, but the Twins scored only six runs while he pitched in his six games. "We hadn't been scoring for Tap, so it was a good day to change the lineup," Kelly remembered. Knoblauch had made five outs on fly balls the previous night, so Al Newman started at second. Lenny Webster, catching his second game since returning from Portland, continued to write a mystery story that befuddled Kelly by homering for two runs in the fifth. "We haven't figured out why he hits so much better at the major league level," Kelly mused. "It's mind-boggling." This was certainly a painless problem for a manager to have. In Webster's starts, he homered twice and the pitchers did well. Tapani worked into the eighth holding Baltimore to one run and six hits before Aguilera relieved with two outs. The Twins' closer was rarely used before the ninth, but having held Aguilera out the day before and knowing a day off was ahead, Kelly felt this move was safe.

With the Twins leading 4–1, Aguilera ended the eighth retiring Joe Orsulak on a ground ball and struck out Sam Horn to start the ninth. But two hitters who would inflict pain on the Twins all season, Randy Milligan and David Segui, homered. Segui's home run was his first in the major leagues, and it bothered Kelly. "We didn't school Lenny well enough," said Kelly. "Segui is a high-ball hitter and Aggie threw the pitch high. That's our fault." Aguilera recovered to strike out Chris Hoiles and Ernie Whitt to close out a 4–3 victory, Tapani's first since April 27. In 12 days, the Twins would have another meeting with Segui and Milligan.

JUNE 7 METRODOME: TWINS 2 INDIANS 0

The lineup card carried the night's first surprise as Dan Gladden batted ninth. He had rebounded from his 1–31 start but had stalled at the .240 mark over the past 10 days. "That move gets a player's attention because he is embarrassed. As a manager, you want the player to get mad. If he doesn't like it, too bad. My job is to do what's necessary to get the best production," Kelly maintained. But Cleveland starter Tom Candiotti would not allow a jump start by Gladden or any other Twins batter. A practitioner of the knuckleball, one of baseball's dying arts, Candiotti's pitch had danced and fluttered through the first third of the season leaving frustrated hitters tied in knots. When his knuckleball was moving well, it was exceedingly tough on a team of hitters as aggressive as the Twins. Domed stadiums with their stillness were the perfect stage for a knuckleball pitcher, although Candiotti would accurately be described as a pitcher who throws a knuckler in tandem with a good curve.

Candiotti's knuckleball proved superb, and the Twins could manage just five hits. One was a Davis home run in the second inning, while another run scored in the eighth on a wild pitch. Candiotti, however, had the misfortune of pitching for a team that had no offense. Cleveland's cleanup hitter and designated hitter was Luis Medina, just recalled from the minors to replace the troubled Albert Belle. The Indians had sent Belle to triple-A after he failed to run out a ground ball, the last in a series of incidents that created an untenable clubhouse situation.

The impotence of the Indians' lineup was a welcome sight for Allan Anderson, who pitched eight shutout innings to win his second straight game. His line looked better on paper as the Indians had nine fly ball outs, several that were blasts to the warning track. Anderson's tensest moment came in the eighth when Joel Skinner led off with a double. Speedster Alex Cole pinch-ran representing the tying run, but stayed rooted as Felix Fermin lined a sacrifice bunt attempt to Hrbek. "Once the bunt didn't work, they had to try and steal third," Kelly remembered. Kelly disagreed with the current baseball wisdom, created largely by the success of Rickey Henderson, that it is easier to steal third base. "But Cole is probably a better second base stealer than third base. You need a special talent to pick up the signs from second and catch a breaking ball to run on." Indeed, Cole picked the wrong pitch and was caught at third by a strong throw from Harper.

Cleveland made no threat in the ninth and the win was the sixth straight for the Twins. Anderson's performance was encouraging as the second trip through the rotation had now been completed with everyone pitching well. The Twins were winning the 3–2, 4–3, and 2–1 games, the tight games that must be won to compile a streak.

JUNE 8 METRODOME: TWINS 2 INDIANS 1

Another classic Erickson performance also featured an effort from Cleveland right-hander Charles Nagy that impressed Kelly. "He can pitch. In fact we like him better than Candiotti or [Greg] Swindell," Kelly said. "We had 11 runners and only two scored. That showed me he could make the big pitches."

The Twins could not get two hits in one inning aginst Nagy until the sixth when Davis doubled home Puckett who had singled. Another omen for this season occurred quietly in the seventh when veteran Jesse Orosco was brought in to face Hrbek. It was June and his bat was awakening, so there was no sign of a pinch hitter. Hrbek delivered a run-scoring single. The managerial moves of April that had caught so many by surprise had begun to pay off in June. In Kelly's parlance, he had grabbed Hrbek's attention, and during this streak he would see results.

A manager who paid no heed to "complete" games, Kelly found himself hoping Erickson could finish as he took a 2–0 lead into the ninth. "Aggie had pitched an inning last night and we had a day game next," Kelly reasoned, keeping in mind his decision to not use Aguilera in three straight games. It seemed a moot point as Erickson easily retired the first two batters. He should have had the final out as Chris James beat a sinking fastball into the ground. Instead of hitting the dirt, this ball went straight down and bounced off home plate so high that no play was possible. The infield hit was followed by two solid singles and Kelly's hand was forced. Cleveland had the tying run at second and the batter, Cole, had three hits off Erickson. Kelly "had to change" to Aguilera who promptly issued a walk to Cole.

Aguilera's career had been characterized by impeccable control, one of the traits that made him such an appealing choice to replace Jeff Reardon. His performance in May was marred by a spasm of wildness, as in one six-inning span he walked seven batters. That problem had seemingly passed, but this walk left him no margin for error as the bases were loaded. Mark Lewis, a rookie second baseman tutored all spring by Hall-of-Famer Rod Carew, was hitting .327 and hit a line drive to right field which, with the good fortune that comes during a winning streak, flew directly into Shane Mack's glove for the final out.

JUNE 9 METRODOME: TWINS 9 INDIANS 2

Aguilera was not needed as the eighth win of The Streak was the first "blowout." Mack struck the decisive blow, a three-run home run in the seventh inning. His return to the lineup was gradual as Kelly sorted out the excess of outfielders, but his production was improving as his average climbed over .250 with two hits in four at-bats. Mack would accumulate more at-bats in June than his combined total for April and May.

Morris breezed through eight harmless innings and Kelly noted, "The competition between Jack and Scott [Erickson] was at a good level. You could see it develop as each strung together three good starts." His fourth consecutive win lifted the Twins into third place, their highest standing to date.

JUNE 10 METRODOME: TWINS 8 INDIANS 5

A new hero arrived in the person of Paul Abbott. He had been something of an enigma to the Twins. Raves came from the baseball department about his "stuff," which some said was the best of the minor league pitchers. MacPhail had predicted at the start of the season that Abbott would be the first pitcher recalled from Portland when most had conceded that distinction to more heralded pitchers Willie Banks and Denny Neagle.

His recall came in late May after Larry Casian failed short relief, and it could safely be said there was no accompanying fanfare. In 1990, Abbott had been a victim of the tension that permeated a team during bad times. He joined the Twins in late August, the time when Kelly acknowledged the players were "gone." His resume showed a 5–14 record at Portland with control problems that were evident in his major league debut at Kansas City, a performance that moved even Gladden to question the front office's motives. Abbott did not appear ready to be a major league starter, so Kelly and Such slotted him in long relief upon his recall. Such is a firm believer in placing rookie pitchers in the long relief role, allowing them to ease into pressure situations. He cites Chuck Finley as the perfect example. As a rookie he rarely pitched with a lead, but within three years had become a premier starter. In closer proximity, there was Morris whose rookie year with Detroit was primarily as a long reliever.

"Suchie thinks Abbott can eventually be a good starter, but he just looks right in the bullpen," Kelly said. "He may be one of those pitchers who works better when he doesn't know he is going to pitch." That had not been a problem for Abbott who had not worked in two-and-one-half weeks.

Mark Guthrie started this game and was dealt a technical knockout at the end of the second inning when Cleveland took a 4–1 lead. Remarkably, it was the first time in the month of June, a span of 74 innings, that the Twins had trailed at the completion of an inning. The time was right for Kelly to call on Abbott. He pitched four scoreless innings, and in total disdain of his 17 days of inactivity, walked no one. While he slowed the Indians, Abbott's teammates roughed up Cleveland's Eric King for six runs.

The game's most important hit came in the fifth inning. Mike Pagliarulo came to the plate with the bases loaded, one out, and a 4–3 Cleveland lead. He also brought an unsightly statistic with him, just seven runs batted in with more than one-third of the season played. Pagliarulo had watched Scott Leius start the day before against a right-hander, Kelly's first departure from his strict platoon at the position. Kelly says he started Leius "because he hadn't played in awhile," but what was unsaid was Kelly's attempt to "get someone's attention," in this case Pagliarulo's. Kelly did feel that "there was a lot of pressure on Pags. He knew there were expectations in taking Gaetti's place."

The Twins were in a stretch where players resembled shoppers waiting for service at the local bakery, each holding a number waiting for it to be called. Pagliarulo's number came up in the fifth, and he lined a double off the canvas in right-center field to score three runs. "There may have been a little extra excitement there because that was Mike's first big hit as a Twin," Kelly admitted. "He worked so hard that everyone would have accepted him even as a .200 hitter. But you want your third baseman to produce some runs, and although they were playing good defense, neither Pags or Leius were knocking the cover off the ball."

A four-game sweep of the Indians was complete and the events of those ten days in June were dizzying. There were nine consecutive wins, 17 runs in the last two days, and good starting pitching. Most significantly to Kelly, Abbott and Pagliarulo delivered one win, Willis and Bush another. With Webster here, Mack there, everyone had contributed, not just the big names. "It was a fun time because everybody was playing," Kelly remembered. "But I don't ever remember things getting out of whack. I had no special meetings. It was only June, and everyone knew there was a game tomorrow."

JUNE 11 METRODOME: TWINS 5 YANKEES 3

For the first time, the end of The Streak loomed near. Scott Sanderson, a veteran pitcher whose career had been resurrected by a year with Oakland and been rewarded with a multi-million dollar contract from the Yankees, was responsible. With the help of three double plays, he took a 3–1 lead into the bottom of the eighth inning, a bizarre inning that neatly forecast the fates of the teams.

Pagliarulo opened the Twins' eighth with a single and Randy Bush was announced as a pinch hitter. The move brought manager Stump Merrill from the Yankee dugout. After a brief conference on the mound, lefty Steve Howe was called into the game. Sanderson had shown no signs of tiring. In the seventh, he had retired the side on three ground balls, so Merrill's move stunned everyone. Kelly, first and foremost a manager who shares with his brethren a natural sensitivity against second guessing, refused to join the chorus. "We don't know what happened in the other dugout. He [Sanderson] may have said he was tiring. For us, it was just thanks that he was out of the game."

So was Bush out of the game, as Mack was inserted to face Howe. He hit a hard low line drive to the left of second baseman Steve Sax, a ball that appeared playable and a certain double play. But Sax inexplicably broke towards the bag for one step and then "he got tangled up," remembered Kelly. "Sax doesn't have the greatest range on turf." The ball went untouched into right-center field for a single.

Right-hander John Habyan was next for the Yankees, and Gladden greeted him with a bunt single to load the bases. Knoblauch then walked to force in a run, cutting New York's lead to 3–2. Habyan recovered, and keeping his pitches outside, struck out Puckett.

Now it was left-hander Greg Cadaret's turn and his mission was to retire Hrbek. A fourth-inning single had extended his hitting streak to 13 games, and his average was up 30 points since The Streak had begun. For the second time in four days, Hrbek won the battle he was not allowed to fight in April, this time with a well-placed bouncer that eluded first baseman Don Mattingly and Sax for a two-run single. After the fifth pitcher of the inning, Steve Farr, walked Gene Larkin to force home another run, the Twins handed Aguilera a 5–3 lead.

Before The Streak could reach double figures, Hrbek had to complete what Kelly regards as baseball's most important cycle by stealing a hit from Mattingly with a diving stop. In one inning, Hrbek had impacted the game with both a clutch base hit and a sterling defensive play, no surprise to Kelly who maintains that the two occurrences are often related, one feeding off the other.

Although Merrill had succeeded in the past by managing with "the bullpen by committee" approach, during this stretch the Twins foiled many previously successful strategies. "When things are going well," Kelly said, "a manager can try a lot of things, and if something doesn't work, the team covers it up and you get away with it. When you're losing, many managers go by the book because they are getting ripped by the media. I just kept trying to do what I thought was right so I could sleep at night. But when you've won 10 in a row, you feel you can get away with anything."

JUNE 12 METRODOME: TWINS 6 YANKEES 3

Pedro Munoz can "flat out hit," said Kelly, the greatest compliment any baseball person can pay to a hitter. Munoz had demonstrated that to the Twins the previous September, and had handled his spring training demotion the way Kelly liked by hitting over .400 in his first month at Portland. Munoz forced the Twins to recall him in mid-May despite there being no real place for him to receive regular playing time.

Kelly spotted Munoz with an emphasis on starting him against left-handed pitchers. Jeff Johnson, a rookie making his second major league start, was the Yankees' choice. Munoz made a first-inning mark with a grand slam home run to center field.

Although the Twins added only one run to the five scored in the first inning, Allan Anderson pitched well enough to win his third straight game. Bedrosian had "his turn to pitch" after Aguilera had saved the last two games. He recorded the last four outs, including a strikeout of Matt Nokes with two runners on in the eighth inning.

JUNE 13 METRODOME: TWINS 10 NEW YORK 3

It hurt to watch Mike Witt pitch, possibly more than it hurt Witt to pitch. Witt had rehabilitated an injured elbow, and made his first start, but would last just four batters. "He shouldn't have been out there," Kelly maintained. "I guess they had to try because he had thrown well on the side, but when he went out to the mound, he was hurting. It's part of the luck that you have during a streak, to catch a guy who's not 100 percent." Before reliever Chuck Cary could end the inning, four runs had scored. With Erickson pitching, even the Erickson who on this night appeared mortal, there was little mystery as to the outcome.

The middle of the Twins' lineup was sizzling. Puckett and Hrbek each had two run-scoring hits and Davis had his second two-home-run game. "Teams still hadn't caught on to Chili," Kelly claimed. "He was such a tough out that the middle of our lineup was hard on pitchers."

The home stand ended at 10–0 and Kelly thought of his first speech of the spring. "We wanted our home field back. That took care of it."

JUNE 14 AT CLEVELAND: TWINS 7 INDIANS 0
JUNE 15 AT CLEVELAND: TWINS 11 INDIANS 7

Wins 13 and 14 saw Cleveland send out starters who were overmatched. The Twins caught the Indians at the number four and five spots in their starting rotation, a black hole for most of Cleveland's season. Right-hander Jeff Shaw started Friday's opener and survived one trip through the batting order before succumbing to a Hrbek home run in the third. Mack greeted reliever Rod Nichols with a grand slam in the first to break open the game, and Morris had an easy seven innings for his fifth straight win.

Kelly made one of those moves that "you can get away with during a winning streak" by resting Davis on Friday. It was just the second game this season that Davis had not started, but Kelly felt

Bush "needed at-bats and had always hit well in Cleveland." Not even the lure of a record winning streak could keep Kelly from "doing what he thought was right."

Jeff Mutis, a left-hander recalled from double-A, made his first major league start for Cleveland on Saturday. His first inning was a revelation as Puckett and Davis hit pitches that "had always been good for him. He thought they were good, and up here, they got ripped. You can see him saying 'What do I do now?'" It seemed to border on cruelty to send a youngster out for his first game against a team with 13 straight wins and a lineup as imposing as any in the American League. Mutis was hit for seven runs in less than three innings, but the Twins needed the offense.

Guthrie had another miserable start, failing to finish the second inning. "What happened to Mark wasn't all his fault," Kelly admitted. "We had to bounce him around since the start of spring training. By this time, he had no curveball, and couldn't hit spots with his pitches like he normally can." The rescue ranger was once again Paul Abbott. His control was shakier but his stuff was overpowering. In six-and-one-third innings, he allowed one run on three hits. Not only did he shut down Cleveland, but he gave the Twins six at-bats against shaky middle relief and the hitters scored enough for a comfortable win.

## JUNE 16 AT CLEVELAND: TWINS 4 INDIANS 2

Prevailing wisdom held that a shutout would be necessary to stop The Streak. Greg Swindell seemed to be a perfect candidate for the role, with a 2.21 earned run average. Matched against Kevin Tapani, the game showcased two of the best control pitchers in baseball and both were sharp.

An error by Puckett gave Cleveland a run in the fourth, but Puckett came back to homer in the sixth to tie the game. Gene Larkin led off the seventh with a double, his third hit off Swindell. The Indians' lefty was on the verge of stranding Larkin when Al

Newman slapped a two-out single to give the Twins a 2–1 lead. It was Newman's first big hit of 1991, the unexpected hit needed to lift a team that had been a more common occurrence for Newman in past years.

Aguilera had not pitched in five days, so Kelly brought him in to start the eighth. Tapani and Aguilera were close, so the pain of a blown save was even sharper for Aguilera when he allowed the tying run. He stayed on, though, as the game moved to extra innings. In the 10th, the five-foot nine-inch Newman adopted his Eddie Gaedel stance, and coaxed a one-out walk from Shawn Hilegas. Puckett singled him to third and Davis hit a fly ball deep enough to left field to score Newman. Harper singled in another run and Aguilera completed his third inning to earn the win that the team craves but the closer despises.

The Streak was at 15 and the Twins were in first place less than 60 days after a 2–9 start. The detractors claimed the accomplishment was achieved against the league's weakest teams. The Twins paid little mind to that shallow view, and MacPhail offered the best perspective. "If a major league team went to triple-A and won 15 straight, it would be outstanding." After all, the Twins had just finished a stretch that represented almost one-tenth of the season without a single loss.

Kelly tried to douse the fires lit by talk of first place. "It's much too early to get wrapped up in standings." He had trouble with the increased attention brought about by The Streak. It hit the Twins in the solar plexus when they arrived at Baltimore's Memorial Stadium on June 17. Their clubhouse was filled with microphones, cameras, and notepads in numbers that might seem normal to the Mets or Yankees. To the Twins, it seemed as if they had just been discovered. The normally unflappable Kelly was shaken. "There seemed to be a lot more pressure once we got to Baltimore. I felt it and usually I'm pretty good about it."

Kelly has little recollection of anything that occurred before the ninth inning of the game against Baltimore. A 3–3 tie was broken in the seventh when Hrbek delivered another run-scoring hit off a left-handed reliever. This time veteran Mike Flanagan was the victim. Newman drove in a run in the eighth and the Twins' defense excelled in protecting the lead. Munoz threw out Mike Devereaux at the plate in the seventh and Hrbek started a 3–6–3 double play to end the eighth.

Aguilera had pitched three innings Sunday but Kelly had no qualms in asking him for one inning with a two-run lead. David Segui was the first batter and rekindled memories of his Metrodome home run with a sharp single to center field. "We just didn't pitch well to Segui," Kelly admitted. Brady Anderson singled and Devereaux sacrificed. Joe Orsulak hit a sacrifice fly, leaving the Twins one out from a 16th straight win.

Kelly was faced with a decision that, in his mind, was a no-brainer. Cal Ripken would not get the chance to tie or win the game. He was intentionally walked as Kelly defied a rule from the "book" that managers hear about but never see by putting the winning run on base. "All our reports said don't let Ripken beat us," Kelly said.

The man who did beat the Twins was Randy Milligan, but he needed a mistake from Aguilera. "Aggie got two strikes on him and the second was a high fastball away from him," Kelly recalled. "Junior [Ortiz] set the target out there again, but the pitch came right down the middle." The ball was quickly sent on a high arc to the left-center-field fence on one bounce. As Ripken crossed home plate with the winning run, the stadium erupted in a wild frenzy. Milligan pirouetted in front of the Orioles dugout with both arms thrust in the air. "The way they were jumping, you would have thought they won the World Series. It showed that beating the Twins was special," Kelly said proudly. Even in the moment of a painful loss, the Twins had found a new measure of respect. It was that kind of year.

Kelly's first concern was for his pitcher. "We grabbed Aggie quick and made sure he was all right," Kelly said. "The attention on our streak made this game hurt a little more than usual. So you have to guard your closer." Once he had consoled Aguilera, Kelly talked to his team. "I emphasized The Streak was a great accomplishment. This had been just one game and was nothing to be ashamed of."

Time hasn't dulled Kelly's sharp sense of how he felt towards that game. "I don't like to lose, but I was actually glad it was over. There was so much extra pressure created by the big number." Kelly has always appeared so impervious to external pressures that this admission would once have seemed unthinkable.

The Twins had won 18 of their last 19 games, and were positioned to contend if they could avoid the pitfalls that snared Texas and Seattle. Both teams had suffered long losing streaks following their winning streaks. Their gains had been reversed by a ride on the roller coaster. Another streak was unrealistic, but good baseball was what Kelly wanted to maintain. Before leaving Baltimore, the Twins would play two games that reassured Kelly.

The night after The Streak ended, old acquaintances were renewed with Roy Smith. He had pitched his way back to the majors and won his first three Baltimore starts. Unfortunately for him, he ran into Erickson and a hot lineup that Kelly felt was prepared. "They had a good idea Roy would keep the ball outside. We were ready, and in Roy's defense, it's tough pitching against your former team." The carnage was seven Twins runs and 11 hits in five-and-two-thirds innings. Erickson was lifted after six scoreless innings, so Kelly could get Carl Willis into the game. "His family was there, and in those cases I always try to get players in the game," Kelly explained. "Family is with you all the time through the struggles early in your career. So it's important they see you play when they make a trip."

The Baltimore series ended on a Wednesday afternoon when

the Orioles "turned back the clock" in a promotion commemorating their 1966 World Championship season. The historical theme of this day could also have applied to the Twins as they played one of Kelly's most memorable games.

It began in the first inning with Orioles starter Jeff Robinson throwing a pitch behind Shane Mack and then hitting Puckett, the next batter, on the hip. "I still don't know why that happened," Kelly said. "They may have been mad about a hard slide Mack put on Billy Ripken earlier in the series. But they were angry about something, because Robinson threw the ball right at our batters."

Now Puckett was mad. After being hit, he pointed, glared, and shouted at Robinson. It was a rare display of anger from the congenial Puckett who plays the game with a perpetual smile, and it fueled the next two hitters. Hrbek singled and Davis crushed a three-run home run, a major "in your face" blow to Robinson. The 3–0 lead was all the Twins would get against Robinson.

Baltimore scored twice in the second inning and again in the seventh, and gave Gregg Olson a 4–3 lead in the ninth when the game entered a twilight zone.

Brian Harper opened with a sharp single to center, part of an amazing run of success Harper had enjoyed against Olson, with four hits in six career at-bats against the Oriole closer. Pinch-hitter Gene Larkin followed with a line drive single between first and second base and Pagliarulo tied the game with a solid single to right field. Kelly was stunned. "Three guys in a row smoked the ball off Olson. I'm sitting there thinking this isn't supposed to happen. We had three quality at-bats to start and that might have shocked him. The first three hitters get all the credit for what followed." What followed consisted primarily of Olson bouncing curveballs in the dirt. Three wild pitches and a throwing error by Olson gave the Twins three more runs, as a disbelieving crowd watched in what looked like a group trance. Olson had never lost a game at Memorial Stadium and he was not just losing, but unraveling before everyone's eyes. "After the three hits, he was trying to throw harder, especially the curve," said Kelly. "He got flustered and the wild pitches were the aftereffects of the first three batters."

The Twins scored five runs in the inning and won 8–4. This was a game Kelly would remember long after the season was over. "They threw at us, then we come back to beat Olson, which gives a team a great air of confidence. We won the series and had an off day next. Add it all up and it was a special win."

The Twins celebrated in an unusual manner. Kelly and Remzi Kiratli had collaborated, planning a special trip to New York, site of the next series. The Twins routinely bussed this trip, but with no game for 48 hours, a second bus was designated to make a four-hour pit stop in Atlantic City, New Jersey. The aftermath of the Pete Rose and George Steinbrenner affairs prevented any boasting of success on the nickel slots, but with 20 wins in 22 games to their credit, the superstitious among the crowd in Atlantic City must not have let any players out of their sight!

# THE GANG OF SEVEN

*"You have to look at players occasionally and evaluate what they can do for your organization down the line."*
***Tom Kelly***

There were only seven survivors. The team that in 1987 had provided an incalculable boost to Minnesota's psyche by winning the state's first professional sports championship, had been dismantled through the attrition that had become commonplace in modern baseball. Some change was natural as role players are routinely turned over according to the annual needs of a team and barely create a ripple of interest. It was the economic ramifications of baseball, however, that led to the loss of many of 1987's impact players. Tom Brunansky, Frank Viola, Jeff Reardon, Gary Gaetti, and Bert Blyleven went elsewhere in large part due to either the money they were earning or the money they wanted to earn. Either way, it was too much money for the Twins' blood. Players dislike the subject, but management maintains that in a market like Minnesota those choices must be made. To sign players at the market prices dictated by New York, Chicago, Boston, and the California teams is impossible. As a result only Randy Bush, Greg Gagne, Dan Gladden, Kent Hrbek, Gene Larkin, Al Newman, and Kirby Puckett remained.

Surprisingly, the Twins were quite normal in having only

seven players remaining from their World Championship team just four seasons earlier. The Twins' World Series opponent that year, St. Louis, had just five holdovers and two were disabled for the entire 1991 season. Detroit, the American League Championship Series opponent in 1987, had six players left in 1991 but one, pitcher Walt Terrell, had been traded away and returned as a free agent.

The seven Twins included four starters, all in their 1987 positions once Puckett returned to center field. Five had never played for another team, and Kent Hrbek joined an exclusive club in August, becoming one of only 12 current players accumulating 10 years of major league service while playing for just one team.

Beyond longevity, these seven ball players had a link with the fans of Minnesota, the extent of which they may not have realized. The events of 1987 on the field can be duplicated, but not the aura surrounding them. It was a time so special that the 25 men wearing Twins' uniforms embodied the hopes of an entire state. Whether it was looking into a sea of white handkerchiefs waved by fans generating deafening noise levels, or being greeted by 60,000 fans at an impromptu celebration of an American League pennant, the 1987 Twins felt more like Olympians than professionals. They were playing for the pride and glory of a state, and when they won the state honored them as conquering heroes.

The fans' emotional investment in that team was deep, and the players will always be remembered for their accomplishments that October. No matter how many other uniforms they wear, numbers they compile, and World Series in which they play, nothing will erase the memories for Minnesotans of Reardon retiring the final batter in all three clinching wins. Or of Gaetti calmly stopping Willie McGee's grounder and, as time seemed to freeze, making the throw of a lifetime to Hrbek to wrap up the series. Or of Viola's indomitable spirit in winning Game Seven. The images of the remaining players forever burned into the minds of the fans are of Randy Bush's instinctive fadeaway slide, or the grand slams by Hrbek and Gladden, or Puckett's series-high 10 hits.

Tom Kelly shared many of these special memories. October was the month every person in baseball dreamed of, and in 1987 Kelly had the month of his professional life. It happened so quickly for him, in just his first full year as a manager, that the passage of time has heightened his appreciation of that month, and fueled his burning desire to experience it again.

## RANDY BUSH

One of the few pictures that adorns the wall of Kelly's office at the Metrodome is a splendid shot of Randy Bush's slide in Game Two of the 1987 World Series. The photograph of what Kelly calls "one of the greatest slides ever," captures the instant Bush's left hand touched home plate while Cardinals' catcher Tony Pena wheeled in vain looking for the runner who should be next to him, but instead seemed to be sliding in the on-deck circle with an octopuslike arm reaching back to score the run.

To Kelly, that slide epitomized much of what has kept Randy Bush with the Twins for nearly 10 years. It was a play "that just sort of came out," but a reaction that many players could not have made. A player who would hardly be classified as a threat to run, Bush nonetheless stole three bases in the five games of the 1987 American League Championship Series. The most shocking and entertaining pair came in Game Two with Jack Morris pitching for Detroit. Bush stole second base because "he's heads-up enough to know when he can steal," Kelly remembered. Bush then made a better play. "We put the sign right back on to steal third, and Randy was smart enough to look into the dugout again. Some guys would have said, he let me steal second, no way will he let me steal third. But he looked in and stole the base."

Among the seven from 1987, Bush's role had changed the most dramatically by 1991. He had been a platoon player for seven years, and close to a regular in 1988 and 1989, seasons in which he fell just shy of 400 at-bats. A hamstring injury shortened his season in 1990, but Kelly had begun to implement a new plan for Bush. Knowing that Bush's long-term value to the Twins was with his bat, which could provide a "professional" hitter with occasional power to confront right-handed pitchers, Kelly decided Bush would be his prime left-handed batter off the bench. There would be occasional starts, but unless a rash of injuries struck, the days of three to four hundred at-bats were over. Bush had to trust Kelly's ability to keep all his players involved, while Kelly knew Bush could make the change and be a younger version of Jim Dwyer, who had compiled a .316 average for the Twins at age 39.

"You have to look at players occasionally and evaluate what they can do for your organization down the line," Kelly explained. "We decided Bush could be our ideal lefty batter for years. We'd like a righty, but are still looking for one. But after the 1990 season, we had to say it wasn't realistic for Randy to be our fourth outfielder. In 1987 or 1988, yes, but not now. So I tried to prepare him by gradually weaning down his playing time until he realized his new role."

Kelly knew Bush wanted to play as he had in past years, but Kelly had been with Bush for a decade, and his manager's intuition told him that Bush would understand. "He's a sharp guy, real bright, and should be the player rep," Kelly said. "And he's a perfect fit in the clubhouse. He knows when to have fun and also when to keep quiet."

The transition for Bush was not without a bump, one that forced Kelly into one of managing's most delicate areas, yet one that he handles with ease. Kelly has the rare ability to befriend players, joining in the clubhouse atmosphere either through verbal sparring or card games, yet still criticize and challenge them when necessary. He doesn't feel compelled to distance himself from his team, but Kelly has developed an uncanny knack of knowing how and when to get "in someone's face."

That time for Randy Bush came in late May. Kelly had started Bush 11 times in the first 28 games, providing the "foundation" for Bush to have a productive season. Bush had not enjoyed any success at the plate in April, and Terry Crowley's attempts to help him were futile. Matters were complicated in May when Pedro Munoz was recalled from Portland. This move did not thrill Kelly who was already juggling playing time for a surplus of outfielders, but the Twins could not ignore Munoz's .400 average. Clearly there was an urgency in Kelly's voice as he called Bush into his office for a pregame "conversation" on May 21.

"I did most of the shouting, although he did some," Kelly recalled. "He said he was trying and I said that wasn't good enough. He had to get working with Crow [Crowley]. I told him it was a disgrace that I had to bat him eighth that night. I was trying to embarrass him and anger him because a lot of people were calling for his head, hollering about Munoz hitting so well at Portland."

For a few emotional minutes, Kelly had to dismiss his own past attachments with Bush. The two had met in 1981, when Bush drove in 94 runs for the championship team in Orlando that Kelly managed. Through the years in Minnesota, Kelly had seen that Bush studied the game and kept himself in good shape. At 32, Bush had many productive years ahead if used properly, Kelly believed. That was why "we had it out. It was a time the manager had to speak up and see if he can generate a response."

Bush had some key hits in June, but his season turned in mid-July. The Twins faced Boston for eight of the first 10 games following the All-Star break. Traditionally, the Twins had stumbled into the break, and this year Kelly was very concerned about losing the gains made during The Streak. A 2–4 trip to Toronto and Chicago was no cause for celebration, but to Kelly it "was better than usual." Despite a series of injuries that sidelined Gladden, Larkin, and Harper, the games were competitive and the trip "was not the catastrophe it had been in the past." It left the Twins, however, percentage points behind Texas at the break.

The important stretch against Boston began. The first game was a good omen for the second half of the season, as Paul Sorrento, recalled when Gladden was disabled, delivered a three-run pinch-hit home run for the game-winning hit. It was another resuscitative contribution from a role player, and it gave hope that what had fueled the Twins during The Streak had not been lost.

The Twins went on to win three games in the weekend series, and after splitting a two-game series in Milwaukee, they faced four more battles at Fenway Park. This historic home of the Red Sox had been the stage for a great deal of Twins' grief in recent years. Perhaps no game better characterized 1990 for the Twins than the July night at Fenway when the Twins turned two triple plays, an unprecedented feat in baseball history, yet lost the game because they could not score a single run. If there were any lingering doubts that 1991 was different and that this team would be a factor in the pennant race, they were put to rest on the weekend of July 18–21.

Eleven runs gave the Twins a comfortable win in the series opener, but Boston's pitching showed more resolve in Friday's game. Jeff Reardon took the mound for the ninth inning trying to hold a 2–1 lead. Reardon relished any opportunity to face the Twins, though not out of personal animosity. The competitive fire that had taken him to the top of baseball's relievers drove him to show the Twins they had made a mistake in allowing him to escape as a free agent.

It was Reardon's third chance to save a win over the Twins in 1991, and he retired pinch hitter Chuck Knoblauch on a fly ball to start the inning. Scott Leius was the next scheduled batter, but Bush was the logical pinch hitter, particularly after he had nicked Reardon for a pinch-homer five days earlier. It would be unrealistic to hope for Bush to duplicate that feat, but if the Twins could get one runner, an at bat would be saved for Puckett.

"He was looking for a fastball on the first pitch, and he smoked it foul," Kelly remembered. Indeed, Bush had turned quickly on the first pitch and hit a line drive that hooked foul past the right-field pole barely three hundred feet from home plate. Hitters often say that in each at bat against a quality pitcher they get only one pitch to hit. If that theory were true, Bush had his chance, or so it seemed. "But Reardon threw another fastball, and Bushie hit the hell out of it," Kelly recalled. It was as if a live instant replay was shown, as the pitch and the swing were replicas of the first offering. Bush launched another line drive towards the right-field corner, but this ball did not hook. As the ball descended, everyone in the Twins' dugout knew this was going to be a game-tying home run. There was no celebrating though—only a sickening moment of disbelief as first base umpire Durwood Merrill signalled the ball foul. The next emotion Kelly felt was rage as he came charging from the dugout followed by half of his team, in a scene reminiscent of a bench emptying to participate in a brawl. In this case, the object of everyone's ire was Merrill, yet Kelly made a beeline to home-plate umpire Larry McCoy.

"I got halfway there, and McCoy pointed fair," Kelly said. "So I went right to Bushie and made sure he rounded the bases." Bush had been so stunned by the call that he had broken out of his home run trot and headed towards the outfield to confront Merrill. Kelly arrived to rescue his runner and escort him most of the way to second base. Watching Kelly's trot soothed those who had worried about his health during an early-season bout with shingles. The worst of that painful virus had passed and the corrected call by umpire McCoy prevented a relapse. "It's so shocking, your stomach goes out when you see something like that," said Kelly. "Durwood made a mistake, but the umpires' mission is to get the play right. I'm just thankful Larry [McCoy] did the right thing."

Bush had struck his most important blow of the season, and the Twins parlayed it into a 3–2 win in 11 innings. It was another victory that heralded a special season, and an at bat that signified the rebirth of Bush. Saturday brought seven shutout innings from Scott Erickson in his second start since returning from the disabled list, and Sunday was a 14–1 rout of Tom Bolton, who started for Boston despite pitching five innings of relief in the series opener. The Twins swept the four-game series, and in the process avoided facing Roger Clemens. "They weren't playing well," Kelly said. "They were plagued by errors and some bad pitching. But sometimes you can play so well that you make the other team look bad. To win a division, you have to hit teams when they aren't going good."

On June 1, Bush sported a .173 batting average and had yet to adapt to his new role. For the final four months of the season, he hit .362 with 13 pinch hits, best in the American League. After the home runs off Reardon, Bush tied a league record with seven consecutive pinch hits. He became the player Kelly had envisioned, "being ready when we needed him, studying the game and being an example for the other players to watch and see how he prepared." Pinch hitting was not completely new to Bush, who led the league in 1984 and 1986. The honors, though, were achieved in years where he played on a semiregular basis. Bush now had to make his mark in half the number of at-bats.

Before 1991 ended, Bush hoped for a chance to relive a career highlight. In what later seemed to be a fit of temporary insanity, Bush went to Kelly during the party in Arlington, Texas, celebrating their clinching the 1987 division title and volunteered to play the next night, thinking Kelly would not remember or would not take the request seriously. That reasoning proved faulty as the lineup card at Arlington Stadium the following night included Bush's name. Charlie Hough was floating his knuckler toward hitters still suffering from the prior evening's revelry. Bush, however, was not fazed by the dancing baseball, and he surprised no one more than himself with a home run. "That's Bush," said

Rick Aguilera addresses the crowd in the celebration after Game 7. On the left is public-address announcer Bob Casey; Jarvis Brown stands alongside.

Jack Morris was the horse the Twins rode in Game 7.

Mike Pagliarulo came to Minnesota with the difficult task of taking over for Gary Gaetti, and was a key contributor to the World Championship.

Kirby Puckett and team spokesman Junior Ortiz.

The Metrodome, as the National Anthem is performed before Game 1 of the World Series.

The Twins' First Family, owner Carl Pohlad facing his wife, Eloise.

Kelly is introduced before Game 1 of the World Series.

A team high-five greets Greg Gagne after his Game 1 World Series home run.

Kelly. "Always making a joke. This year, when he played nine innings, he'd ask for a game ball and then announce he was not available for the rest of the week." His emergence as a deluxe pinch hitter enhanced the Twins' odds of needing another Bush "volunteer performance" in 1991.

## GREG GAGNE

Greg Gagne should have played in the All-Star Game in 1991. Always a steady if unspectacular shortstop, Gagne's defense had been airtight. Gagne finally appeared to be conquering the part of baseball that tormented him—hitting. On June 3, after the Twins had played 50 season games, Gagne owned a .319 batting average, rare air for a .247 career hitter. Gagne's combination of hitting and fielding impressed American League All-Star Manager Tony LaRussa.

"Tony told me that he was going to take Gags as the backup shortstop to Cal Ripken," Kelly insisted. "All he needed to do was keep up some resemblance of decent batting and he'd have been an All-Star." Instead, Gagne fell into a maddening slump that robbed his average of 70 points by the break. After hitting over .300 in each of the first two months, Gagne endured a 32 at-bat stretch without a hit. For June, his average was .160.

As nightmarish as June was for Gagne, who cared passionately about contributing with his bat, Kelly was resigned to his slump. Kelly had seen this in each of the seven years that Gagne played everyday shortstop, and he "had exhausted all avenues" in the search for preventive medicine. Terry Crowley had heard about the "Gagne slump" from Kelly over the winter, was prepared for it, and still was unable to halt its progression.

Kelly knew all hitters, with the possible exception of Kirby Puckett, hit bad times. What perplexed him about Gagne's slumps was their length. "It was never just a week or 10 days, but they stretched over a long period of time. When this happened, Crow couldn't help, and it went so long that he lost his All-Star spot."

It pained Kelly to see Ozzie Guillen selected as an All-Star ahead of Gagne, not out of any animosity toward the Chicago shortstop, but because the standards by which shortstops are measured seem to be hitting and flashy defense. To watch Gagne every day was to appreciate the steadiness with which he fielded the game's most demanding position. Kelly described Gagne as "playing the hell out of shortstop, with fielding that gets more consistent every year." Baseball should demand less of a "play of the day" approach and more of a "make the plays every day" approach, but the proliferation of videotapes and television programs featuring highlight plays did a disservice to Gagne's type of player. Baseball was becoming likened to the entertainment business where flash sells, and Gagne did not bring flash to the table. "When you break down the game, Gagne plays great shortstop. But a Ripken does a lot of damage swinging the bat, and Ozzie Smith makes fabulous plays that add a charisma to the game. Those are the players that end up being thought of in the superlatives," Kelly admitted.

Kelly was even more troubled by Gagne's struggles at the plate because the manager had long looked at Gagne as a player with unlimited offensive possibilities. A wiry five-foot, 11-inch, 172-pounder, Gagne had the speed to steal bases and the strength to hit with power. Over the years, Kelly had seen flashes of each from Gagne, but never together consistently enough to make a major impact. Gagne demonstrated his power in the 1987 postseason when he hit three home runs, and in two different seasons he compiled 45 extra-base hits, a total few shortstops attain. Before the 1991 All-Star break, he had homered off Nolan Ryan, Dave Stewart, and Dennis Eckersley. The speed was evident also, in his high number of triples, and a stolen base total that reached 15 in 1988. Kelly had managed Gagne in double-A and saw all of the necessary tools for someone "I predicted would be a .290 to .300 hitter. That's why his slumps are a shame."

By 1991, Kelly had reached internal peace with Gagne's offensive contributions. "I always dreamt he'd be a leadoff or number-two hitter," said Kelly. "But he strikes out a bit too much for that. Gags just seems more comfortable down in the lineup. He seemed much better there this year, and with Gladden and Knoblauch up top, we kept our speed bunched together." In fact, Gagne did start 11 games as the leadoff hitter, including three games during The Streak. While anchoring the ninth spot in the order, however, Gagne rebounded with a strong second half to finish at .265, an improvement of 30 points from the previous season.

What made Gagne's season was his ability to separate his fielding from his hitting. By contrast, Chuck Knoblauch had difficulty in keeping his anger over an at bat from affecting his play in the field. The Twins lost to a Milwaukee ninth-inning rally in July where the key hit resulted from a ball Knoblauch reacted to slowly. Kelly saw the "non-play" as a carryover from an inning-ending double play Knoblauch hit into during the top half of the ninth. While Knoblauch was watched carefully in the field, there was never any concern about Gagne. Even when Gagne had his greatest problems at the plate, he played errorless shortstop. There were no errors in the month of June, and in fact there had been none since May 1. "You have to give Gags a lot of credit for that," Kelly said. "He held his fielding together beautifully while his hitting went south."

Kelly knew that the slumps bothered Gagne. The Twins leaned on Gagne for his reliability in the field, but he had an inner drive that constantly pushed his focus toward hitting. A comfortable relationship developed in 1987 between Gagne and Don Baylor that eased some of Gagne's anxieties towards batting, but nothing since then. Yet Kelly had seen a maturation in Gagne over the past few seasons. "He has taken on more leadership in the infield. This year, he helped Knoblauch quite a bit. His arm is strong, he turns the double play well, and we all know his value to us in the field."

The All-Star Game didn't happen for Greg Gagne in 1991, but he hit well in the last two months and fielded with precision. The errorless streak he began on May 2 did not end until August 12, a span of 76 games, second only to Cal Ripken's 95 games in 1990. Gagne played with new infielders on each side, yet committed just nine errors all season. His near-flawless defense coupled with five good months of hitting made his season a resounding success. If June hadn't interfered, there would have been an All-Star Game berth, but Gagne had to "settle" for the opportunity to play baseball in October instead.

## DAN GLADDEN

Other than Kirby Puckett, no player has gripped the fans of Minnesota in recent years like Dan Gladden. Anyone who has played baseball at any level looks at Gladden and says, "That's the way I played" or "That's how I would play if I had the talent." Gladden is truly the people's ball player, with his blond mane flapping in the breeze as he runs full tilt for a batted ball. Despite playing his home games in a stadium covered with artificial turf, Gladden has the knack of getting his uniform dirty. The sum of the parts, the long hair, facial stubble, skinned knees, and dirty uniform, epitomize a working-class player that the paying customers adore. They loved the 16 hits in the 1987 postseason, the grand slam in Game One of the World Series, as well as hitting safely in each series game, and the memorable performance in the 1988 home opener with a pair of home runs and a steal of home.

Gladden's biggest contribution to the Twins has been largely overlooked for five years. The aforementioned image is "part of the show and great for the fans," Kelly concedes, but means little in playing the game. Gladden excels playing left field, particularly at the Metrodome. "I think left field at the Dome is harder than center field," Kelly maintains. "The lights are tough and there's so much room, plus the foul area. Danny catches an awful lot of balls and covers a lot of ground." A persuasive argument could be made that Gladden's defense in left field has been as critical to the Twins as Gagne's play at shortstop, although Kelly maintains that Shane Mack could also play left field well if needed.

Gladden's image as baseball's version of a rebel plays well with fans, but within the team, Kelly says "his bark is worse than his bite." Indeed, teammates appreciate Gladden's spirit in the dugout, even during games that he is not playing. Kelly is not big on cheerleading, but "daydreaming for nine innings doesn't work" and he likes Gladden's involvement in "rooting everybody on."

Gladden always tried to maintain a "presence" in the clubhouse, but on some occasions his mouth roared him into trouble. One instance occurred in August of 1990 when he criticized the recall of rookie pitcher Paul Abbott to a team in the midst of watching its season collapse. Questioning management in print may be acceptable in New York or other major markets, but it did not play well in Minnesota. Kelly remembers having several talks with Gladden because no one was happy with a player criticizing the organization or one of its leading prospects. "Danny was wrong," Kelly maintained. "A lot of people were embarrassed by what he said, including Paul Abbott. No player should ever embarrass someone who's trying to help the team. The front office was mad at him. I was mad at him because statements like that to the press are just wrong. There's nothing good that can come from that kind of statement."

The first contribution Gladden ever made to the Twins was to bring a "new look" to the batting lineup. On the wall of Kelly's office is framed his first lineup card as manager of the Twins. The date was September 12, 1986, and Kelly's leadoff hitter was Kirby Puckett. "That season, I had talked to [former manager] Ray [Miller] about hitting Puckett third. But he probably felt we really didn't have another leadoff man." Kelly's logic on Puckett's proper place in the order was sound. He believed the team's best hitter should bat third. But Miller's conclusion was also sound, because there just was no one else. With the arrival of Dan Gladden the scenario changed.

Gladden was not a leadoff hitter in the Rickey Henderson mold, but he was an aggressive hitter who swung often and rarely walked. What Gladden did was "steal bases and turn singles into doubles," Kelly said. The formula worked well in 1987 and 1988, but as the Twins' run production dropped, first in 1989 and then dramatically in 1990, attention focused on the leadoff spot. Over the winter of 1991, Gladden heard a lot about improving his on-base percentage, and his efforts towards that goal clearly led to his miserable start (one hit in 31 at-bats). "That's just not the way Danny plays. It's like trying to change the stripes on a zebra," said Kelly. "He tried to change, it wasn't working and I told him to just swing the bat like he always had. I'd love to have a prototypical leadoff guy, but that's not what Danny does best."

Gladden's average surged to .259 before he strained abdominal muscles during an at bat on June 28. Nearly a month on the disabled list followed, and the Twins survived with a 12–10 record as Kelly masterfully pieced together lineups using six different players in left field and seven different leadoff hitters. Gladden's return on July 25 was accompanied by pregame drama as space on the 25-man roster was created by sending pitcher Allan Anderson to the minors. After winning 33 games and a league earned run average championship in his first two years as a Twins starter, Anderson's stock had fallen so badly that he was relegated to mop-up relief. In his last five starts, he had allowed 10 home runs.

Although Gladden wore a stomach wrap to support his injured abdominal muscles in the first game, he wasted no time making an impact. Facing left-handed pitcher Scott Aldred, Gladden had driven in four runs by the fourth inning, sending the Twins to a 9–3 getaway night victory in Detroit. Returning to the

Metrodome, Gladden wreaked havoc with Milwaukee's staff. He broke a 3–3 tie in the series opener with an eighth-inning bases-loaded double, and the next night sent 47,632 fans into a frenzy with a three-run game-winning home run in the ninth inning. Gladden's score card read three games played with five hits and 10 runs batted in. "That was a real spark for us," Kelly said. "The injury Danny had is tough to come back from, but he came back with some game-winning hits that picked up everybody."

The home run off Milwaukee's Bill Wegman won a Saturday night game, but its true impact was not felt until Sunday morning. Gladden came to the ballpark and saw his name on the lineup card. It was a day game after a night game, and everyone with the Twins knew that Gladden rarely played on these days. Gladden's hot bat had forced Kelly to deviate from his routine. "When Danny first came here, I kept trying to play him in day games and it always ended up with me banging my head against the wall," Kelly remembered. "I would swear I wouldn't do it again, and then I'd give in. It wasn't until last year [1990] that I held him out of day games, unless the matchup dictated he should play the day game, and then I'd hold him out the night before."

Gladden was understandably peeved by this characterization, and he occasionally dropped subtle hints to the beat writers about his unhappiness. Kelly heard it from Gladden directly several times, but all the manager did was to "pull the stats out of my desk." In 1991, Gladden hit .265 in night games and .182 in day games.

After his loud reentry to the lineup in late July, Gladden slumped and hit barely over .200 for the last two months. Kelly was concerned about Gladden's injuries that "seemed to start creeping up" on a player who depended on his speed and had just turned 34.

### KENT HRBEK

When Kent Hrbek reported to Fort Myers for spring training, Tom Kelly had no concern about Hrbek's readiness to face major league pitching. Instead, the Twins had spent the winter of 1991 monitoring the left ankle that Hrbek fractured in a clubhouse horseplay incident late in the previous season. Injuries were hampering Hrbek's career, but this was the first mishap that was not directly related to a play on the field. "There's a harness driver and trainer by the name of Del Miller who I talk to," Kelly said. "Del has been around horses his whole life and he's now in his seventies. Del believes you can relate his experiences with horses to athletes. The ones who try hard and give you that extra effort are the ones who get hurt. If you look at Hrbek's career, every injury, except for the fooling around in the clubhouse, has been from playing hard and diving at balls."

The issue of injuries is unavoidably tied to Hrbek's weight. Kelly refuses to make it an issue because "he plays his butt off. His numbers speak for themselves." Yet the manager was nothing if not a realist. "I won't lie and pretend I wouldn't like him at 235 pounds. We all know it would be better for him, and he knows that. But he's not going to get there, so am I going to fight with him?" On Sundays, the Twins weigh in, and Kelly watches these figures closely. If Hrbek's weight heads the wrong way, Kelly will issue "a few subtle sentences" but nothing else.

Kelly values durability in a player and in each of the first five years of his career, Hrbek had more than 500 at-bats. Over the second five-year span of his career, the toll of injuries showed and he reached that same number of at-bats only once. "Herbie has a lot of legitimate injuries, his knee hurts or his shoulder hurts, and I need to give him a day off here and there," Kelly admitted. "Now add them up for a season and he misses a lot of games. It hurts our team because we can't survive more than a few days without him. And it hurts him in the Gold Glove voting."

Hrbek is a large man whose size is natural, not the product of exercise machines and growth powders. He reminds a longtime baseball observer of a Boog Powell or a Frank Howard in physique, yet watching Hrbek for any time opens one's eyes to his defensive excellence. No throw from an infielder was too tough for Hrbek who simply smothered even the toughest hops. Despite his size, Hrbek has no peer in ranging down the right field line, with his back to home plate, to catch foul pop-ups. Jim Kaat, a 25-year major league pitcher who played with Keith Hernandez and broadcast Yankees games in Don Mattingly's prime, maintains Hrbek is the best defensive first baseman he has seen. Kelly has watched Hrbek every day for nine years and simply says, "He's the best, better than Mattingly [the 1991 Gold Glove winner] and that's not taking anything from Mattingly, but Hrbek is that good. But [Mark] McGwire won last year [1990] because he had more assists, and more putouts from playing in more games. If Herbie could play 150 games in a season, I think he'd win one."

Hrbek's ankle was fine in the spring and the six weeks in Florida were simply his countdown to Opening Day. He was someone who loved playing the games. "He's not much for practice," Kelly admitted. "But he has a gift. One week of spring is all he needs to be ready for the season. Puckett needs the whole spring and then maybe some of the regular season, but Hrbek needs one week and he's ready to hit. That's one reason why Herbie doesn't like to practice. He has enough natural talent that he can not practice much and still play at a high level. We've learned that playing the game is what keeps him going."

Only winning surpassed playing for Hrbek, who has an inner fire that fuels a thorough dislike of defeat. "He really wants to win, probably more than anyone on the team," Kelly observed. "Losing bothers him, it eats at him. It's something a manager senses, and you can see it in his face, his eyes, and his reactions. That's another reason why we can't play more than a day or two without him."

Hrbek's drive lurks beneath a smiling, relaxed exterior that was an original component of the Twins' fraternitylike behavior during the 1987 postseason. Probably the least recognized facet of

Hrbek's personality is a sensitivity that Kelly would see unveiled in a most unfortunate way later in the season. Many have seen the caring Hrbek who willingly travels the region every winter to meet fans on the Twins' caravan and who runs his wildly successful charity golf tournament every June.

Over nine years, Kelly and Hrbek formed a friendship away from baseball that has never been threatened by the player-manager relationship that ensued. The first memory Kelly has of Hrbek is the 18-year-old first base prospect in his first spring training lying on the ground in the batter's box clutching Kelly's leg. "He had just taken a swing and his knee went out," Kelly remembered. "I ran out there and he just lay there and he wouldn't let go of my leg."

That injury cost Hrbek all but 17 games of his first professional season. Rick Stelmaszek managed Hrbek at Wisconsin Rapids in 1980, and in the spring of 1981 Hrbek hoped to jump past Visalia, the higher class-A team, in order to play for Kelly at Orlando. "I wanted Herbie real bad," said Kelly. "We already had a hell of a team [Viola, Gaetti, Bush, and Tim Laudner among others] and he would have made it really something. Herbie had a great spring, but [minor league director] George Brophy wanted him to go to Visalia, which I understood.

"The funny thing is that Herbie still is mad at me for that. He thinks I had something to do with it. One night that spring, Gaetti and Hrbek came back to the hotel in Melbourne after curfew," Kelly recalled. "I was rooming right below them, and they started wrestling. After a while, I couldn't take it any more, so I went up and knocked on their door. They got the message. The next day, we finished our morning session, and as everyone was filing off the field for lunch, I said you two [Gaetti and Hrbek] stay with me. Then I just about killed them, hitting slow rollers to make them charge the ball, making them go to their left, then their right. They did everything, and by missing lunch they got the message. It was a gift for keeping the manager awake at night."

Kelly smiles at the reminiscence. He takes no pleasure in punishing players, but like a parent, he revels in the success they all have enjoyed since the days when discipline was necessary. Both Kelly and Hrbek have matured in their respective jobs to the point where the player-manager relationship can function, as it did in Seattle in April. Hrbek had to speak his mind after being lifted for a pinch hitter twice in the first two weeks, and Kelly had to explain his rationale. "If the player respects you as a manager, then you can say whatever is necessary and it will be accepted," Kelly said. "You don't like to do it with any player, but it's your job and the most important thing is to have some rapport with your players. Problems begin when I say something to a coach and it gets out. Then the player thinks you're talking behind his back."

Kelly did not like lifting Hrbek in April, but honestly felt it was necessary to inspire Hrbek. As a young player, Hrbek made a lasting impression with his ability to hit left-handed pitching with an effortless stroke to left and left-center field. Somewhere through the years, Hrbek became an easier out for lefties, and Kelly began batting him seventh, if he played him at all. This surprised many people around the league who could not understand why a vital member of the Twins did not play against left-handed pitchers that were not overpowering. Kelly saw this as something Hrbek could overcome, but he felt the predicament was part of a player's natural evolution. "All good young hitters come to the majors hitting the ball well to the opposite field," said Kelly. "As they play more, they learn what they can do with the bat and more about what pitchers throw. Then they start to pull the ball, and hit it over the fence. When Herbie came up he hit well to left field, but after awhile, he learned what he could do and became more of a pull hitter. Unfortunately, he does much better against lefties when he takes them the other way."

Kelly was intent on seeing Hrbek hit lefties more effectively in 1991, and the April episode served a purpose. He ended the regular season with a .281 average and six home runs against lefties. Included was a stirring blast to deep left-center field off Chicago's Scott Radinsky, a young thrower whose repertoire was hard, harder, and hardest, to win a game in early July. Although the events do not compare in magnitude, the home run in Chicago reminded some of Hrbek's grand slam off Ken Dayley in Game Six of the 1987 World Series. It was a strong swing with the intent of driving the ball, though not necessarily pulling the ball. "That was a huge hit and it was the result of our scouts' preparation," Kelly believed. "We were told Dayley liked to throw fastballs on the first pitch. Herbie knew it, Dayley threw it, and Herbie smoked it. To Herbie's credit, he still had to hit it and it was the way he had always hit left-handers." Hrbek came back to hit them "the old way" in the second half of 1991, and there would be moments when he would get the chance to duplicate his memorable swing against Dayley.

GENE LARKIN

Early in the 1991 season Gene Larkin and Jack Morris reminisced about a prior meeting. The incident took place in 1988 and Larkin lay prone in the Tiger Stadium batters' box, unconscious after a Morris pitch struck him squarely on the batting helmet. It was Larkin's first full year in the major leagues and the trade of Tom Brunansky had made him a regular player. Now he was victimized for the first time by the inside pitch that all hitters must conquer to flourish in the majors. Bush had just homered for the fourth Twins run, so Larkin, Morris, and everyone else in the stadium knew the intent of the pitch. Now that they were teammates, Larkin needed to hear from Morris that the pitch was thrown not at his head, but at him.

The conversation confirmed Larkin's suspicion, but three years earlier Larkin had been the one who had been carried off the field on a stretcher, and after gaining medical clearance, came back to play two days later. "Geno's a tough guy," remembered Kelly. "After someone's hit by a pitch, you need to get him back in there. The longer you wait, the worse it can be."

Larkin's toughness paid off as he showed no aftereffects from the beaning. He was a living embodiment of the clichéd "strong, silent type." For Larkin, major league baseball was much more of a job than a game. Although he was not averse to his share of fun and laughs in the clubhouse, he approached each day at the ballpark as a serious day at work. His stringent exercise regimen, both during and between seasons, clearly made him a more versatile player, and in turn a more valuable one.

A self-made major-leaguer, Larkin was drafted by the Twins primarily as a right-handed-hitting first baseman. By 1991 he was a switch hitter who was considered a better threat batting left-handed, and a decent right fielder. Both changes were initiated by Larkin, who began to hit left-handed in 1981 in his first year in college, and first tackled the outfield during the spring of 1989. "Gene came to us and said he wanted to try right field," Kelly recalled. "He knew he was jammed behind Hrbek for playing time at first base, so he worked hard and made himself an outfielder." Observers were surprised and somewhat skeptical as Larkin began taking fly balls at Tinker Field, trying to learn a position he had never played. What they did not know was that Larkin made it to the big leagues after being a 20th-round draft pick and "one of the hardest working guys I've ever seen," said Kelly. If playing right field would keep him in the majors, then Larkin would make himself a right fielder.

As he gained confidence in his ability to play the outfield, Larkin found himself starting games in the Metrodome's right field, a smaller field that Kelly felt better suited Larkin's skills. The arrival of two players, however, conspired to thrust Larkin into a reserve role. Shane Mack's emergence in the second half of 1990 gave the

Twins a third starting outfielder, and for 1991 Chili Davis was signed as the everyday designated hitter. Throw in two injuries that sidelined Larkin for a month of the 1990 season, and Kelly sized up Larkin for 1991 as an "excellent player off the bench. You like to have a switch hitter on your bench and he can play first well when Herbie gets hurt, and go to right field once in awhile."

Gene Larkin found himself filling a role in 1991 that was very similar to his 1987 rookie season. A man without a position, he still played in 98 games as Kelly practiced his managerial preaching by finding playing time for everyone. The only difference for Larkin was the change from designated hitting in 1987 to right field in 1991. He could hit well from either side, although Kelly felt he was a better left-handed hitter in this season. Larkin's selectiveness and ability to make contact with few strikeouts endeared him to Kelly. "We don't get too caught up with power," said Kelly. "Now, there's nothing wrong with the long ball, and we wanted to hit more homers this year, but the numbers clearly show that when we out-hit the other team we win [with a 82–11 record in 1991]. So we play hit and run, move runners, and figure that if we put up 10 hits, we'll win. In Geno's case, we try to identify what a player can do and use that. You can't change someone who isn't going to knock the ball over the fence."

Larkin's strength was tested by a most unlikely source, the Minnesota fans. On September 18, the Twins lost to Kansas City when the Royals scored six runs in a sixth inning that featured several misplayed balls and a throwing error by right fielder Larkin. The self-made outfielder had a nightmarish day at the ballpark, and was soundly booed by the crowd. Some observers and even some Twins players were stunned that a member of a first-place team who worked tirelessly at his game could receive such treatment. Kelly understood. "It's not surprising, it's just the nature of a fan," he explained. "If things aren't going good, and they paid their 10 or 12 skins, they have a right to boo. Geno had a bad day, but he wasn't alone. Anyone in the game long enough has experienced it. And Geno was fine. He said he deserved it, and heck, I was booing too," Kelly said with a chuckle.

Gene Larkin finished the year strongly with a career-high batting average of .286, and he took one hope into October. In this gang of seven, Larkin was the only one to not get a base hit in the 1987 World Series. Little did he know in what manner his wish might come true.

## AL NEWMAN

A man Tom Kelly called "one of the league's best utility players," Al Newman, also became a man without a position during 1991. Newman, like Bush and Larkin, watched more baseball in 1991 than in any previous Twins' season. Chuck Knoblauch filled the team's black hole at second base, so Newman lost the hope of much playing time at the position he had played most frequently. The platoon at third base was successful and Greg Gagne was playing exceptional defense at shortstop, so Newman simply lost at-bats. Kelly felt the title "utility" can be misleading because that player, as Newman had shown in prior seasons, often winds up as a regular player. It became clear, however, that Newman would be a "true" utility man in 1991.

Kelly became inventive in his attempt to keep Newman active. The Twins traveled to Toronto in the week prior to the All-Star break. Early July had been a terrible time for recent Twins teams, and Kelly was concerned about a repeat. His concern was fed by disabling injuries to Gladden and Larkin, and a series of minor injuries to Hrbek. On July 4, Kelly's dilemma was finding a first baseman to face Toronto starter Jimmy Key. Randy Bush and Paul Sorrento were the only active players with experience at the position, but both were left-handed batters. In a move that was part Dr. Frankenstein and part Dr. Doolittle, Kelly chose Newman to play first.

"We had no other choice," Kelly explained. "Newman is a versatile guy, a good athlete, and I felt he could adjust. It was a day game, so Stelly [Rick Stelmaszek] and I took him to the Skydome early in the morning and gave him a crash course. We got there so early that the ground crew had to come out and remove the tarps. But we hit him grounders, made throws from all the positions, and showed him the footwork."

There was a method to Kelly's apparent madness. "We had just lost two games in Toronto and five of the last six, so what did we have to lose?" Kelly explained. "This was a little trick to get the infielders to bear down. It's not like Herbie and Geno are over there and can catch anything they throw. It makes the infielders play with some extra intensity, and it shows that the manager is not afraid to make moves to win a game." Newman handled two chances in the first inning and played seven flawless innings in a game the Twins won 1–0.

Later in July, the Twins traveled to Milwaukee and the attention shifted to an unlikely source, Newman's power. Or more accurately, his lack of power. Brewers' infielder Jim Gantner had pulled about even with Newman in a new statistic, the most consecutive at-bats without a home run. While Newman made the best of the publicity he received for his nonpower, Gantner resented it and refused to participate in a home run hitting contest with Newman suggested by the Brewers. Not long after that Gantner did homer, leaving Newman far ahead of the pack for the dubious distinction. (At season's end, Newman's streak was at 1725 at-bats.)

"I think the home run thing bothered him," Kelly admitted. "When Gantner homered, we started seeing Newmie take big long swings, pulling off the ball. His swing would be fine in batting practice and a mess in the games. It's just my opinion, but players have a lot of pride, and I think that once this home run deal was made into a big issue, it really bothered him."

What concerned Kelly was seeing Newman's average listing at .200 for much of the season. Newman never had gaudy offensive numbers, but had always produced in critical situations. "I can remember many times over the years," said Kelly, "where we'd have a threat going and [Dick] Suchie would say, 'We're right where we want to be. Newmie's up.' I tried to create some situations this year for him, but he had a rough time with the bat."

In 1989, Newman had stolen twenty-five bases, but that total dropped to four in 1991. That alarmed Kelly, who said it was "obvious Al was a step slower. I don't know whether it's from a lack of playing time or just getting older [31]." The combination of sliding average and loss of speed left Kelly in a predicament as the season moved into the final stages. A valuable player for five years who excelled at third base in 1988 during Gary Gaetti's knee injury, and who was virtually a regular second baseman in 1989 when he hit a respectable .253, was fighting declining production and reduced playing time. "He knew what was going on," Kelly admitted. "I talked to him about it a couple of times." Newman knew that the "utility" player had to combat a perception that left him less room for the error of a bad season. Kelly firmly believed this about all role players, not just Newman, when he said, "I don't think you can play him for many days in a row. Things will slow down."

KIRBY PUCKETT

The tale of Kirby Puckett's arrival to the Twins in 1984 has been told so often it is now legend. The young outfielder recalled from triple-A joined the Twins at Anaheim Stadium after a cab ride of $80 from Los Angeles International Airport for which he could not pay. Traveling secretary Mike Robertson provided the cash, and for the next eight years Puckett has provided the play of a Hall-of-Famer.

Four hits in his first major league game signaled Puckett's

arrival loudly and clearly. The circumstances surrounding his recall, however, have faded from the fans' memories. When the 1984 season began, Jim Eisenreich was in center field for the third consecutive year. There was lingering hope that this charter member of the "young Twins" who, like Hrbek, had jumped to the big leagues from the class-A Midwest league could overcome the medical problems (later diagnosed as Tourette's Syndrome) that had prematurely ended his first two seasons. After just 12 games, it was clear that Eisenreich could not continue, and he would never again play for the Twins. Next in center field came journeyman Darrell Brown, who was clearly a short-term solution.

Tom Kelly felt the long-term answer was a "roly-poly guy who I first saw in the instructional league doing terrific things on the field. He could do everything, hit, run, throw, catch, and bunt." Puckett's body was always the first image. From his earliest days in baseball, observers had difficulty matching the body with the plays it made. It was undeniable that Puckett, regardless of his looks, made more plays and collected more hits than most others.

By 1984 Puckett had earned a promotion to triple-A after he hit .314 at Visalia in 1983. The major league team needed a center fielder by early May. Kelly, although just the third base coach at the time, spoke his mind. "We were in Seattle and there was a meeting in Calvin Griffith's suite," Kelly recalled. "Stelly [Rick Stelmaszek] and I campaigned to bring up Puckett. We had worked with him in the instructional league and we knew he would be an improvement over what we had. There was resistance from George Brophy, who wanted Puck to play a full year at triple-A. But we felt he could make us a better team." Puckett had played less than two full seasons of professional baseball, but Hrbek, Gaetti, and Viola had all skipped triple-A. With the precedent set, Puckett was recalled on May 8, 1984.

Looking at his rookie year, it is jarring to see that Puckett had only 12 doubles, no home runs, and 31 runs batted in. The next year saw him hit four home runs, but in 1986 he exploded with a power that had not been foreseen. Puckett hit 83 home runs in the seasons from 1986 to 1988. "When he swings the bat, you just never know what's going to happen," Kelly marvelled. "At that time in his career, his swing was geared to hit the ball over the fence. For all I know, he may turn around and do it again." In the seasons from 1989 to 1991, Puckett's home run total dropped to 36, and suddenly Kelly was hearing "people wonder if he's going to hit those home runs again. But I look at a guy hitting over .300 every year, so why am I going to mess with that? You leave that alone." Puckett wished the fans and media would have followed suit in 1989, the year in which he hit .339 to win the American League batting championship. It seemed to Puckett that his achievement was overshadowed by constant questioning of his season total of only nine home runs. There were 45 doubles, 85 runs batted in, and 215 hits, but Puckett was disappointed by the harping on his power. Kelly, unconcerned by the lack of home runs, was genuinely excited by the prospect of managing a "batting title race" through the final day of the season. "I remember that we all wanted to make sure Puck won the championship," Kelly admitted. "It was a new experience for me at the major league level, so we had [former media relations director] Tom Mee on the phone to Oakland checking on second place batter Carney Lansford. Then Puckett hit a ball off the right-field wall in the first inning and we knew he would hang on."

The batting championship capped a four-year period in which Puckett was the league's most productive hitter. His lowest average in the span was .328, his lowest hit total was 207, and in the first three years his power numbers ranked among the league leaders. In 1988, Puckett put together a season that will forever have a place in baseball's lore as one of the best performances that did not win Most Valuable Player honors. Remarkably, his .356 average (the highest by a right-handed batter in the American

League since Joe DiMaggio in 1941) and 121 runs batted in were runner-up totals as was Puckett in the MVP voting, second to Jose Canseco. Kelly's memories of that period are of "a player who could get 10 or 12 hits faster than anyone. He was swinging good almost every game, and when he does that, a pitcher has little chance. No matter where he throws it, Puckett's going to hit it."

Much has been made about Puckett's "swing hard in case you hit it" theory. Kelly, however, sees more to Puckett's prowess than something that simple. "He's a gifted player," said Kelly. "When Kirby hits a dribbler, often it's a hit. For a .240 hitter, the same ball is an out. The majority of the times he swings the bat, something good happens. He has good speed, and he bunts well which helps him get those kinds of hits. But if he hits three balls on the button, he has a good chance for three hits. A .250 hitter can swing the bat well and have nothing good happen. Puck reminds me of Tony Oliva as a hitter. Tony could swing at a pitch down and in, and hit the ball to right field one time. Then, in his next at bat, he would get the same pitch and hit it to left. You can't explain things like that. He's just gifted."

Relying on his "gifts" has never been Puckett's modus operandi. Like Hrbek, he thoroughly enjoys playing the game and the competition it spawns. Puckett enjoys practicing and works endlessly at his game from the first day of spring training. "I worry during the year that he is taking too many swings and he's going to leave the best ones in the cage," Kelly admitted. "Sometimes we try to shut him down after a few minutes of batting practice. But it's hard to discourage somebody from working hard."

Until the 1990 season, Kelly never noticed that the hours of practice and the daily grind of playing center field on artificial turf had any negative effect on Puckett. From 1985 to 1989, Puckett missed just 11 games, and when Kelly became manager, he followed an unwritten rule of giving Puckett his rare days off on the road. Aware that the Twins attract fans from a large region, Kelly would never deny anyone who traveled many miles, perhaps to only one home game each year, the opportunity to see Puckett play.

By the middle of the 1990 season, Kelly was confronted with the reality that Puckett "is probably losing a step in the outfield." This was not shocking in the objective analysis of any player, but the name "Kirby Puckett" suggests a certain immunity to the ravages of time. Yet Kelly was strong enough to separate his admiration for the player "that I've been blessed to have had a chance to manage" from the player "who should be the Twins' right fielder." The Puckett-Mack shift was simultaneously logical and courageous, and so was the return of Puckett to center field after only 10 games of the 1991 season. He started the season in right field, yet played most of the year in center field, and it was there that he won his fifth Gold Glove. Applying the same reasoning that Kelly attributes to Greg Gagne's failure to win the award, Puckett added "charisma to the game. He does damage at the plate, so he is one of the special players that is always thought of in superlatives."

Despite the special attention, Puckett never changed in his interaction with teammates. If he is deified throughout the state, then he finds the clubhouse a place for solace and sanity. "He's such a great guy in the clubhouse, the camaraderie he enjoys with everyone is special," Kelly said. "It's quite a change to see him get a tremendous amount of respect outside, and then come inside and be just one of the guys. At the park, he'd just as soon enjoy the clubhouse atmosphere, play the game and go home. And he's learned how to escape well after a game. But he doesn't need the attention." The intense scrutiny that started after 1987 has made Puckett a more private person, but he still is heavily involved in community affairs, including hosting a celebrity pool tournament that raises money to fight heart disease in children.

The lone irregularity in Puckett's 1991 season was a tendency to bunt in questionable situations. Bunting was one of Puckett's strengths, and Kelly recalls as a third base coach "how rewarding it was to flash Puck the sign that gave him a green light to bunt, and have him bunt for a hit." In those days, however, Puckett was a leadoff hitter. Manager Kelly had moved Puckett, the team's best hitter, to the third spot where he was expected to produce runs and strike fear in opposing pitchers. "He had good intentions in trying to reach base, but there are times that we need him to swing the bat," Kelly said. "We talked about it, he knew it, but he always thought of the ballclub. What he had to do was think of the big picture, who is pitching, and what the score is. Sometimes what's a good play in the eighth inning is a bad play in the third inning. But Kirby's first priority is always what's best for the team."

The bunting affair was the only blip in a stellar season for Puckett. He missed only 10 games, while batting .319 with 195 hits. His year contained its trademark consistency, as he had just one month, September, with an average below .300. And the return to the familiar surrounding of center field produced a team-leading 13 outfield assists. Not bad for a player who is "a lot bigger" than his early years and "may have lost a step in the outfield," according to Kelly. Perhaps he is truly "gifted," but the season appeared to be yet another case of Puckett defying the odds.

Puckett has been accorded a unique place in Minnesota sports history. The state has had the honor of watching two Hall-of-Famers in Harmon Killebrew and Rod Carew, and two whose careers warrant serious consideration for the Hall of Fame in Tony Oliva and Jim Kaat, but no one has approached Puckett's place in the hearts of Minnesotans. The atypical physique and the never-ending smile are permanently recorded in the memory banks of Twins fans, while the barrage of hits and leaping catches have sent Puckett well down the road to Cooperstown.

# OAKLAND

*"We have always had such tough games in Oakland that it was nice to have them chase us once."*
***Tom Kelly***

## THE BUILDUP

For five years, the Twins regarded their games with the Oakland Athletics as baseball's version of Muhammad Ali fighting Joe Frazier. Like classic heavyweights, these teams never just sparred. Rather, they engaged in fierce battles alternating the roles of champion and challenger. Looking back, the Twins players, like the boxers, appreciate that Oakland brought out the best of their abilities. The Twins treated each series with Oakland with a high regard rarely felt in baseball's regular season.

As their teams competed, managers Tom Kelly and Tony LaRussa developed a friendship rooted in a mutual respect for the approach each took to his job and their respective teams took to the game. Success helped breed this rivalry. Since 1987 each series (except the season openers in 1990 and 1991) saw one of the teams residing in first place. As Oakland succeeded the Twins and ruled the division with a rapidly growing fame, they became targets. As the '90s began, it was no longer New York or Boston, but rather Oakland that was the leading attraction on the Twins' home schedule. Many came to see Oakland—some came to boo them.

Even during bad times the Twins could always count on healthy crowds during the Oakland visits.

Tom Kelly could also count on spirited efforts against the Athletics, regardless of his team's standing. Refusing to subscribe to any one theory, Kelly acknowledged that his teams might have "risen to the level of the competition." Indeed, in the dark years of 1989-90, the Twins won 12 of the 26 games played against the league champion Oakland Athletics.

The current cast of characters first became familiar with each other in 1987. Each manager was in his first full season with his team, and although neither team excelled, they found themselves in a critical series of games in August. First place was the prize. Both teams thirsted for it because the winner would end a championship drought of over a decade. The Metrodome generated an aura of electricity as for the first time it hosted a baseball series with pennant race implications. The Twins scored a convincing knockout with a four-game sweep, taking first place, and leaving the Athletics in a position from which they would not again challenge.

The Twins' 1987 World Championship prompted some Oakland personnel changes that would alter the balance of power in the American League West. The overhaul brought Bob Welch, Dave Henderson, and Dave Parker to Oakland in 1988, and added Rickey Henderson the following year. The Athletics were serious about winning, despite the high monetary cost, and their three consecutive pennants brought them as close to a dynasty as is possible under the current baseball labor structure. The Twins competed well in their head-to-head meetings with the Athletics, but as 1991 dawned there were no signs that a reversal of fortunes was ahead.

Kelly and LaRussa had met in 1983. Both spent more years than any player should at triple-A, and neither man was given as many as 200 major league at-bats. Yet both were major league managers at a young age. The White Sox hired LaRussa when he was 34, and the Twins hired Kelly when he was 36. When Kelly joined the Twins as third base coach, he found LaRussa "personable." Tony always stopped by to say hello to other coaches, unlike many other managers. Over time, Kelly became a manager. The two kept in regular contact and shared information they gleaned from their trips throughout the league. Kelly and LaRussa shared an admiration bordering on reverence for Sparky Anderson. Kelly visited regularly with both managers, and the resulting relationships became important as Kelly entered his new fraternity. He was no different than a newcomer to any business, striving for acceptance from his coworkers. For Kelly, that arrived when LaRussa and Anderson asked him for opinions about players. He felt validated as a major league manager, and the pregame conversations became a ritual whenever these teams met.

Many people admired LaRussa's managing during the three years he guided Oakland to American League pennants. He balanced delicate and fragile egos with strong personalities. He managed many wealthy players, and some who were angry because they wanted more money. During a time when it was virtually impossible to field the same 25 players in successive years, he managed to hold a talented nucleus together.

But no previous challenges prepared LaRussa for what he faced in 1991. Economics sent Scott Sanderson, a 17-game winner as Oakland's fourth starter in 1990, to New York, and sent Rickey Henderson into a spring training funk, searching in vain for a renegotiated contract. Carney Lansford suffered serious injuries in an off-season accident and would miss at least the first half of the year. Finally, LaRussa's most potent weapon, the league's best bullpen, was thinned when Mike Pagliarulo's opening night line drive into the dugout broke Gene Nelson's pitching hand, sending Nelson to join Rick Honeycutt on the disabled list. The men who had smoothed Dennis Eckersley's path to stardom as a closer were now missing. Their absence would be felt severely when Oakland faced the Twins.

Oakland received no sympathy from its competitors. After all the injuries were accounted for, this was still a team loaded with talent and impact players. Three premier starters in Dave Stewart, Bob Welch, and Mike Moore were backed up by Eckersley, the game's preeminent closer. Pitchers still stared at a tough lineup with Dave Henderson, Rickey Henderson, Jose Canseco, Harold Baines, Mark McGwire, and Terry Steinbach. Even though Oakland fielded a team with Lance Blankenship at second base, former Twin Fred Manrique at shortstop, and Ernest Riles at third base against the Twins in late April, they were still winning more than they were losing. Oakland had the league's best record in April at 13–7, and stayed above .500 in May at 15–12. People already applauded LaRussa for the best managing job of his career, but he could see this year would be different. Texas had ripped off its 14-game winning streak in May, and the Twins followed with The Streak in June. In the past, LaRussa had the pitching necessary for a similar run. This year, when LaRussa needed them to offset the bullpen woes, Stewart and Welch became merely human. On a late June visit to Fenway Park, LaRussa reflected about the season to date. Although Oakland trailed the Twins by just three games, he feared the pace needed to keep up with the division would tax his team. Three months still remained, and LaRussa was concerned about his team being tired.

The Twins and the Athletics split six games in April and the managers did not meet again until the All-Star Game, where Kelly served as a coach for LaRussa. "Most people gave me the usual clichés about how we were doing great," Kelly recalled. "I don't think anybody expected us to stay there. But Tony said we had a chance. I felt he was being sincere, in part because he realized where his team was."

Their dominance over Boston propelled the Twins into first place by the end of July. Oakland was still 10 games over .500, but trailed the Twins by five games. The teams were headed for seven games against each other, three in Oakland on the first weekend of August, and four at the Metrodome two weekends later. The Athletics were in the position they had left the Twins in for most of 1988, needing to win the head-to-head battles in order to retain hope of defending their title. For the Twins, these games presented an opportunity to deliver a knockout punch.

The American League's efforts to devise a balanced schedule (a misnomer, as teams play more games outside of their division) often lead to illogical road trips. The Twins faced this inexplicable itinerary leading to the Athletics: Minnesota to Oakland, via New York. A two-game series at Yankee Stadium preceded nine games on the west coast. After this road swing, the Twins would play 30 of their final 50 games at home. It was reasonable to expect the Twins to stay in the race until the end if they could survive these 11 games on the road.

Kelly downplayed the trip's significance. "There's too many games to go, still two months to play," Kelly said. "I had two concerns. First, I wanted to win both games in New York to get the trip off to a good start. Second, we had a history of playing well in Oakland and then going to Anaheim and losing. I wanted to put a stop to that."

Kelly did not achieve his first goal. The Twins split the New York games, and endured a six-hour flight to Oakland for a series that began the next evening.

"Tony and I talked before the first game," Kelly said. "I said I thought the race would be close, and I wasn't sure how our kids would hold up. Tony then said that we had already played four months, so why did we think we couldn't play two more. I remembered that statement later. He was right."

## FRIDAY NIGHT AT OAKLAND

On August 2 the Twins were 61–42, leading the division by two games over Chicago and by four games over Oakland. The roles had reversed, as for the first time since 1987 the Twins were in first place for an important series between these teams. "That was nice," Kelly recalled. "We have always had such tough games in Oakland that it was nice to have them chase us once."

Oakland fans felt the urgency, and created an atmosphere surrounding the series that no manager, not even Kelly, could defuse. With two months yet to play, Oakland needed wins now. Meanwhile, the Twins position was similar to Oakland's in June of 1988, when Plunk knocked down Gaetti sending a message that his team would not be easily beaten. The Twins needed to show Oakland that they would compete as hard with first place at stake as they had when pride was their only goal.

The Oakland team awaiting the Twins had changed. Walt Weiss, the shortstop and the glue of the infield, had a season-ending injury after just 40 games. "That hurt Oakland, because it forced them to play [Mike] Gallego every day," Kelly explained. "Like Newman, Gallego has been a fine utility player. When you have to play him every day, he may slow down a bit. Losing Carney [Lansford] was the biggest blow, but Weiss hurt as well." Lansford's premature comeback from a devastating knee injury lasted only five games. The team had acquired Brook Jacoby from Cleveland to play third base for the rest of the season.

Oakland's bullpen was also unstable. Honeycutt and Nelson were active, but neither had regained their past form. Joe Klink had bypassed Honeycutt as the left-handed short reliever, and Nelson, whose confidence was shaken, had been relegated to long relief. Eckersley was having another fine season, but had been hit just enough to strip away the aura of invincibility usually accompanying him to the mound.

The series in Oakland promised to feature wonderful pitching, as Jack Morris and Bob Welch were paired in the opener, and Dave Stewart and Scott Erickson would pitch the finale. The

Twins were healthy following the return of Gladden and Larkin from the disabled list, and they looked forward to the cool weather of northern California to provide a refreshing break from the humidity of summer.

Friday night was the 104th game of the season, and Kelly sent an immediate message to his counterpart. He lost the first battle as Oakland threw out four Twins on the bases, but Kelly had his mind on the war. "We took a lot of heat for running and getting the four guys thrown out," Kelly said. "But we were trying to play aggressively and take the game to Oakland." This was only one game, and Kelly knew that for the remaining months his team had to play with the same feistiness demonstrated by his refusal to change his game plan. After the first two runners were thrown out, Kelly continued running when a logical situation presented itself. Kelly showed that he and his team would not back down. "Twice, we had runners thrown out on 3–2 pitches when our batter just didn't put the ball in play," Kelly said. "We struck out fewer times than any team in the league. Add it up, and we had to run to try and stay out of the double play. I think if you asked most managers, they would run in the same situation. I had no qualms about that."

Bob Welch was the beneficiary of the Athletics' victory in the baserunning battle. With catcher Terry Steinbach eliminating four runners, Welch cruised through nine innings, allowing just seven hits while raising his career record to 6–0 against the Twins at the Oakland Coliseum.

As had been the case on Opening Night, two-out base hits were Morris's downfall. Dave Henderson delivered the first Oakland run in the third inning, and Mark McGwire drove in the second run in the fourth. Both hits occurred when Morris needed only one out to escape the inning unscathed. Morris went the distance, but Welch prevented the Twins from "putting the ball in play" when runners were on the move. The result was a 3–1 Oakland victory.

Oakland was one of four American League teams (along with Boston, Cleveland, and Toronto) to play home games on Saturday afternoon. After losing the series opener on Friday night, Kelly welcomed the opportunity to "come back to the park quickly. That was good."

## SATURDAY AFTERNOON AT OAKLAND

Through seven innings on Saturday, the Twins looked weak. A barrage of five solo home runs left Oakland with a 5–0 lead, with Joe Slusarski thwarting the Twins as unaccountably as he had in the third game of the season. "We were absolutely dead in the water," Kelly admitted. "There were guys jumping up and down and hollering, trying to stir something up. I remember Suchie saying, 'We're just going to have to ride out the storm. When the boys decide to start hitting the ball, we'll be fine.' We just had to wait a long time."

Kelly smiled at the remembrance, but at the time only Oakland was smiling. Flexing their ample muscles, the Athletics had zeroed in on reducing the Twins' division lead to two games. Dave Henderson homered in each of his first three at-bats against David West, who otherwise stopped Oakland for five innings. After each homer, Jose Canseco starred in a baseball version of "Can you top this?" Trying not to be upstaged at his game, Canseco kept swinging harder and offering at bad pitches. The pride of the power hitter took over, but the results were two strikeouts and a harmless groundout.

McGwire led off the sixth inning with a solo homer to center field, ending West's afternoon. In the seventh, Canseco faced reliever Steve Bedrosian, and hit a ball that most big league hitters could only dream about. He whipped a line drive with heavy topspin that flew quickly to deep left field. The ball rode a flat plane to the fence, and it robbed the fans of the anticipation usually felt when an apparent home run climbs in its flight, and the joy felt with the realization that the ball will descend over the fence. As Canseco's line drive hurtled towards the left-field fence, the only question seemed to be whether it had the necessary height to clear the wall. Suddenly Shane Mack, playing left field in a day game following a night game, streaked towards the fence. Mack and the ball converged at the wall simultaneously. Bracing himself with his right leg halfway up the padded wall, Mack soared over the barrier just as the ball crossed. There was a split second of disbelief in the stadium as the ball ripped into the webbing of Mack's glove, which extended a foot behind the fence. Then, almost gingerly, the ball fell out as Mack's body hit the fence and he recoiled his arm into the field of play.

It all happened so quickly that it took several seconds to decipher the results. Canseco had hit a home run, not a majestic fly ball but a lashed drive that exemplified the brute strength he had helped make commonplace in baseball. Mack had made a breathtaking play simply getting near the ball. No matter how many times it was replayed, Mack's quick reactions were astonishing.

Canseco's home run gave Oakland the 5–0 lead that Slusarski took to the mound in the eighth inning. The pitcher limited the Twins to six singles, and with Eckersley in the bullpen there was absolutely no cause for optimism in the Twins' dugout.

With one out in the eighth, Greg Gagne walked, Mack singled, and Knoblauch doubled to produce a run. Suddenly, the Twins' bats were alive for the first time in the series. They were still trailing 5–1, but the Twins had two runners in scoring position and the middle of the batting order ahead. At this juncture a bolt of reality struck the Twins. Joe Klink and Kevin Campbell were warming up in the Oakland bullpen. For three years, the Athletics had been invincible in games where they led after six innings. Controlling a stable of pitchers both talented and deep, LaRussa could always orchestrate the matchups to his liking with Greg Cadaret, Eric Plunk, Todd Burns, Nelson, and Honeycutt. The set-up men needed only to finish the eighth inning, for Eckersley was as close to "automatic" as any closer in baseball history.

Now, Cadaret and Plunk were in New York, Burns was in the minors, and Nelson and Honeycutt were struggling. Opponents could harbor some faint glimmer of hope in the late innings. In the misery of their 2–9 start, the Twins inadvertently struck one damaging blow to Oakland when Nelson was injured on Opening Night. "Tony got messed up with his bullpen right there," Kelly maintained. "In his position, you have to try and piece together a staff and it just didn't happen for him."

In a departure from the norm, LaRussa let Slusarski pitch to Puckett, who singled home the two runners. With Hrbek next and the lead narrowed to two runs, LaRussa summoned Klink from the bullpen. Kelly flashed back to the last two season openers, where he had lifted Hrbek for a pinch hitter in late-inning situations against Klink. Briefly a Twin in 1987, Klink had developed into someone Kelly felt was "pretty tough on left-handed batters." It was early August with more than 50 games to play, but this was a "pennant race" series. Hrbek had improved against lefties, so he strode to the plate and coaxed a walk out of Klink.

Chili Davis singled home the fourth Twins run, and with Brian Harper due up, right-hander Campbell received the call. A product of the Dodgers' system, Campbell had never pitched above double-A until the Athletics acquired him in January. After fewer than 20 innings of major league experience, he was brought in to face a .312 hitter in what was a very significant game for his team. The moment screamed for one of Oakland's experienced hands, but LaRussa's only alternative would have been Eckersley, and the decision had been made not to use him before the ninth.

All the Twins knew about Campbell was that he threw a fastball and a slider. With two runners on, one out, and his team behind by one run, the expectation was that Harper would try to put the ball in play. Later Harper, who made himself into a .300

hitter in the majors by abandoning a concern for home runs, would say this was a rare at-bat where he thought about "going deep."

"Harp put a good swing on a fastball that the pitcher didn't get inside enough," Kelly recalled of the fly ball that Harper lofted into the left-field bleachers for a 7–5 Twins' lead. With one swing, Harper had capped the Twins' most satisfying and important inning of the year. The contrasting moods in the ballpark were memorable. The crowd sat in stunned silence, as did the Oakland dugout. The Twins emerged, ecstatic, to greet Harper. Both sides, however, realized there were still six outs remaining in a game that had lost all pretense of normalcy.

Kelly was playing a "game of outs" with his bullpen. The rally had been so shocking that the thought of using Aguilera had never occurred until Harper's home run. But Kelly wanted at least two outs in the eighth before using his stopper. Terry Leach did that for Kelly, retiring Willie Wilson and Ernest Riles, before Harold Baines was announced as a pinch hitter. Kelly had Mark Guthrie ready in the bullpen. Guthrie was breaking into the specialized role of left-handed short reliever and this presented Kelly with a perfect opening to use him. Baines did not represent the tying run, and with the two outs in his pocket, Kelly had Aguilera ready. Guthrie threw his eight warm-up pitches, and then one pitch in anger that Baines knocked over the right-field fence. "It was a fastball right down the center of the plate," Kelly recalled. "I went out there and we were sort of laughing that this move hadn't quite worked."

Baines' home run was Oakland's sixth of the game, all coming with no runners on base, and the Twins still led 7–6. With Rickey Henderson due to bat, Aguilera came in to pitch. With Dave Henderson looming on deck and already having homered three times, it was imperative for Aguilera to retire Rickey. For a split second, it appeared that Rickey would reach base as he sent a low liner up the middle. Before the ball cleared the mound, however, it struck Aguilera on his right foot, which was still swinging on its follow-through. For a split second the focus was on Aguilera and his possible injury. Then, surprisingly, Aguilera sprinted off the mound to retrieve the ball that had rolled 15 feet towards home plate. He reached down, picked up the ball in his bare hand, and fired a strike to Hrbek that barely beat the fleet Henderson. The play was every bit as amazing as Mack's effort on Canseco's drive, and not only did Aguilera get the out, but he walked off the field unassisted.

Kelly remembers the play as a "good sign that we were supposed to win the game," one of those signs that he wholeheartedly embraced. Yet, the play was a much larger indication of the Twins' season. In 1990, Kevin Tapani's promising rookie season had been curtailed by a line drive to the shin. This was the third time in 1991 that a Twins' pitcher had been struck by a batted ball and survived (Morris was hit twice, in the All-Star Game and on July 23 at Detroit.) The same analogy that Kelly always applied to Kirby Puckett's hitting could be applied here. A last-place team loses its best starter on a hit, while the first-place team can have two important pitchers get hit a total of three times and not have them miss a start.

In the ninth, Mack homered to restore the run lost to Baines' home run, and Aguilera calmly retired Oakland to close out what Kelly called a "storybook game." There [illegible]as nothing calm about the visiting clubhouse at the Oakla[illegible]hat Saturday afternoon. In the closest the Twins w[illegible]ome to really celebrating a regular-season win, Tom Kelly drank a beer, a sight not easily forgotten. "Actually, it was half a beer," he remembered. "I very rarely do that. But to go into Oakland and win a game like that makes you feel like you robbed a candy store and got away with it."

Oakland hit six home runs in a nine-inning game and lost. The Twins had overcome a five-run deficit in the eighth inning, and Eckersley had never risen in the bullpen. "The way we came back, it may not have mattered who came in. It may have been one of those days where we were just meant to win," said Kelly.

The mood in the clubhouse came dangerously close to the state of giddiness that Kelly so aggressively fought to avoid. This, however, was a win that Kelly equated with the June win in Baltimore as the most special of the year. "A lot of what a manager does in a clubhouse is directed toward the players," Kelly said. "When you act a certain way, you're trying to convince your players of something—in this case, that this win was great. It was a fun day, so why not enjoy it for a short time after the game?"

The manager was also able to enjoy a free Saturday night on the road. There was no worry about salvaging a win in the series, or awakening slumbering bats. What Kelly truly hoped for was a carryover from this emotional high to the series finale on Sunday.

## SUNDAY AFTERNOON AT OAKLAND

The first inning Sunday granted Kelly his wish. After Dave Stewart retired the first two batters, five consecutive Twins reached base, producing three runs. In a flashback to May and June, Scott Erickson took those runs to the mound and left no doubt as to the game's outcome. He wasn't the dominant pitcher the league had previously seen, but it was his best start since his injury. Over six-and-two-thirds innings, he held Oakland to two runs and allowed only four fly balls. Carl Willis finished for his second save in a 6–2 Twins' victory.

Round one went to the Twins, two games to one. One inning had clearly swung the series to the Twins, and made an indelible impact on their psyches. They were perilously close to allowing Oakland a foothold in the inevitable pennant race, along with the emotional benefits of a win in direct combat. Instead, they reestablished themselves as the team to be chased, and kept Oakland in the unfamiliar role of the pursuers.

## THE SEPARATION BEGINS

Kelly addressed his second concern about the 11-game, four-city trip. "Our biggest fault as a team over the years has been struggling right before the All-Star break," he contended. "Second to that is our history of doing well in Oakland, then going to Anaheim and playing poorly. That's what worried me."

Something else that worried Kelly since the day The Streak had ended was what he called the "separation." At some point in every season, Kelly believed division contenders create space between themselves and the remaining teams. When this separation occurs, you must be in the lead group to have any realistic hope of winning the division. The Streak, Kelly felt, left the Twins in position to contend. He stressed consistent baseball from day to day and series to series, to insure his team would be in the lead group during the separation of the American League West in 1991.

By the time the Twins went to Anaheim, the separation was in its embryonic stages. The Angels and Royals had fallen 10 games off the pace with five teams between them and first place. For those teams, it was getting late early.

Not only did the Twins have a carryover from Saturday to Sunday in Oakland, but it continued into Monday in Anaheim. Battering starter Joe Grahe for five runs in the first inning, the Twins won the opener 7–4. Randy Bush started in right field, and lined two doubles to the left-field corner. A left-handed hitter who pulled everything, Bush joked that he had probably cost some advance scouts their jobs with his unintentional opposite-field hitting. He also provided what was becoming a daily sign to Twins' watchers that what they were seeing unfold was definitely out of the ordinary.

The fourth consecutive win on the trip was posted by Willie Banks Tuesday night. In his first major league start, he displayed a curve ball that Ron Gardenhire, who managed Banks at Orlando in 1990, called "the best he had ever seen from the pitcher."

Banks's eight strikeouts included an impressive dismissal of Dave Winfield immediately after Wally Joyner had touched Banks for a two-run double.

Winning the series in Anaheim just as in Oakland, two games to one, soothed Kelly. What he termed a "great trip" was finished with two wins out of three in Seattle. The Twins had won all three series on the West Coast, and split the pair of games in New York. They went 7–4 on the trip that seemed so critical, but while he was happy with his own team, Kelly saw the Chicago White Sox constructing their first extended streak of good baseball. While in Seattle, Kelly was a guest by telephone on WFAN, the all-sports radio station in New York. Kelly said he anticipated a multi-club race in September. He looked at the standings and saw Chicago creeping closer, and knew he couldn't discount Oakland. On August 11, Wilson Alvarez of the White Sox pitched a no-hitter in Baltimore just as the Twins took the field in Seattle. A Twins' loss would leave the teams tied for first place, and the momentum that the Twins had seized in Oakland and carried through their trip would likely shift to the White Sox. Kevin Tapani responded with a four-hitter, and the Twins went home still alone at the top of the division.

Before Oakland came to the Metrodome for a long-anticipated four-game weekend series, the Twins had four games with the Angels. They turned out to be highly forgettable games after the opener, which the Twins won by a run on an eighth-inning home run by Hrbek. The Angels followed with victories by scores of 8–3, 7–4, and 9–1. "We just had a couple of days where we didn't pitch or play well," Kelly admitted. "I couldn't panic because we had played so well on the road, and we had the best record in baseball since May. It's hard to put a finger on why we lost those California games, although maybe we were looking ahead to Oakland."

Despite losing their first home series since May, the Twins took solace in the fact that their pursuers stumbled. Chicago lost three out of four games to Detroit, and Oakland was swept in a three-game series at Seattle. The Twins actually added a half-game to their lead. When the Athletics arrived in Minnesota on August 16, second-place Chicago was one-and-one-half games behind, and Oakland trailed by four games.

## FRIDAY NIGHT AT HOME

Four night games were scheduled in a series commanding great attention in Minnesota, where over 190,000 fans would attend the games. Sunday night's game was scheduled for national telecast on ESPN. While Minnesotans did not attach the urgency to this series that Oakland felt, it was clearly the most glamorous weekend of the summer for fans at the Metrodome.

The pitching rotations for the teams aligned Mike Moore and Kevin Tapani to start the Friday game, neither of whom had pitched in Oakland two weeks earlier. From the first inning, Kelly noticed a trend that he watched closely. "It seemed to me that Moore was complaining about pitches to the umpire [John Shulock]," Kelly remembered, "and [catcher Jamie] Quirk looked to be doing some arguing." There was no indication that Moore needed help, as Oakland's best pitcher in the second half held the Twins to two runs, only one of which was earned, through eight innings.

The Twins had taken an early 2–0 lead, but Canseco and Quirk erased that by the sixth. Canseco led off the fourth and sixth innings with long home runs to the opposite field. Tapani had a habit that neither Kelly nor Dick Such could explain of allowing hits in bunches, and in the innings where Canseco homered, Quirk added run-scoring hits. With a 4–2 lead, the game proceeded in a more orderly fashion for Oakland as Moore and Honeycutt carried the Athletics into the ninth.

At that point, the Teflon roof was nearly blown off the Metrodome by a most astonishing baseball inning. The Twins faced Dennis Eckersley, a matchup that the closer had previously dominated. Since becoming Oakland's full-time stopper in 1988, Eckersley had been perfect against the Twins, saving 15 games. For three years, the Twins could not even score a run off Eckersley, a streak that ended in April of 1991, when he surrendered a solo home run to Greg Gagne while pitching with a three-run lead. Kelly believed the Twins were "dead in the water" during the Saturday game in Oakland. Now, 50,000 fans shared that sentiment as they watched Eckersley enter the game. Few dared to think the Twins could repeat their earlier comeback that took place in Oakland.

Chili Davis was the first to face Eckersley, pitting a batter with patience against a pitcher with impeccable control. The result was an at-bat containing all the elements that constitute baseball's best drama. The count went to 2–2 when Eckersley fired a pitch towards the outside corner against the left-handed-batting Davis. The only thing more surprising than seeing Davis take the pitch was seeing Shulock call the pitch a ball. American Leaguers have been conditioned to accept that any close pitch thrown by Eckersley will be called a strike. It is an unspoken, unwritten honor earned by players who excel, and is accepted universally. Eckersley expected to reap the benefits on this pitch, and when he did not, his knees buckled in disbelief.

The count was now full, and Davis lined the next pitch to right field. Canseco attempted to field the ball on a short hop off the artificial turf, but it skipped past his left shoulder and bounced to the fence. Davis ended up at third base, and the Athletics gladly conceded the run when Harper grounded out.

Still, Oakland led 4–3 with one out and the bottom of the Twins' order coming to bat. If Eckersley could compose himself and forget the pitch to Davis, Oakland would have the victory.

Kelly wanted left-handed batters to face Eckersley, so he pinch-hit Randy Bush for Shane Mack. Bush jumped on the first pitch and lined a double into the right-field corner. People stood and the noise rose in a crescendo reminiscent of the Metrodome of 1987. For the first time, Eckersley appeared merely mortal in front of Minnesotans, and the Twins needed only one more hit to tie the game.

No one had the chance to even sit back down before Mike Pagliarulo lined Eckersley's first pitch into left-center field, easily scoring pinch runner Scott Leius. The crowd roared at the unprecedented feat. The Twins had denied Eckersley a save. The Oakland dugout roared at Shulock, while Eckersley and Quirk tried to suppress their rage. The game went to extra innings after Gagne struck out and Gladden flied out.

Steve Bedrosian pitched for the Twins in the tenth, and began the inning by hitting Dave Henderson with a pitch. Canseco came to bat, and after his earlier home run, there was fear that he could dampen the heightened spirits of the crowd with one swing. Bedrosian responded to the challenge, however, getting Canseco to pop out to Hrbek. Harold Baines was next, and he sent a line drive to left-center field that Gladden caught. Henderson, who had just stolen second base, tagged up and tried to advance to third, a questionable play since there were already two outs. Gladden's throw to Pagliarulo was on target, and Henderson was caught.

As the Twins left the field listening to the roaring crowd, a confrontation began at home plate. Quirk and Shulock were engaged in a violent argument, one that was expected an inning earlier but had begun unnoticed in the inning break. Quirk, it was later learned, had flung his batting helmet from the on-deck circle after Henderson had been called out at third, and was ejected by second-base umpire Tim Tschida. He came out to catch the bottom half of the inning, and when informed of his ejection, went berserk, throwing a tantrum any third-grader would be proud of. He flung his catching gear in all directions, and had to be physically restrained from Shulock.

After Quirk was escorted from the field, LaRussa replaced him with Terry Steinbach. Within moments, Kelly was out of the dugout to talk with Shulock. "My understanding of the rule was that when a player is ejected, the new man gets five throws," Kelly recalled. "Steinbach had his five, so I went to John [Shulock] and asked him how many throws does a man get when he comes in to replace an ejected player? Those were the only words I said. Shulock took over, and Tony got mad about that."

LaRussa later claimed that Kelly had administered a cheap shot, a charge that bothered Kelly and one he denied. "I did what I thought was best for any club. Danny [Gladden] made a big play, my team was excited about playing. We had the momentum going our way, and the game was being slowed down. I was actually trying to get the game going. I'm sure Sparky Anderson or any other manager would have done the same thing," Kelly said, evoking the name of the manager both he and LaRussa admired.

Kelly felt an odd mixture of competitiveness and compassion running through him as the ugly scene unfolded. As manager of the Twins, he had to respect LaRussa's will to win, and be alert to a deliberate attempt to delay play. Kelly remembers "standing in the dugout, and feeling bad for what was going on over there [in the Oakland dugout.] "I know I wouldn't want to be in that situation," he said. Oakland was on a losing streak, their closer had allowed the tying run, and a player had completely snapped before 50,000 fans. No wonder Kelly believes that "Tony was mad in general about this game, and what had happened before the series. He may not have liked my move, but I think there were numerous other things about that game he disliked more than what I did."

After the game resumed, the bullpens "matched zeroes." In the 12th, LaRussa turned to Nelson as his sixth pitcher of the long night. After retiring Gladden on a fly ball, Nelson surrendered a double to Knoblauch. Only 180 feet of base paths from a win, the Twins had Puckett and Hrbek batting. Never could a fan have predicted that Knoblauch would score on a pair of dribblers to the left side of the infield that together did not travel the distance he ran to score the winning run.

It was another Twins-Athletics classic, a game replete with drama and quality plays. Yet in the end, the game was decided in the Twins' favor by a couple of infield hits.

Kelly hoped to meet LaRussa before Saturday's game. He had read and heard of LaRussa's "cheap shot" references in postgame comments, but LaRussa's priority was to meet with the umpires to clarify his statement "Someone has decided we've won too much." "I'd have probably done the same thing," Kelly admitted. "You have to make sure everyone is on the same page and can forget about yesterday." Kelly waited in the Twins' dugout during batting and infield practice, hoping to catch LaRussa's eye after he arrived on the field for his pregame press briefing. (LaRussa dealt with the traveling media en masse, much like a politician.) In fact, LaRussa did not arrive in the dugout until shortly before first pitch, and the two managers did not speak.

## SATURDAY NIGHT AT HOME

Saturday featured another Morris-Welch matchup, and Oakland struck quickly as the first four batters singled to produce three runs. Welch was handed a lead, and hoped to shake his past problems at the Metrodome, but the Twins' hitters never let him settle into the game. "I have no idea why we have success against him at the Dome," said Kelly. "But, in this game, the players came back at him well."

A run in the second plus three more in the third, coupled with an additional Oakland run off Morris in the third, left the game tied at 4–4. The hitters had taken early control of this game, and the Twins' goal was to finish off Welch while he was scuffling.

It happened in the fifth. Shane Mack was the batter, with the bases loaded and two outs. Welch was facing his third tough inning, but LaRussa's bullpen had been used the previous night, and like Kelly, he knew that any hopes for his team revolved around the efforts of his top starters. Mack stepped to the plate a much more relaxed hitter than the man who had faced Welch in April. Since the All-Star break, Mack had been the Twins' best hitter. His average was pushing .300, and he had more home runs than anyone except Davis. His return to the lineup in May had been gradual, and in the second half he made Kelly's handling of the whole outfield affair appear masterful. Mack now had an opportunity with one swing to further distance himself from the days of April. With that one swing, he lined a low drive into the right-field corner for a double that easily cleared the bases for a 9–4 Twins' lead.

Welch had another Metrodome start unravel, and this was particularly distressing as his team had staked him a three-run inning before he took the mound. Meanwhile, Morris breezed through the middle innings. "This was one of those games in which Jack may not have had his best stuff at the start, but he got much stronger as the game moved along," Kelly maintained. After the three-run first inning, Morris allowed just four hits, one being Canseco's 34th home run of the season. Once Mack's hit gave him the lead, Morris was indomitable, allowing only two balls to leave the infield in the last four innings. His 15th win, by a final score of 12–4, pushed Oakland six games behind the Twins.

Kelly finally had his moment with LaRussa on Sunday morning. The two managers had committed to appear on a taping of Bob Costas's national radio program in downtown Minneapolis. LaRussa was understandably grim about the first two games of the series, and what had become a six-game losing streak for his team. "I told Tony what I did and why," Kelly said. "Deep down, I think he was still mad about the whole series."

## SUNDAY NIGHT AT HOME

Sunday night's game focused the national spotlight on this wonderfully entertaining series. Stewart was the Oakland starter, and Banks was making his third start for the Twins. Pitching a second game against California had been a rude awakening for the rookie, who was pounded for six runs in less than four innings. Tonight, he would regain the unfamiliarity that gives a pitcher an extra edge in his first meeting with a team.

Certainly the rookie faced a formidable foe in Stewart, with tension added by national television and a huge crowd. Banks was a long way from St. Elizabeth High School in Jersey City, New Jersey, where the Twins had scouted him endlessly before drafting him in 1987. This night would be one that Banks could chalk up as a baptism to the big leagues. "Willie didn't hit the corners very well with his pitches," Kelly admitted. "His ball was over the center of the plate. So after three innings he had enough. And we had Train [Carl Willis] ready to pick us up as he did all year."

Willis entered in the fourth with Oakland already leading 3-1, and Stewart doing his best to imitate Morris's performance of Saturday night. However, Stewart, who had been bailed out by three double-play ground balls, was struggling with his control. After walking his fifth batter with one out in the seventh and a 4–1 lead, LaRussa began to ready his bullpen. The Twins struck quickly, though, and tacked up two runs before Honeycutt retired Hrbek to end the inning.

Oakland went out in order against Willis in the eighth, the fifth inning for the veteran who had provided the Twins all year with the kind of relief pitching that LaRussa was accustomed to but lacked in 1991. Nursing a one-run lead, LaRussa hoped for a return to form with Honeycutt pitching the last of the eighth, and Eckersley the ninth. The Twins' hitters would not allow that to happen.

In order, Honeycutt surrendered a single by Davis, a triple into the right-field corner by Harper, and singles by Mack and Pagliarulo. Before Steve Chitren could end the inning, three runs scored for a 6–4 Twins' lead. When Aguilera retired the Athletics in order, Oakland had lost seven consecutive games for the first time under LaRussa. Seven games separated the teams, and the decisive way in which the Twins had won these games firmly established them as a team capable of handling first place.

## MONDAY NIGHT AT HOME

Oakland had one last chance to salvage some pride and a win from this series on Monday. This game was the most entertaining of the weekend. Oakland won 8–7 on a two-out single by Terry Steinbach in the ninth inning, but not before another emotion-driven comeback by the Twins had overcome a 6–1 deficit. Puckett, Pagliarulo, and Hrbek homered for the Twins offense, and the defense shone by throwing out Rickey Henderson twice at the plate.

An interesting byplay developed between Rickey Henderson and Puckett. In the sixth, Puckett nailed Henderson at the plate on a perfect strike from center field. The next inning, Henderson threw Puckett out at second as he tried to stretch a single. After his throw, Henderson ran towards Puckett, pointing at him as if to say that they were now even. This action, while shocking had it come from Puckett, was not surprising coming from Henderson.

This game did not end until the season's most memorable foul ball had been hit. After Steinbach's single, Eckersley appeared for the first time since Friday's fiasco. Pagliarulo struck out as the first batter, then Bush followed with his second pinch-hit double of the series off Eckersley. The stopper appeared to be avoiding a repeat of the series opener as he retired Knoblauch for the second out. Gene Larkin was the Twins' last hope. The Twins' left-handed hitters had been enjoying some success against Eckersley, and what Kelly still recalls first about this superb game was the "unbelievable swing" Larkin put on Eckersley's pitch. Turning on the pitch with power he did not often show, Larkin smashed the pitch towards the right-field upper deck. For those watching, there was a brief instant of ecstasy and even disbelief as the ball left Larkin's bat. Could the Twins beat Eckersley twice in a series? The improbability of that occurrence hit home as Larkin's drive hooked several feet to the foul side of the right-field screen. It was as long a ball as any Twin had hit off Eckersley in his career as a closer, and it served to send another jolt of energy into a crowd drained by the events of the weekend. Eckersley regrouped and retired Larkin on a pop to the shortstop.

"It was a fantastic series, and I was happy to win three out of four," Kelly recalled. Many of Kelly's fears were allayed as his younger players performed well, led by Knoblauch's nine hits. After trailing in all four games, the Twins had rallied in each to tie and eventually win three. Oakland now knew that the Twins were the team to beat, and so did the rest of the American League West.

After the conclusion of the series, Kelly felt more comfortable about his relationship with LaRussa. On Monday afternoon, the Twins hosted a luncheon at the Metrodome for season ticket holders, and both managers had committed to attend. As Kelly waited outside his office for the program to begin, he professed no doubt that LaRussa would show. "I knew Tony would be there, and he put on a very entertaining show," Kelly remembered. "Afterwards, we went into my office and talked. I showed him a few things about some pitchers he would be facing, and we exchanged some secrets. It's something of a professional courtesy that we've always done."

With the showdown complete, Kelly wasn't completely sure he could write off Oakland's chances entirely. "You can't be sure about any team with hitters like they have," Kelly warned. "I didn't look at it that way then. But now, if you look back, I think Tony would say that series might have done them in."

There were 42 games left to play, but these teams were finished with each other. It seemed a shame, after seven games of such quality baseball filled with quality plays. As had happened in past years, playing Oakland had brought out the best in the Twins. They had faced their biggest challenge to date, and had prospered. In doing so, the Twins left the legacy of a series at the Metrodome that will live on in baseball lore. "There was controversy, arguing, home runs, comebacks, extra innings, strategy, packed houses, and drama. It was filled with everything baseball has to offer," marvelled Kelly. "It was the best regular season series I've ever been involved with."

# MORRIS AND THE FINISH

*"When Seattle won, I grabbed the intercom and just said, 'Congratulations, 1991 West Division Champions.'"*
***Tom Kelly***

JACK MORRIS

"I can't help but wonder though. Do Twins fans really think Jack Morris will make their boys a winner?" Mike Gelfand, *St. Paul Pioneer Press,* February 10, 1991

Tom Kelly believed Jack Morris would make the Twins a winning team. He actually had no other choice, after posturing to Carl Pohlad and Andy MacPhail over the winter that Morris's presence was vital. Kelly knew that Morris would be the foundation of his pitching staff, always taking the ball for his turn, allowing the bullpen an occasional day off, and allowing Kevin Tapani and Scott Erickson to develop further in a less intense spotlight. Morris's performances toward the end of the 1990 Detroit Tigers' season had convinced Kelly that he could pitch, and an incentive-loaded contract based on innings convinced Kelly that Morris would pitch.

There was still concern that the unique contract Morris had signed could present thorny moments for the manager. The Twins had hired Morris to pitch a large number of innings, and he earned more money as that total climbed. The contract structure could conceivably lead to conflict between Kelly's obligation to remove a pitcher at the proper time for the sake of his team, and Morris's earning power.

With Morris, the Twins inherited a pitcher who had established his own pitching tradition. In eight of the previous nine seasons, Morris had pitched at least 235 innings, a total achieved yearly by only a handful of other pitchers. Sparky Anderson never removed Morris if there was any question as to Jack's ability to continue. Morris often said he had "earned the right to stay in those games." Kelly, however, was unconcerned about the routine in Detroit. He had established his own tradition in handling pitchers, one that did not include permitting his starters to pile up a large number of innings. Complete games meant little to Kelly, and he always had his mind set on making a move when he walked out to the mound.

It was obvious that the manager, whose pitchers praised him for his care and handling, and the pitcher, who detested coming out of any game, had to set some ground rules. "We talked in the spring," Kelly recalled. "Jack told me, 'You're the manager. If you have to take me out of a game, do it. Don't expect me to like it.' And we never had a problem. Now, Jack didn't always like coming out. That's fine. You want a guy to want to stay out there. But you can't have any productions on the mound when you make a change, and we never did. In fact, about halfway through the season, Jack was angry about coming out of a game. But then he said that Sparky always left him in these games and he would end up losing. He was not a guy you liked to take out, but he realized we were doing the right thing."

Morris had played for just one major league manager, and Kelly had only managed one pitcher, Bert Blyleven, at a comparable stage in his career. It was perfectly normal to expect each to need an indoctrination period, but Morris allayed any fears about his assimilation into his new team with an outstanding spring. Kelly could not have hoped for a better approach to the often monotonous drills and exercises of spring training. "I saw why Jack is such a good athlete, and why he fielded his position so well," Kelly explained. "He was always first in line for the drills, and he did everything properly."

While Morris's pitching presented no serious worry, Kelly did carry concern for Morris's ability to handle all of the changes this year brought into his life. Not only was Morris pitching in a different city for the first time, but he was in the early stages of a particularly painful divorce, which also separated him from his sons. "We all knew Jack was going through a lot personally," Kelly said. "There were some days when he came to the park, and we could tell from the look on his face that something was wrong. I was worried about his mood swings. But the clubhouse atmosphere here helped Jack. When he had tough days, the other players really seemed to help him."

Nothing helped Morris on his first trip back to Detroit in May. The Twins were scheduled for a three-game weekend series, and Sunday was Morris's turn to start. "We made a mistake," Kelly admitted. "His day was Sunday, but that meant he had three days of nonsense before he worked. There was too much going on, to the point where he was being hassled on parking tickets. Then Jack decided he was going to trick his old buddies. It was awful." The trick was on Morris, as Cecil Fielder hit a three-run home run in the first, further inciting a crowd that was poised to harass Morris. Rookie Milt Cuyler hit a grand slam to complete a seven-run first inning, seemingly bringing the stadium Morris had excelled in crashing down on the pitcher. It would have been easy for Morris to be emotionally crushed by the heckling of a crowd that had once cheered his every pitch. Instead Morris kept pitching, completing four innings. Before he left the game, Morris made a lasting impression in the dugout. As disappointing as the memory of the game was for Kelly, he smiled at the reminiscence of Morris refusing to hide or sulk after the first-inning pounding. "Jack gives up seven runs, and he comes in the dugout and says, 'Just get me 10 runs, boys. I've never lost a game with ten runs.'"

The veteran Twins began to form a vastly different opinion of Morris as a teammate. Opposing him through the years, many Twins had developed a disdain for Morris's mound antics, in particular his attitude towards errors behind him in the field. That was another topic that Kelly addressed with Morris in the spring. "Jack had a train of thought that he was out there busting his butt to pitch, and had trouble accepting errors," Kelly explained. "We were a little worried about that because we couldn't have that attitude here. I understood what Jack said, but I didn't agree with it. Fortunately, we never had a problem." Morris did not react to Puckett's error in the season opener, which quelled many fears.

Kelly did not just have to be concerned with Morris's pitching, but he was also wondering about Morris's presence in the clubhouse. Here came a successful veteran with a strong personality into a clubhouse, where the first commandment was that all occupants were equal. Kelly was thinking about ways to insure that the tone set by Puckett and Hrbek would not be disrupted by the addition of a prominent player from another team. "Jim Wiesner and I talked about where his locker should be," admitted Kelly. "In Detroit, he had an end locker, sort of buried in the corner. There is a science to this, and you have to be very careful who you put in the corners. Wies had a good feel for this, and after we talked we decided to put Jack's locker toward the middle of the room. That way he would be involved in all the joking and ribbing."

Morris was indeed involved in the clubhouse. He quickly developed a good rapport with the pitchers, most notably Kevin Tapani. Morris acquired the nickname "Fossil," which was respectfully bestowed upon him by his fellow pitchers at every turn. His wardrobe, featuring a loud mustard-yellow sport coat, was a frequent target for verbal abuse. "Jack was real vulnerable to a good ribbing," Kelly remembered with a smile. "It was too easy. But he was a great guy to have in the clubhouse."

Morris's mood brightened significantly as the season progressed. His pitching improved dramatically as the team's fortunes rose. Kelly believed Scott Erickson's excellence served to prod Morris. "I thought it was a challenge to Jack, and as he saw Scott string together wins, he had to try to keep up," Kelly maintained.

Morris proved himself true to the test by winning eight consecutive games after that Sunday massacre in Detroit. It took Morris nearly 10 starts to conquer his inconsistency and run off a streak of top-calibre games. Kelly recalls a turning point when Morris pitched in Texas the night after Erickson stopped the Rangers' 14-game winning streak. "I remember sitting with Tony [Oliva] in the dugout, watching Jack's forkball work," Kelly recalled. "We looked at each other and said Texas had no chance." Morris pitched a four-hitter to beat Nolan Ryan, and won the second game in his streak of eight. From that point in late May until October, his vaunted forkball was again a weapon. "Jack's fastball may not be quite what it once was, but it's still pretty good," Kelly said. "What separates Morris is his forkball. If it's working, he's devastating, and won't get beat."

The theme of Morris's return to Minnesota was first sounded on June 30. Chicago was visiting the Metrodome for the first time. The White Sox captured the first two games, the second being the game that ended Erickson's winning streak and sent him to the disabled list. On Sunday afternoon, Morris was matched with Chicago's ace, Jack McDowell, before a sell-out crowd. Morris's goal was to stop a losing streak that stood at four, and stem any Chicago hope of establishing control of their series with the Twins. Paul Abbott was scheduled to start Monday's final game, and no one wanted him to take the mound with the burden of a long losing streak.

Now was the time for Morris to give the Twins a return on their investment. His response was a four-hit shutout that White Sox manager Jeff Torborg labeled as "vintage Morris." "This was the day we got Jack for," Kelly admitted. Morris wrapped up into one performance a scintillating shutout that stopped a losing streak, rested the bullpen, removed pressure from a young pitcher, and slowed a charging competitor. It was the first time a game had been designated as the kind Jack was supposed to pitch. That refrain would be heard again.

Chicago stopped Morris's winning streak in his next start. LaRussa then honored Morris with the starting assignment at the All-Star Game in Toronto. Even Morris admitted that the start belonged to Erickson, who was disabled. Yet Morris took justifiable pride in the honor, as it served to validate his ability to compete at the highest baseball level at age 36. "I think he knew he could still pitch, and he knew we were confident in him," said Kelly. "Maybe he felt he had to prove it to others."

Taking the mound wearing his stirrups low in the style popularized by Erickson, Morris was on the national stage for the first time since facing the Twins in the play-offs four years earlier. He was tested immediately, as Bobby Bonilla ripped a line drive off his right foot. The hearts of an entire region stopped, beginning with Kelly's in the American League dugout. The Twins had yet to learn about Morris perseverance and tolerance of pain, qualities that carried him through more than 3,000 innings. Morris had told Kelly in the spring never to expect him to ask out of a game, and the All-Star Game was no exception. He finished two innings and made his next scheduled Twins' start.

The shining example of Morris's resiliency came two weeks later. In his encore performance at Tiger Stadium, he was hit on the right arm by a Cuyler line drive. The sound of ball hitting arm was sickening, and Morris immediately walked off the field with a visible welt. It would have been no surprise had an announcement been made that the arm was broken. Instead, Morris escaped with a deep bruise that seemed certain to do what the All-Star Game blow to the foot did not cause Morris to miss a start.

Two days later, early arrivees at Tiger Stadium saw and heard a personification of competitive athletics. Morris was on the bullpen mound doing his normal throwing between starts. The sight was stunning given the injury, but more memorable was the sound emanating from Rick Stelmaszek's glove as he caught Morris's efforts. "It was amazing to watch," Kelly recalled. "He's a tough son of a gun. When it's his turn to pitch, he pitches unless he's on his deathbed."

Morris took his next scheduled turn, and although it lasted less than three innings, he demonstrated a reliability that his manager and teammates came to depend upon. They also came to admire Morris's sheer love of winning. Morris was a baseball player's version of Vince Lombardi. He loved to play and compete, but he needed to win. As the Twins won more games, and it became clear they would contend down to the wire, Morris relished his role as the leader of the staff. While the fourth and fifth spots in the rotation became a "mix and match" process for Kelly, on every fifth day came a soothing calm with the knowledge that Morris would start. To those who had seen Jack over the years, he seemed happier in the clubhouse. On the good days, there was relaxed repartee with his teammates, and on the bad days, the same people were there for support. The fans knew nothing of Morris's personal life, but they fell in love with the pitcher the franchise had desperately needed, who made fantasy a reality by finally pitching in his hometown.

As the season moved towards its increasingly inevitable conclusion, Jack Morris was in professional nirvana. He was the acknowledged leader of a staff heading towards a championship. Eighteen wins would be his highest single-season total since 1987, and he matched his career norms with 35 starts and 246 innings pitched. Kelly knew that Morris had been "everything we got him for," but still felt frustrated because "Jack could easily have won the Cy Young Award. He let a couple of games get away that could have given him 20 or 21 wins."

Kelly found the experience of managing Jack Morris "enjoyable" and very similar to what Sparky Anderson encountered. "Sparky said that Jack could be moody, arrogant, self-centered, things like that, and at certain times that was true," admitted Kelly. "But Sparky also said that Jack was the best pitcher he had ever managed. And that was also true. Jack can pitch the baseball. When his mind is on it, he's as good as anyone."

## COUNTDOWN TO OCTOBER

Tom Kelly had a nagging concern through September that left him perplexed. Each morning, he looked at the newspaper and saw his team edge closer to what had been unthinkable nine months earlier. September began with a seven-game lead over Oakland, which effectively eliminated the Athletics, as the teams had no games remaining with each other. Chicago's hope rested primarily in six games with the Twins in the final two weeks. For the Twins, the goal was simple. They just had to "win our games" to avoid any semblance of a division race.

Still this anxiety that Kelly could not name haunted him in September's early days. It took some time, but he was finally able to pinpoint the cause. "After 1987, I knew what a great thing it was to participate in the play-offs and the World Series. Suddenly it's September, we have a seven-game lead, and I had an awful time understanding why I was so concerned. But I finally realized that I didn't want to miss that opportunity. The thought of missing out on October when we were so close scared me. Once you've been there, you don't want to miss the chance to go back."

Kelly was relieved that he saw no such concern in any of the players, so he focused on hiding his own worries. His team never

Kirby Puckett watches his home run leave the park in Game 6 of the World Series.

Agony becomes ecstasy as Gladden scores the World Championship run.

The look of a champion . . . Puckett sends the Twins to Game 7.

The moment every player dreams about . . . World Champions!

Kirby Puckett after the Twins win the World Championship.

The rookie played like a veteran in October; Chuck Knoblauch proudly wears his World Championship shirt.

Kirby Puckett leads a World Championship salute.

Wearing their World Championship hats and shirts are (*left to right*) Carl Willis, Steve Bedrosian, David West, Tommy Kelly (Tom's son), Chili Davis, and Scott Erickson.

allowed anyone close enough to cause Kelly's fears to surface. After a 12–7 start in September, the Twins' lead on September 22 was eight games, identical to the margin on September 1. Now just 12 games remained, including six with Chicago, and the magic number count was in full swing.

The White Sox had waited since the All-Star break for a shot at the Twins, but by their first appointment at the Metrodome, the Twins were reveling in the comfort of an eight-game lead. Chicago approached all six games knowing that winning was necessary for survival.

"They set up their pitching for us with [Jack] McDowell and [Alex] Fernandez at the Dome," Kelly recalled. "We were three starters, and then some mix and match. But McDowell didn't throw well and we beat him around pretty good. That picked us up with a huge crowd there."

Two runs in the first inning and four in the second, punctuated by a Hrbek two-run homer, drove McDowell from the game and the crowd of 43,450 into a frenzy. As the game moved into the middle innings, there was a celebratory air about the Metrodome. The noise level was high for a regular season game, and it seemed to be tinged with an extra jolt of energy as these fans realized they were the first to witness the crowning of a champion. They had watched the elimination of Oakland from serious contention in August, and now they saw Chicago's hopes, the last team with a threat, fading.

Scott Erickson took the gift of six early runs and pitched like his older teammate Morris. When he would get an early lead, he pitched better with that comfort. Erickson did not allow a baserunner until the sixth inning, or a hit until Dan Pasqua homered with one out in the seventh. "He pitched a great game, his best since he was disabled," Kelly maintained. "It wasn't a devastating performance like he put on early in the year, but he kept the ball down with good movement. I was thrilled he gave up a hit, so I could get him out of there." The seven innings Erickson worked matched his longest outing since June 24.

Mark Guthrie completed a one-hitter with two shutout innings. The Twins, in reducing their magic number to three, enjoyed a victory that placed them on the brink of a division title.

Chicago denied the Twins the pleasure of clinching a tie at home with a 6–1 win the following night. Toronto was the next stop, and the Twins hoped to wrap up the division there to strip any significance from a four-game series in Chicago which followed.

Juan Guzman, a rookie right-hander who had burst onto the major league scene with a fastball that regularly topped 90 miles per hour, stopped the Twins on Friday night, but Chicago also lost to Seattle. On Saturday afternoon, with the magic number at two, Morris strode to the same SkyDome mound that he had last left at the All-Star Game. It was another game that Jack was meant to pitch. The result was his 26th career shutout, a suspense-free six-hitter that clinched a tie in the division.

In a season that had seen so many omens of good fortune for the Twins, this clinching was the first troublesome venture, albeit a pleasant problem. Every man in uniform wanted to clinch on the field, by winning their game and celebrating in the appropriate manner. But as Kelly realized, "It's not a perfect world. I wanted to clinch Saturday afternoon, so I could enjoy relaxing Saturday night at the racetrack." Instead, a team gathering was planned at a Toronto sports bar owned by hockey personality Don Cherry. There the Twins could watch Chicago's game via satellite. It quickly became awkward as the players watched uncomfortably, many secretly hoping for a Chicago win that would enable the Twins to win the last game themselves. Television cameras watched the players for reactions. The affair ended mercifully and quickly as Chicago scored early and proceeded to win.

Given the chance they wanted, the Twins fell by a 2–1 score

on Sunday. "We played a good game, but just came up short," Kelly recalled. "We had a discussion and some thought was given to staying and waiting for the Chicago game to end. [At this point, the White Sox game was in the middle innings.] But that didn't sound right to me. I'd rather go with the program we used all year. Sitting around and waiting for somebody to lose wasn't right."

So the Twins showered and dressed for their 75-minute bus ride to Hamilton, the city whose airport was used by American League teams to expedite the customs and immigration process. Kelly's attitude was to prepare to beat the White Sox the next night and clinch the title on their field. Halfway to Hamilton, the news came by cellular phone. "Remzi [Kiratli] had his phone and was on with the press box in Chicago," Kelly explained. "When Seattle won, I grabbed the intercom and just said, 'Congratulations, 1991 West Division Champions.'"

The news was relayed by radio to the second bus in the Twins' party, and one of the oddest clinchings in baseball history had transpired on the Queen Elizabeth Way in Ontario. The team allowed television cameras and newspaper photographers on the buses, and their presence restrained the celebration on the bus ride. There were handshakes, high fives, and lots of smiles, but this was a far cry from the typical clinch scene that players dream about. On the tarmac at the Hamilton airport, some emotions were unleashed as the buses unloaded. For fifteen minutes, the Twins were able to mingle among each other with hugs, and accept the realization that they had accomplished something no one outside their group dared to think was possible at the beginning of the year. Just as in 1987, at this moment, a bond was formed among these players that will never be broken. As their careers and lives move in different directions, they will forever be linked by six months and a championship in 1991.

Tom Kelly was relieved. After handling media obligations at the airport, he was able to share a few moments of joy with the coaches and players. He needed to fear no more, for he would not miss the opportunity that he craved to repeat. He would be around for a seventh month, the month of October.

Nearly four hours after they became champions, the Twins finally celebrated. When the arrived at the Westin Chicago, champagne was awaiting in a banquet room. The team had their clubhouse party, and with no cameras or reporters present, it was an uninhibited, unrestricted affair. Players, coaches, trainers, and staff, all people of varying backgrounds and interests, partied as one. If they partied hard, there was good reason.

"This was the biggest relief because it's the toughest title to win," Kelly believed. "Winning a championship decided over 162 games is unbelievably difficult, so it's such a relief to have it over. We needed 95 wins for the division. It seems so small to need just four wins to reach the next step."

Indeed, no championship in team sports compares to winning a baseball division. The mental grind of 162 games, crammed into a schedule that permits an average of three days off per month, is at least the equal of the physical demands of major league baseball. Kelly often talked about the sight of adults jumping around like children, when a team wins a championship. That is usually a group release of the mental tension a baseball season breeds. In a Chicago hotel on a Sunday night, the Twins let all their tensions loose in one wonderful night.

Kelly was there for the party's beginning. "I wanted to be there for a short while," said Kelly. "It's probably just a personal preference. I just felt I should stay for a bit, then get away and let the team have the party to themselves."

Reflecting on his 1987 experience, Kelly knew his team would avoid one question. This club had already clinched a winning road record, the one failing that his 1987 team could not live down. "That didn't mean much to me," Kelly claimed. "It was just something that the writers could use when they needed something to write." More importantly, there was one parallel between the teams. "We worked hard to get in position to clinch with six or seven games left in the season," said Kelly. "In 1987, we were able to rest people, unlike the Cardinals. So it's not our fault when people got hurt for St. Louis. It was a tribute to our club that we got in position to rest people and get them healthy. This year I had the same chance to get rid of the fatigue factor."

Seven games remained in the regular season and Kelly would use them as a "fall training." The starters would get enough at-bats to stay sharp and enough rest to be fresh. The reserves would get a chance to play in their postseason roles. The pitching would be structured to align everybody around the expected start by Morris in the play-off opener.

Before the regular season ended, some bizarre business had to be concluded in Chicago. On the first night, tradition from 1987 was repeated as Randy Bush homered. A wise man who learns a lesson quickly, Bush did not volunteer for duty in this year's "after the party special." Yet he was in the lineup, and not even any residual effects of the celebration could slow his torrid bat.

Then there was the Kent Hrbek-Hawk Harrelson battle. As a White Sox television announcer, Harrelson had adopted a unique style that was long on enthusiasm for the home team, and in the eyes of virtually everyone outside Chicago, short on professionalism. In his haste to boost the fortunes of "his team," Harrelson often sounded as if he were demeaning the efforts of opposing players. In the satellite era, other games are always showing in clubhouses throughout baseball. Thus the Twins were able to monitor Harrelson's utterances all season long. To a team that prided themselves on treating baseball with respect, Harrelson's approach grated on the Twins. The sentiments, however, were not voiced until after the emotional win of September 24, when Hrbek told writers how much Harrelson's comments irritated the Twins. Harrelson responded the next day on a Twin Cities radio station, with an attack on Hrbek's productivity that received considerable play in the newspapers of both cities.

Kelly wanted the feud to end. "When we got to Chicago on Monday, I told Herbie that I didn't want to hear any more. It's over with." It was, until Thursday. The first rain out of the Twins season occurred on Wednesday night and forced a doubleheader for Thursday afternoon. Plans for an airport rally upon the Twins' return from Chicago were altered. No one could foretell that the day would be played as if it had been scripted by Rod Serling.

Chicago won the first game by scoring three runs off Aguilera in the ninth and 10th innings, a rally that cost Morris his 19th victory. The Twins led the nightcap 6–1 in the fourth inning, but the pitching staff had an uncharacteristically rough day. By the ninth, Chicago owned a 12–8 lead. After two runs had scored, Bobby Thigpen came from the bullpen in search of the final out. Tom Kelly called on Hrbek to pinch hit. The teams had arrived in the morning, and it was now evening. A mist blew in the air, and rain was forecast for the nighttime hours. The players already used by the Twins were showered and ready to leave. There was just the matter of Hrbek versus Thigpen. Over 30,000 fans attended the first game and fewer than 3,000 remained to witness the incredible sight of Hrbek driving a Thigpen fastball into the left-field bleachers for a game-tying home run. Hrbek ran the bases with an uncontrollable giggle, and as he touched home plate, he pointed to the broadcast booth occupied by Harrelson, and repeated the salute when he reached the dugout. Kelly felt the players "took some of the announcer's words too literally," and he wasn't much in agreement with Hrbek's display. However, the emotion of the moment was undeniable.

Unfortunately, the Twins could not push across one more run. Chicago finally ended the game in the 12th inning, sweeping a doubleheader that lasted over eight hours. The games meant nothing, yet were both maddening and entertaining. An airport rally scheduled for six o'clock in Minnesota would not happen until midnight. But the craziness of the day in Chicago forced the Twins to look at the bright side. Five minutes after the second game ended, the skies opened in a downpour.

Going home for the Twins meant recognizing the true magnitude of their accomplishment. There was a different joy than in 1987, in large part because this team had played so well that the division championship had seemed inevitable for a month. The Twins had earned this championship by outplaying baseball's strongest division, and the region sensed both how unexpected this had been, and how rewarding it is to have two title winners in five years.

For Tom Kelly, the last weekend of the season meant three meaningless games against the champion of the East Division, Toronto. As he managed to prepare for the play-offs, he could reflect on the decisions made in Fort Myers and piece together the elements of a division winner.

Kelly had fought for Morris and those results were obvious. Easily forgotten were the contributions of the Pagliarulo-Leius platoon. Kelly stuck his neck out for the veteran Pagliarulo. While he did not rediscover his power, Pagliarulo hit .279, 40 points above his career average, and fielded well. Meanwhile, Leius handled his new position cleanly and hit .286. Knoblauch started the year as a rookie and ended it as one of the team's foundations. Kelly finally found a number-two hitter and a fluid second baseman.

Bush became a premier pinch hitter, while Larkin was an exceptional role player, hitting .286. Shane Mack became the everyday player Kelly had hoped for after the All-Star break. In the last three months, Mack was the team's best hitter, with a .356 average and 44 runs batted in.

The veteran hitters produced. Davis had a career-high 29 home runs and 93 runs batted in, and added a professional presence to the clubhouse. Puckett and Hrbek were in danger of being taken for granted, yet both had fine seasons. One of this team's strengths was that it did not need to be carried offensively by one or two players. There were so many who took turns, like Brian Harper, who was the league's best hitting catcher at .311.

Not only did Morris contribute his 18 wins, but as Kelly had hoped, his presence permitted Erickson and Tapani to develop into top-flight pitchers without the burden of being a staff leader. Erickson won 20 games, more than any pitcher except Detroit's Bill Gullickson. Tapani was the quiet member of the rotation who stifled opponents with consistency. He won 16 games, but more importantly, pitched 244 innings while never missing a start.

Aguilera ended the season with 42 saves, the third best total in the league, as he issued a stamp of validity to his conversion to the bullpen.

In the league rankings, the Twins finished first in batting average, second in fielding, third in pitching, and fourth in runs scored. The construction of the team by MacPhail and Kelly and the foundation laid in spring training proved true. The Twins had demonstrated a balance that left opponents frustrated by their inability to focus on one weakness in the Twins' game. They put the ball in play better than any team in the league (first in hits), yet could win with power (sixth in home runs). Their defense was airtight, and if you could knock out a starter, the long relief was vastly improved.

The only vulnerable spot on the Twins' roster at the end of the season was depth in their rotation. After the top three starters, Kelly had shuffled bodies for the last two months. He had survived, however, and with the play-offs ahead, only three starters were needed.

Kelly had all winter to look back with pride at 1991. More immediately, Toronto was ahead in the play-offs. The Twins' 95 wins had led the league, but now the goal was to get four more.

# TORONTO

*"I just felt the games would be so tight that whoever made one mistake in a game would get beat."*
***Tom Kelly***

Never before had the participants in a League Championship Series played each other to end the regular season. The American League's attempt to play a balanced schedule conditioned teams to expect scheduling oddities. With its membership of 14 clubs, the schedule guaranteed that at least one interdivision series would be played on the final weekend. Toronto was the designated "swing team" for 1991, meaning they would play West Division teams for their final 23 games with the last series at Minnesota.

Neither the Twins nor the Blue Jays were enthralled by the schedule. Playing each other six times in 10 days meant there would be "no secrets" by the time the play-offs began. It also seemed to rob the postseason of some of its mystery. The players readied themselves over the final weekend with the primary goal of avoiding injury.

Tom Kelly spent the final weekend completing the play-off preparations that he had begun over a month earlier. Managers and players on first-place teams take caution to the extreme state by avoiding any comments about postseason play until an official clinching occurs. In reality the planning begins long before the title becomes a formality. Scouts are assigned to follow potential opponents. Travel plans are made, and hotel rooms are booked in opponents' cities.

Baseball's rules dictate to management that a roster of 25 players for postseason play be chosen by August 31. Kelly met with management in late August to determine who would fill those spots. Basic decisions were made first. The Twins would carry two catchers and nine pitchers. "That's the way we went in 1987," Kelly said. "In reality, if you need more than nine pitchers, then you're probably going to get beat." Eliminated from contention for October were Lenny Webster, who would have been the third catcher, and Allan Anderson, who might have been the fourth starter. Morris's presence meant that only three starting pitchers would be needed.

There were two openings available, and Kelly and the baseball department chose Jarvis Brown to fill one spot. A rookie outfielder who had spent part of the summer with the Twins after Gladden's injury, Brown added a dimension that had been missing from the Twins for much of the year. "We basically added Jarvis in place of the tenth pitcher," Kelly explained. "He gave us the dimension of speed that we could use as a pinch runner or for late-inning defense."

The choice for the other opening was narrowed to Paul Sorrento or Pedro Munoz. Had a poll been taken, public sentiment would likely have sided with Munoz, who had influenced the media and fans with his strong hitting. Kelly, however, had to look at the available role. This spot was for a pinch hitter. Pedro didn't show us enough coming off the bench," Kelly said. "He didn't have the knack for pinch hitting. Sorrento seemed to be more accomplished as a pinch hitter, and with Larkin and Bush, we had good left-handed bats ready for pitchers like [Tom] Henke and [Duane] Ward." Even in August, the Twins were planning on Toronto as their play-off foe.

Two health concerns surfaced in October. Steve Bedrosian was bothered by a circulatory ailment that frequently left the middle fingers of his pitching hand numb. "That was a question, but our doctors got it better late in September," Kelly recalled. "If he was healthy, then it was right for him to be on the postseason roster, because he had been with us all year."

Larkin was slowed by tendinitis in the knee that worsened in the days immediately preceding the play-offs. Again, the trainers and doctors worked to keep Larkin healthy enough to hit, but he would not run the bases or play the field against Toronto.

The only performance-related concern for Kelly revolved around Dan Gladden. The veteran left fielder had faded at the plate, batting just .195 in September. Kelly knew an effective Gladden was needed to win the play-offs, but the manager was looking for some sign of life from Gladden's bat. "I hoped some days off in the last week would help because Danny was not in a good groove," Kelly admitted. "He was swinging so poorly that there was a question as to whether he could contribute."

Analyzing the Blue Jays was more important than scouting them. Playing 12 regular-season games against Toronto, coupled with the reports compiled by advance scout Jerry Terrell, left Kelly feeling that he "knew what was going on with the Blue Jays." In the days leading up to the play-offs, Terry Crowley and Kelly pored over videotapes of Toronto's starting pitchers. "Crow did a great job dissecting their pitchers," said Kelly. "Our hitters went into the series with a good plan to use against [Tom] Candiotti, [Juan] Guzman, and [Jimmy] Key."

What proved difficult for Kelly was devising a plan to stop the top of Toronto's batting order. The Blue Jays had rebuilt the top of their lineup before the season began, and by the play-offs their threesome of Devon White, Roberto Alomar, and Joe Carter had established themselves as Toronto's best offensive threat.

White and Alomar were always on base, stealing more bases

(53 by Alomar, 33 by White) and scoring on hits by Carter. That formula had led the Blue Jays to a 9–3 season series win, as White had 14 hits and Alomar added 13. Kelly knew the Twins had to find some way to slow down the leadoff duo in order to win the playoffs.

"White had changed quite a bit and become a much better hitter, and tougher out than he was in California," Kelly said of the fleet-footed switch-hitter. "He shortened his swing, so he could wait a fraction of a second longer before swinging."

"We had reports from the National League on Alomar," Kelly added, "but to this day, I'm still not sure we have figured him out. Sometimes, you have to take chances with a guy and throw strikes in the hope he hits the ball at someone."

Kelly knew he could not adopt that theory over a seven-game play-off series, so he tapped into his own scouting network. During the final road series of the season, Kelly sat in his Comiskey Park office before a game and telephoned LaRussa. "I asked him for some information on a couple of guys we were stuck on, guys that we had seen for a full season and still couldn't retire. So I asked Tony if he had any success against these people, and if so, where did he throw the ball to get them out."

For Kelly, this was a natural part of the manager's job in preparing for a key series. "You explore every avenue, and do everything you can to be ready," explained Kelly. "It's part of my job, and I've been on the other end of those calls at times. I don't know how many managers do this, but it's common for me."

Carter was a player that Kelly had a better line on, but after driving in 100 runs for the third consecutive year (in a major league first, it had been accomplished with three different teams), his opportunities had to be limited. There was inside baseball knowledge at work in Kelly's summation of the Toronto lineup. "We had to keep White and Alomar off the bases. First, they were both capable of stealing second *and* third base. And if they get to second, they can create a lot of situations for Carter. It's well known in baseball that Joe likes to get the pitch and location tipped to him by a runner on second. Now, Joe will also get the location from the on-deck batter if he has to. The on-deck batter just whistles when the catcher shifts because Carter wants to know if the pitch is coming inside. But if you keep those two off the bases, you're in better shape."

There were indeed no secrets between these teams, and because they had current knowledge of each other Kelly expected this series to be played with a slim margin for error. "It's unfortunate that the schedule happened as it did," admitted Kelly. "I just felt the games would be so tight that whoever made one mistake in a game would get beat."

As the series moved towards the Tuesday night opener, the conventional wisdom said that Toronto had a decided edge in speed, with White and Alomar, and in the bullpen, anchored by Henke, Ward, and rookie Mike Timlin. The Twins had a better-balanced lineup, and as in 1987, the advantage of opening at home with Morris, a veteran of postseason play, opposing Tom Candiotti, pitching in his first October series.

Toronto manager Cito Gaston's choice of Candiotti as his Game 1 starter raised some eyebrows in Minnesota. Most speculation had centered around either Juan Guzman, a rookie but the Blue Jays' best starter in the second half, or Jimmy Key, a veteran left-hander who had three prior postseason starts. Even though it meant facing a knuckleball pitcher, many Twins were relieved not to see Guzman first, as he had stymied them in three starts. Meanwhile, the Blue Jays faced the possibility of three starts by Morris.

A recurring theme around Minnesota in October was the comparison of this postseason to that of 1987, a most unfair process that shortchanged the achievements of this team. The Metrodome would be loud and intimidating, but would it resemble the lunacy of 1987? Kelly was realistic about his expectations. "Nothing will ever match for me the emotions of the 1987 crowds," Kelly admitted. "But the people were ready and the atmosphere was exciting. It might have been a bit more dramatic if we hadn't just been playing the Blue Jays for a week."

GAME 1

The crowd was ready for Morris. He warmed up for Game 1 in the left-field bullpen, as the crowd filed in earlier than normal for the pregame ceremonies. When he was finished, he turned and began to walk down the foul line towards the Twins dugout. As he walked, the crowd along the third base line began to cheer and rise. Slowly, the rest of the Metrodome joined in until Morris was engulfed by a roaring wall of noise. Morris was living out a childhood dream, and the same crowd that he pitched against in 1987 was now letting him know he was truly home.

The first inning was exactly what Kelly had hoped for, as Morris retired White, Alomar, and Carter in order. There was no first inning trauma for Morris, something the manager always watched for with the veteran pitcher. Candiotti took the mound with no early advantage.

The preparation by Terry Crowley and Kelly paid immediate dividends, as the Twins greeted Candiotti with singles by Gladden and Knoblauch. Everyone knew right away that the Twins were ready for Candiotti. "We knew he started hitters with the knuckleball," Kelly said, "then when he fell behind in the count, he threw breaking balls. If he went 3–0, then he mixed in a little cutter [moving fastball]. We had the right idea on what he was going to throw."

Gladden's leadoff single provided several positives, not the least of which was showing the manager that he was ready to contribute. The painful abdominal injury that cost him a month of the season occurred when he swung mightily at a Charlie Hough knuckleball. In his first play-off at-bat, facing a pitcher who specialized in knucklers, Gladden had delivered. Clearly, the Twins were determined to run at every opportunity.

"They came in advertised as going to run and run," Kelly said. "So I thought we would dispense with that and see if we could get someone's attention. We did our homework and knew what he would throw in certain counts."

Kelly does not like to start runners with his best hitters at the plate, so after the first two singles, he let Puckett and Hrbek hit. Candiotti rebounded by striking out Puckett, and retiring Hrbek on a fly to deep center with Gladden advancing to third. However, he could not get the third out, as Knoblauch stole second, and Davis dumped a single to left field, scoring both runners.

In the second inning, there were four more singles and two more stolen bases to raise the lead to 4–0. The fourth run was driven in by Knoblauch, who in his first two play-off at-bats, singled twice and stole second twice. "In the second half of the season, you could see his all-around play improving," said Kelly. "His play in the field got better, and he became more confident. He stayed away from injury and the excitement of winning picked up his play in September [when the length of a major league season normally takes its toll on rookies, Knoblauch hit .330 in the month]. He really believed he could play the game at this level."

Davis walked with one out in the third, and true to form, was running with Harper batting and stole second. Davis had stolen just five bases all year, but Kelly was consistent in his managing. In one game of the Oakland series of early August, he kept sending runners even though four had been thrown out. It was a matter of principle as the Twins let everyone, even themselves, know they would play aggressively. In the play-offs the same standard applied, so Davis stole the fourth base for the Twins in three innings.

Shane Mack followed with a two-out double to score Davis for a 5–0 Twins lead. Candiotti was lifted after a shattering outing in which he surrendered eight hits and five runs, while seeing those four bases stolen by a team that was not expected to run. "He didn't change his pattern until he faced Puckett in the second inning," explained Kelly. "By that time, seven of the first eleven batters had hit safely. Crow really deserves credit for a great job of preparing our hitters."

All season, Kelly had seen Morris pitch better with runs, and now the Twins had staked him to a five-run lead after three innings. Everyone in the Metrodome was programmed to believe this game was over.

Yet the fourth inning opened with a single by Alomar. Carter then followed with a double to right-center field. As Alomar came to third, he and everyone else watching was stunned to see third base coach Rich Hacker waving him home. The ball had been fielded by Puckett, and the relay throw by Gagne to Harper arrived to easily retire Alomar. Trailing by five runs, the Blue Jays had a runner caught at the plate for the first out of the inning.

"He [Hacker] was trying to get something going," maintained Kelly, a major league third base coach for four years. "But if you try too hard sometimes, it gets thrown back in your face. To me, he made a mistake. It seemed like he got caught up in the excitement of the game, trying to create a positive. Once he was sent home, we should have thrown Alomar out."

Carter moved to third base on the play at the plate, and scored on a ground out by John Olerud. Only one run scored in an inning that began with great promise for Toronto, but that was curtailed by the first mistake in a series that Kelly promised would be decided by such plays.

David Wells had relieved Candiotti and stopped the flood of runs by the Twins. The score was still 5–1 as Toronto batted in the sixth. Morris opened with a strikeout of Manuel Lee, but White followed with his first hit, a single to left. Alomar then popped up a Morris pitch with White running. "Knobby [Knoblauch] went for the deke with the runner, and then when he looked up, he couldn't find the ball," Kelly said. "That happens in the Dome. If you take your eye off the ball to look at the runner, when you look up, you'll lose it." The ball, which appeared to be an easy out, fell untouched behind second base.

Toronto capitalized on the Twins' first mistake as Carter, Olerud, and Kelly Gruber ripped consecutive singles to produce three runs. The crowd was stunned by the rapidity of the Blue Jays' strike, and a game that seemed so comfortable for the Twins was now at 5–4 in the sixth inning.

This was the moment when Kelly had to make a decision that could be complicated by Morris's track record. It was only the sixth inning, and this was a "game we got Jack to pitch." Had Alomar's pop been caught, Morris may well have escaped the inning without a run scoring. Kelly, though, had a rule about starters that he stood behind. "We draw a line at four runs for our starters," stated Kelly. "That's enough for me unless there has been some atrocious fielding. The fact is that after the pop fell in, they hit three shots. Our bullpen was rested and it was their time to pitch. Let's go ahead and use them."

Kelly's choice was Carl Willis. When the season began, Bedrosian was the man tapped to bridge the game from the starter to the closer Aguilera. By October things had changed, due to the injury to Bedrosian and the outstanding season turned in by Willis. At age 30, and staring at the end of his career, Willis had taken this last chance and parlayed it into a key role for a division champion. He won eight games with a 2.63 earned run average, and despite the presence of a former Cy Young Award winner in Bedrosian, Kelly said "there was no question about that move. Willis was obviously pitching better."

Arriving with the tying and lead runs on base, Willis retired Candy Maldonado on a fly ball, and Rance Mulliniks on a ground out to end the inning. "He threw the ball like he had all year," Kelly said. "It was rewarding for him, and for all of us, to watch someone who had been on the verge of retiring hang in there and then get to the postseason."

An intriguing emotional swing occurred at this point. The Metrodome crowd was overjoyed at Willis's performance, which kept the Twins lead intact despite their first mistake of the game. However, in the bottom of the sixth, Wells and Timlin kept the Twins from scoring. Suddenly there was an uneasy feeling as a string of zeroes appeared on the home team's line. The joyous postseason atmosphere that filled the stadium as the Twins roared to an early lead had changed to a gripping tension. White and Alomar would bat in the seventh and eighth innings, and the Blue Jays' bullpen made sure the Twins would not add to their five runs.

Willis took the mound for the seventh amidst a noise level that rose with each out. As Pat Borders grounded out to second and Manuel Lee lined to left, Willis arrived at his second critical juncture. He had escaped the jam of the sixth inning, and now he had to prevent another. If White reached base, the stolen base threat would reappear with Toronto's best hitters due to bat. After eight years of surviving in the minor leagues, many of those years tantalizingly close to the majors, Willis had arrived at his moment to shine. White was retired on a swinging third strike, and Alomar looked at a called third strike to begin the eighth inning. After Carter hit a fly ball to left, Willis was removed for Aguilera, and left the mound to an ovation that for one precious moment made the years at triple-A seem worthwhile. It was easy to imagine hundreds of pitchers like Carl Willis watching the game on television across America and using the scene as their inspiration to give baseball another chance.

The Twins did not score a run after the third inning, but the flawless work of Willis and Aguilera made the fifth run hold up for a win. Aguilera recorded the final four outs, two by strikeouts, in a 5–4 victory. "We heard a lot about their bullpen coming into the series," said Kelly. "But starting with the first game, our bullpen was unbelievable. They won it for us."

There were other signs from Game 1 that bode well for Minnesota. Four stolen bases in the first three innings introduced the thought to Toronto that the Twins would run. Gladden singled in his first two at-bats, a signal that the catalyst of the offense was prepared. Finally, the sixth-, seventh-, eighth-, and ninth-place hitters for Toronto had combined to go hitless in 15 at-bats, a performance that underscored the importance of stopping White and Alomar. If you could throttle the top of their order, Toronto would have difficulty scoring runs.

The first game was scheduled for Tuesday night, requiring a quick turnaround to the second game on Wednesday afternoon. Not only would there be little sleep for some of the participants, but unwinding from the pressures of the first game was nearly impossible. For players, coaches, and managers, the postseason games blend together into one unfolding story, with the starting pitchers serving as the only discernible change from one day to the next.

## GAME 2

Juan Guzman, a 21-year-old rookie right-hander, was Toronto's choice for Game 2. His rapid development in his first year created a strong push to have him start the opener. Instead, Toronto hoped his fastball would seem more devastating to the Twins' hitters who had just faced Candiotti. In addition, there was a postseason mystique surrounding the Metrodome that Toronto hoped Guzman could shatter. The Twins were now 7–0 in postseason games at their indoor home. To many, that fact served to override Toronto's 10–2 mark at the Metrodome in the last two seasons.

Guzman had pitched a three-hit shutout for seven and two-thirds innings at the Metrodome in June, and in his three subsequent starts, the Twins had not scored many runs. Yet Kelly was convinced that the familiarity his hitters had gained with Guzman's repertoire would work to the Twins' benefit. "We knew what we wanted to do," Kelly maintained. "Again, Crow's preparation gave us a good plan. But sometimes a good plan doesn't work because it can't be executed."

That was readily apparent in the bottom of the first inning. Gladden led off with a walk, an early confirmation that Guzman's nerves could lead to a recurrence of the wildness that plagued him in the minors. Kelly disagreed, saying, "You don't put together the season he had [10–3, with a .197 opponents' batting average] by being wild. He throws enough strikes that you couldn't look for a walk."

Knoblauch was the next batter and he struck out swinging, a sign of Guzman's explosive fastball, as Knoblauch had struck out only 40 times in the regular season. Gladden stole second just before Puckett walked. Without hitting a ball, the Twins had a threat alive that forced the Blue Jays to change the pace of the game. Borders, Gaston, and pitching coach Galen Cisco orchestrated trips to the mound that slowed play noticeably, short-circuiting the enthusiasm of the crowd and, Toronto hoped, the Twins' batters. "Guzman was getting out of whack. They had to go out there and settle him down," Kelly remembered.

Meanwhile, there was the anticipation of a big inning with Hrbek and Davis due to hit. Visions of the previous night's carnage against Candiotti, though, were quickly doused as Hrbek fouled out to third base, and Davis struck out swinging. Guzman's first inning was clearly his most important. Despite the walks and the intimidating atmosphere of a hostile Metrodome crowd, Guzman had allowed only one batter to put the ball in play. Kelly saw the trend established in the first inning. "He was too powerful. Our hitters had an idea, but they just couldn't catch up to his pitches." Then there was the manipulation of the first inning by the Toronto bench. "Give their staff a lot of credit. With the emphasis on every pitch so magnified in the play-offs, they were on top of him and pulled him through. In the summer, if that happened, he probably couldn't have made it. We stepped out and did some things to try and disrupt him, but he hung in there," recalled Kelly.

While Guzman survived his first inning with no scoring, his opponent, Kevin Tapani, did not. Tapani was a familiar foe to the batters he faced, and the Blue Jays started the game with their familiar attack.

Devon White opened with a single to center. Signaling that they wanted a lead, and that they had confidence Guzman would not need many runs, Alomar watched White steal second, then sacrificed White to third. Carter stroked a single to center, scoring White for Toronto's first lead of the series.

Tapani advanced to the third inning where he was stung by the same batters. White sliced a double into left field, and moved to third as Alomar beat out a roller to third base. The runners held as Carter hit a soft line drive to shortstop for the first out. Alomar then stole second, but Tapani struck out Olerud for the second out. Now, a critical at-bat loomed for the Blue Jays. Kelly Gruber represented the last chance to cash in on the success of White and Alomar. In a 1–0 game, Toronto's leadoff hitters had done their job, and if the middle hitters could not deliver the runs, the Twins would receive a tremendous boost. Tapani watched in disbelief as Gruber splintered his bat and dropped a lazy looping ball into right field for a two-run single. Kelly remembered his own reaction. "They broke three or four bats early in the game, and Gruber shattered his bat for his hit. There were a bunch of bloopers, but that's all that a team needed to win the way these games were going."

The momentum the Twins had gained in winning Game 1 disappeared after Guzman's first inning escape. He did not walk another batter until the sixth, and the Twins found themselves unable to generate a sustained rally. What the fans saw was an endless parade of trips to the mound by Borders, and an endless string of Guzman pitches fouled straight back by Twins batters. "We just couldn't get the bat to the ball," admitted Kelly. "There used to be a theory that when a ball was fouled straight back, the hitter was on time. I look at it as the hitter is late. It looks like a nice swing, but they're always a fraction late, and the bat doesn't get on top of the ball."

Puckett singled home a run with two outs in the third inning, and with a 3–1 lead in the sixth, Guzman showed his first signs of tiring. He walked Knoblauch, the leadoff hitter, and then walked Davis with two outs. Harper singled to center, narrowing the deficit to one run. Gaston quickly called for Henke. "They got Guzman out at the right time. He was done," Kelly said.

It was Gaston's hope that Henke and Ward could end Game 2 as decisively as Willis and Aguilera had ended Game 1. Their roles had reversed due to a bout with shoulder tendinitis that limited Henke's availability in the final month. The veteran had pitched two innings in the final regular season series, and declared himself fit for the play-offs. Gaston, though, would use Ward as the closer and Henke in the largely unfamiliar role of set-up man. Both were rested, as neither had pitched in Game 1.

Shane Mack was the batter, with two runners on base and two outs. One base hit could turn the game in the Twins' favor, but Henke, who was not throwing as hard as in the past, had brought his nastiest weapon to the mound, a forkball as potentially devastating as Morris's. Mack chased a forkball out of the strike zone, and hit a weak ground ball to the mound that Henke easily relayed to first base for the third out.

After that the Twins had no chance. Toronto's script played itself out perfectly, as Henke struck out two batters in the seventh and Ward finished with four more strikeouts in two innings. Just as the Twins left an imprint on Toronto's minds with their running attack in Game 1, the Blue Jays answered with an awesome pair of relievers in Game 2. "We didn't get close to either guy," admitted Kelly. "Henke threw some forkballs that were not strikes that we chased. But when his forker is working, you have no chance. Ward was well rested, and he threw extremely hard."

Two Toronto runs in the seventh off Tapani and Bedrosian were irrelevant as the story of Toronto's 5–2 victory was their pitching. After the exit of Candiotti in the third inning of Game 1, the Twins scratched out just two runs. The big guns, Puckett and Hrbek, were silent guns at the Metrodome, as they combined for just two singles in 15 at-bats. "These guys are eligible to hit, just as Toronto's guys are eligible to come out and pitch," Kelly said. "That's why in a short series you focus on pitching and good defense, and hope everything else falls into place. But we were confident they would hit." More astonishing was the transformation of the Metrodome, in the space of 12 hours, from revelry to skepticism. Suddenly, as the Twins lost a postseason game at home, fans felt their advantage in the series had disappeared. There was doubt that the Twins could bring the series back to Minnesota, particularly without contributions from the big bats.

Fortunately, that feeling never invaded the players, who left immediately after Game 2 for Toronto. Everything about baseball in October was slightly different, and that included travel. Normally, the Twins chartered their airplanes with 150 to 200 seats for a traveling party that rarely exceeded 50. In the postseason, spouses were invited, and ownership, management, staff, and media filled every remaining seat. This presented an interesting dichotomy. The uniformed personnel traveled strictly for the business of playing the most meaningful games of their careers. For many others in the group, the trip was a wonderful opportunity to enjoy one of North America's most entertaining cities. One of the true tests of October baseball for players is maintaining their focus on the game amidst ticket requests, family distractions, and media demands.

Tom Kelly had no idea that Junior Ortiz would handle the latter department in Toronto. On Thursday afternoon, a casual workout was held at the SkyDome that allowed the media hordes their best access to players. Midway through the workout, Kelly was taking throws near first base when he noticed Ortiz entertaining a small group of writers. Within moments, the "lemming syndrome" that afflicts the media at large events took over, and Junior was surrounded by a sprawling mass of cameras, microphones, and notepads.

Kelly and Ortiz's teammates genuinely liked Ortiz for his ability to laugh at himself as well as at others. He was a perfect fit in the close-knit clubhouse. At times, Ortiz became his own press agent. Early in the season, a team broadcaster gave Ortiz a newspaper article about veteran pitcher and former teammate Rick Reuschel. Mentioned in the story was an anecdote about Reuschel's dislike of visits to the mound, and of a particular instance where he swore at Ortiz. Junior, as the story went, looked back at Reuschel, and addressing him by his nickname, said, "Ooh, Big Daddy, I love when you talk dirty to me." For the remainder of the season, Ortiz kept the clipping in his locker, and would show it to any party, whether or not they were interested, in the search for some publicity.

The media loved Ortiz because he was friendly and talkative. A baseball season is so long that reporters covet cooperative players. There are so many dull days, be they unspectacular games or off days, that can only be saved by easily obtained quotes. Junior was a player who flirted with a .400 average early in 1990, and adopted the nickname "Ted," as in Williams. A year later, fighting to stay above .200, he announced that "Junior" had been sent to the minors, and henceforth, his name was "Joe" Ortiz. On this team, Ortiz and Al Newman were the friendly faces that writers could always approach for usable material. Ortiz's charm and ease with the media was unusual in light of his stutter. Rather than withdrawing from the limelight, Ortiz often poked fun at his own speech, and took no offense when others followed.

Now Ortiz was in his first postseason, and Friday's third game promised a story with Scott Erickson pitching. This qualified Junior to speak with the eloquence of a baseball Aristotle. "It was quite humorous to see Junior there speaking for Erickson," Kelly chuckled. "Junior is so full of garbage, joking constantly, saying one thing and meaning another. I still don't know if the media knew they were getting conned."

As the series venue moved to Toronto, the game moved from an indoor football stadium to a theme park. The SkyDome is truly a national attraction throughout Canada, and as such brings crowds (four million paying customers in 1991) but not necessarily baseball fans. It is impossible to visit the facility without admiring the construction. The unique retractable roof allows sunshine and fresh air to enter on appropriate days. While a hotel, restaurant, and two levels of private suites ring the perimeter of the building, the game of baseball retains some integrity. The playing field contains no oddities and the seats offer viewing comfort. If one can procure a ticket and handle the exorbitant concession prices, a SkyDome visit for baseball can be a novel experience.

The Twins stepped into this atmosphere with the knowledge they were facing a very good team in Toronto, and with the comfort of knowing the Jays did not play before an intimidating home crowd. Toronto is first and foremost a hockey city, and their baseball fans are both spoiled and cynical. The Blue Jays have enjoyed remarkable success. In fact, they have been the model expansion franchise in professional sports. Yet there has been nothing but heartbreak in late-season games, with a seventh-game loss to Kansas City in the 1985 play-offs, a loss to Detroit on the final day of the 1987 regular season that cost the Blue Jays a division title they seemingly had locked up a week earlier, and then an Oakland steamroll in the 1989 play-offs. The World Series had never been played in Toronto, and there was supreme confidence that the Blue Jays' time had arrived. After all, the obstacle was not the mighty Athletics, but just the Twins. Hadn't the Jays owned the Twins over the last two seasons? Winning Game 2 meant a sweep at home ended the series, and no trip back to Minnesota's raucous Metrodome would be needed.

## GAME 3

Jimmy Key was Toronto's starter for Game 3. The left-hander had only faced the Twins once in 1991, losing a 1–0 decision to David West on July 4. Not only did Toronto save Key, their most experienced postseason starter, until the third game, but his preparation for the play-offs had been pitching a simulated game in the Metrodome bullpen on the final day of the regular season. Scott Erickson was the Twins starter, and there was cause for optimism based on his finish to the regular season. Three consecutive strong starts, two against the Blue Jays, included a six-inning performance that earned him his 20th victory on October 5.

Kelly made an unexpected batting order change as he hit Gagne seventh and Scott Leius, in his first postseason start, ninth. After the fact, Kelly did not remember a specific reason for the shift. It may have been career success for Gagne against Key, or to relieve Leius of some pressure. But it was unusual, as Gagne had not hit seventh all year, and it would turn out to be meaningful.

The early advantage in Game 3 went to Toronto, despite Erickson's ability to retire White and Alomar in the bottom of the first. Carter followed with a long home run to center field, a blast that had to shake up Erickson, who all year had allowed only five home runs by right-handed batters. Suddenly, Erickson appeared mortal as Olerud walked, Gruber singled, and Maldonado doubled to left (for the first run driven in by Toronto's 6–9 hitters). The Blue Jays were one hit away from blowing open the game in the first inning when Erickson induced Mulliniks to fly out, the first of four crucial at-bats that determined the outcome of this game.

Key cruised through four innings and Erickson, although plagued by wobbly control, regained his balance as Toronto's 2–0 lead carried into the fifth.

Shane Mack led off Minnesota's half of the fifth, with a long fly ball to right that carried to the wall. Carter retreated and tried to brace himself against the padded fence with his right leg, but instead turned his ankle. The ball caromed off the fence towards the right field line, with Carter hobbling in pursuit. Mack had an easy triple in an at-bat that permanently altered the course of the series. Carter refused to leave the game, but his ankle was badly sprained and his effectiveness impaired. "He tried to make a real good play and it backfired," explained Kelly. "You never want to see a player get hurt, especially in these important games where people are paying a lot of money to see stars play. I was just glad he had hightops on. Otherwise, he might have snapped the ankle."

The massive SkyDome was silenced as if the crowd was already mourning the loss of Toronto's top run producer. Carter, however, refused to leave the field. Hrbek was the next batter, and he sent a bouncer towards second base which Alomar fielded and fired to catcher Borders. Mack had a good jump off third base, and easily beat the throw. "I thought that was wrong," maintained Kelly. "Alomar tried to make a Superman play, instead of getting the out you are supposed to get. We teach our players to avoid those plays."

The play caused no damage to Toronto, as Key escaped further trouble by coaxing a double-play ground ball from Ortiz, but a pattern established in Game 1 had continued. There was a line between aggressiveness and foolishness, and the Blue Jays had crossed it a second time. Kelly strived to have his team respect that difference, and truly believed this series would be determined by lapses in judgment as well as physical error.

In the last of the fifth, Alomar led off with a walk. The third crucial at-bat of the game followed. Carter was heroically trying to stay in the game, and he was trying to deliver the one hit that everyone knew the Blue Jays needed to seize control. It was the hit that Mulliniks could not produce in the first inning, and here Erickson found himself fighting a worthy foe for the third time. Carter had homered in round one and struck out in round two. Now he seemed "zeroed in," smashing two foul drives, one into the left field upper deck.

The count went to 1–2. "I remember putting the sign on for Scott to throw over to first," Kelly recalled. "He threw once or twice, but then he kept throwing over. It was somewhat uncharacteristic of Scott, and I felt he was losing sight of the hitter." No one was prepared to see what occurred next. Erickson made four throws to first base, and out popped Kelly from the dugout. He would not say anything at the play-offs, in order to protect his pitcher, but it was obvious that Erickson was hesitant to throw another pitch. So Kelly made the call for David West, who had been warming up in the bullpen.

"Surely that was a decision that could be second-guessed," admitted Kelly. "I'm bringing a lefty in to face Carter. If he hits the ball over the fence, I could get crucified. But it didn't seem to me that Scott was going to get him out." This easily appeared to be Kelly's most baffling maneuver of the season, but it was a decision forced upon Kelly by the events taking place on the field.

A bizarre pitching change was followed by an absolutely mind-boggling series of events. West threw a wild pitch, but rebounded to strike out Carter. He walked Olerud, a left-handed batter, threw another wild pitch, and then struck out Gruber and Maldonado. In his Twins' career, West's success had come as a starter. There had not been enough consistency, however, to allow Kelly the luxury of using West as a fourth starter in the postseason. Now here he was in relief, entering in an unexpected situation filled with postseason pressure, and pitching out of a delicate jam.

"He bounced a couple of balls in the dirt [the two wild pitches]," said Kelly. "After that he threw well, mixing sliders down and in with fastballs up. They swung at some bad pitches. But what we liked was that he went after hitters without backing off." West's effort highlighted one of Kelly's points of emphasis. The pitching had shut Toronto down after the first inning, and now the hitters were beginning to solve Key.

In the sixth, Knoblauch lined a one-out double into the left-field corner. Puckett then lined a sharp single to right. The initial reaction upon seeing the hit was that Knoblauch would not be able to score. The next sight was Ron Gardenhire waving home Knoblauch. Carter's throw was strong, but tailed slightly to the third-base side of home plate. Olerud cut the throw, pivoted, and relayed it to Borders, well before the arrival of Knoblauch. Kelly felt Knoblauch was a sure out, but the rookie did a wonderful imitation of Bush's 1987 World Series slide, fading into foul territory, but still able to reach the plate with his extended left hand as he avoided Borders's tag. "Gardy took a real chance sending him, but Knobby made a great slide," conceded Kelly. "I guess those slides are part of our good fortune in the postseason. But even if Carter was hobbling from the injury, it was still a gutsy play by Gardy."

Another part of the postseason good fortune was surviving questionable judgment, and the Twins had done just that. A game that Toronto should have owned was now tied, and with Key out after six innings, and Carter removed in the seventh for a pinch runner, the Twins' hopes brightened.

Game 3 became a battle of the bullpen, and the off day preceding the games in Toronto meant both pens were ready and able. Willis relieved West with two outs in the seventh, and retired Gruber on a ground ball with two runners on. Meanwhile, the Twins posted no threats in innings seven, eight, and nine against Wells and Henke. The top of the ninth was emphatic as Henke struck out Davis, Mack, and pinch hitter Sorrento. Yet the Twins answered as Willis and Mark Guthrie closed the door on Toronto to send the game to extra innings.

In the top of the tenth, Gaston called on Timlin. Henke had recorded four outs, and surely could have worked another inning were it not for his late-season tendinitis. Ward was available, but Kelly could only surmise that "he was being saved," although the home team never faces a save situation in extra innings. It is undeniable that Timlin was impressive in his Game 1 outing, and his hard sinker seemed ideal for preventing the long ball (he had allowed only six home runs in 108 regular-season innings).

Ortiz was scheduled to start the 10th, but Larkin pinch hit for the catcher and grounded to second baseman Alomar. Next up was Mike Pagliarulo, pinch hitting for Leius and batting ninth in Kelly's new Game 3 order. Had the lineup followed the regular season norm, Leius would have batted in the ninth and Gagne, who was pinch hit for by Sorrento, would be facing Timlin in the tenth. Instead, Pagliarulo missed Henke and faced Timlin.

On a 1–0 count, Timlin threw what he later called a "horrible pitch." Kelly called it "a high sinker down the middle of the plate." Pagliarulo drove the pitch on a line to right field with the "hope it would be high enough." Rob Ducey, the replacement for Carter, ran to the warning track and watched helplessly as the ball easily cleared the barrier. He had hit only six home runs in the regular season, but Pagliarulo had delivered a blow that shocked his own manager as much as anyone. "You hope for a home run there, but you never expect one," Kelly mused.

Had Larkin reached base to start the inning, Pagliarulo would not have batted. Kelly would have chosen between a Leius bunt or a pinch hitting appearance by Harper, who entered the game in the bottom half for Ortiz. In addition, no one knew where Ward was at this point. The fates had clearly conspired to benefit the Twins in the fourth crucial at-bat of Game 3. Had any one of the four at-bats ended differently, the winner would likely have been Toronto. After Aguilera calmly set down Toronto in order in the bottom of the 10th, the Twins had registered yet another improbable victory. Kelly's immediate goal was to attack the jubilance of his clubhouse. "I sat everybody down in the clubhouse and told them we had to focus on tomorrow's game," recalled Kelly. "We had to put a stop to the flip-flop of these games, and to back this win up. I knew we were up 2–1 with Morris pitching Game 4. That's not a bad position."

In Toronto, Pagliarulo's blow stirred the dust off unpleasant memories. Moments came to mind such as Jim Sundberg's three-run double in Game 7 of the 1985 American League Championship Series that sent his Royals to the World Series. Or Larry Herndon's home run off Jimmy Key for the only run in the final game of the 1987 season, one in which the Blue Jays won 96 games but finished second to Detroit. Or Jose Canseco's majestic home run to the fifth level of the SkyDome in the 1989 American League Championship Series, the signature moment of Oakland's victory.

## GAME 4

The overriding question mark going into Game 4 was Toronto's ability to rebound from the emotional jolt inflicted the previous night. Morris was the Twins' starter, and Carter's availability was limited to the designated hitter role. The two met in the third inning, and the result demonstrated to Toronto that their Game 3 problems had not been solved.

The Blue Jays led 1–0 when White and Alomar each singled and executed a double steal. Carter batted with runners on second and third. It was yet another at-bat that meant survival for the Twins. In the play-offs, Twins pitchers had excelled in these battles, and Morris continued that trend. Carter would strike out, waving feebly at a 1–2 pitch in the dirt.

"It was obvious that Carter was hurting," admitted Kelly.

"He couldn't reach the ball down and away. It was very similar to Bo Jackson in September. When someone can't use their legs to hit, you need to throw the ball down, and you'll be in good shape."

After West had bailed the Twins out of trouble in Game 3, they had scored the tying run in the next at-bat. A better rally was produced after Morris struck out Carter and followed by getting Olerud on a groundout.

Puckett opened the fourth by driving Todd Stottlemyre's second pitch into the center-field bleachers, one prodigious swing that tied the game. With two outs, Davis was on second courtesy of a double, and Shane Mack worked out a walk that Stottlemyre said afterwards was the inning's most critical at-bat. "Shane fought back from behind in the count. That at-bat probably took a lot out of Stottlemyre," Kelly admitted.

Pagliarulo singled to break the 1–1 tie. Gagne was hit by a pitch, and then Gladden broke his bat as he dumped a curveball into right field for two more runs and a 4–1 Twins' lead. Stottlemyre, whose father Mel had pitched a World Series game for the New York Yankees 25 years before to the day, had his second career postseason start unravel rapidly. "He's an emotional guy, and I think he got worn out by the emotions of the game," Kelly conjectured. "Even though he hung a couple of pitches in that inning, he has the pitches to succeed. I think he'll settle down after going through that experience."

Gladden's hit was maligned afterwards by Stottlemyre, but the Twins immediately recalled Gruber's shattered-bat hit that helped win Game 2 for Toronto. What mattered was that the Twins had come through with the big inning that had eluded the Blue Jays in Game 3. "If Toronto had put up four or five runs in the first inning in the third game, Key might have gone right through us," Kelly said. "We gave Jack the four runs, and all year he was a much better pitcher with the lead."

On this Saturday night, Morris was also a healthier pitcher.

Slowed by a bronchial infection in Game 1, he was close to full health, and with four runs he was indomitable. "He relaxed and just threw the ball well," said Kelly. "In a scoreless game, he'll try to make the perfect pitch. Here, he got real tough."

Toronto had nine hits and their leadoff man reached base in four of the last five innings, but they could score only three runs. Carter went hitless in five at-bats, stranding six runners. At the same time, the Blue Jays made two errors and looked lackluster in stark comparison to the Twins, who featured a sparkling stab of a line drive by Pagliarulo in the fifth.

The final was 9–3, for a 3–1 Twins' lead in the series. "I had to pull out the same speech I had used the previous night," recalled Kelly. "We didn't know if we would be able to wrap it up the next day, and we had to focus on that game. I did feel the Blue Jays were waiting to get beat towards the end of these games. Even in Game 2, if we had been able to do something late, we could have won that game. We believed Toronto would be ready for Game 5, as they had to pack their suitcases and be prepared to go back to Minnesota."

GAME 5

Cito Gaston again faced questioning over his choice of a starting pitcher when he tabbed Candiotti for Game 5. In Toronto, the media sentiment was to bring Guzman back on the fourth day, but Gaston, in a move Kelly could identify with, would not deviate from his program.

Unlike Kelly, though, Gaston would not be in the dugout to manage his team in a game they had to win. After two innings were completed, Gaston was ejected by home plate umpire Mike Reilly. "It looked like Cito disagreed with Reilly's strike zone," Kelly observed. "Some pitches that are borderline high for most umpires get called strikes by Mike. You know that going in to the game, so it's no big deal. But the magnitude of the game had something to do with it."

At the time of his ejection, Gaston's team was behind 2–0. Puckett had homered in the first inning, and Mack singled in a run in the second. They scored some runs, but there was one difference in Candiotti, evidenced by the trouble Borders was having behind the plate. "We hadn't seen Borders miss the ball, just not be able to stop it," Kelly remembered. "Candiotti must have a super-duper knuckler that he can really make fly at times."

While the SkyDome had been silent since Carter's injury in Game 3, the early Twins' runs added an air of finality to the atmosphere. Unexpectedly, Kevin Tapani was not sharp, and Toronto found hope with five runs in the third and fourth innings. "I really think the familiarity factor hurt Tap against the Jays," Kelly remarked. "His location wasn't good, but they seemed to have a good read on him the second time around."

Candiotti took the 5–2 lead given him and carried it into the sixth inning. He had been questioned by his manager for not throwing enough knuckleballs in Game 1, and he responded with a dancing knuckler. Yet Kelly maintained that, except for a few adjustments, Candiotti pitched to the Twins' scouting report.

After Mack and Pagliarulo opened the sixth with singles, Gene Tenace, managing for Gaston, summoned Timlin from the bullpen. Kelly did not use a pinch hitter for Gagne, and the shortstop fouled out. With runners on first and third, Gladden chopped a ground ball at Gruber. With a three-run lead, the prudent play seemed to be at first for the sure out. Instead, Gruber fired the ball home. Borders had stepped up to block the plate from the onrushing Mack, but the throw came in high to Borders's glove side. It was in plenty of time, but as Borders caught the ball, Mack slid inside the catcher on the fair side of home plate. Borders then inexplicably reached out at Mack with his bare hand, allowing the Twins' runner to score. "If the throw was better, things might have flowed better for Borders," Kelly admitted. "The throw was up and away, and that got Borders out of whack. Not giving excuses or blaming anyone, but there's no substitute for going to first and putting an out on the board."

Three times in Toronto, a Twins' runner had scored when Toronto thought they had him out. As Kelly had forecast, this series was being determined by mistakes. Toronto was making them, and the Twins were capitalizing.

After Gladden reached base, Knoblauch smoked a Timlin pitch into the right field corner. Gladden scored from first to tie the game at 5–5. The rookie second baseman had played the five play-off games with savvy and poise. The double was his seventh hit and left his postseason average at .350.

If Kelly's feeling about Toronto waiting to get beat needed justification, it was provided in the home half of the seventh inning. Alomar led off by drawing a walk from reliever West. With 53 stolen bases in the regular season, and a pair in the play-offs, it was fully expected that Alomar would at least try to swipe a base, particularly with Carter, who liked the aid of a runner on second, at the plate. Carter, again the designated hitter, had doubled home a run in the third inning, but was still not himself. Firing high fastballs, West popped up Carter, then Olerud, and finally Gruber. All the while, Alomar stood at first, never once making a move towards stealing second.

Ward had entered for Toronto in the sixth inning, after Knoblauch's double. He had not pitched at all in the dramatic third game, and now in a game of desperation, he was pitching in his third inning. With one out in the eighth, Gagne singled to left, but Borders gunned Gagne down as he attempted to steal second. Gladden followed with a single to left, and successfully stole second base. The contrast was startling between Alomar's hesitance and the Twins' boldness on the bases.

There was also a startling change in Ward. Both Gagne and Gladden had pulled fastballs on the outside part of the plate. "He wasn't throwing good," Kelly said. "The third inning was too much for him. He was trying to do more than he was capable of doing."

Still, Ward needed only one more out, but Knoblauch prolonged the inning by walking to load the bases. In the first two games, Puckett and Hrbek had been dormant. Now they had a chance to send their team to "the Big Dance," the players' term of endearment for the World Series. Puckett lined a single to right field scoring Gladden for a 6–5 Twins lead. It was the eighth hit by Puckett in the three games at Toronto. Wells replaced Ward, and Hrbek stroked a pitch from the left-hander into left-center field for a pair of insurance runs. Kelly had seen the hoped-for response from Hrbek ever since the pinch-hitting episodes of April. "He put up better at-bats against lefties than he had in the past," said Kelly.

The hits by Puckett and Hrbek cleared the SkyDome of everyone but the diehards and the Twins fans. Yet every bit as important as the hits was the relief work of West, who sparkled with three hitless innings. It had been the weekend of West's dreams, two sterling outings from the bullpen that saved his team.

Willis pitched the eighth, and for the ninth Kelly called on Aguilera. The ultimate closing assignment gave Aguilera the chance to purge the memory of the 1988 World Series. In the tenth inning of Game 6, Aguilera had surrendered a home run to Dave Henderson that, were it not for Bill Buckner's misplay, would have won a championship for Boston. Aguilera has never watched a tape of that game. He now had a chance to star in a show he could pass on for generations.

While Aguilera took his warm-up pitches, Kelly felt compelled to take care of some unfinished business. Randy Bush had been ready to pinch hit, but the Twins' half of the ninth inning had ended before his turn arrived. "I walked over to Bushie at the end of the dugout," Kelly said. "I felt bad that I couldn't find a spot for him. [Only Bush and Terry Leach did not participate in a play-off game.] He looked at me and said, 'Just get me to the Big Dance.' To hear such a professional statement at that moment meant a lot to me."

Attention turned to the field where the home ninth was over quickly. Wilson popped to short and White struck out swinging. Aguilera fell behind Alomar 3–0, worked the count back to 3–2, and finally induced a well-hit drive to left that Gladden camped under on the warning track. As the ball settled into his glove, the incredible weekend in Toronto sent the Twins' journey onward to the World Series.

While the players hugged on the field, Kelly actually left the dugout. He worked his way to the first base foul line where he embraced each player as they filed by. In the clubhouse, Jim Wiesner was prepared with shirts and hats bearing the inscription "1991 American League Champions" and Remzi Kiratli had prepared the champagne that the players would spray, shoot, and partially consume.

Many players kept repeating the phrase "the Big Dance" in their postgame comments. "There's a lot of pressure lifted by getting to the World Series," Kelly explained. "A lot of players will tell you that there's more pressure in play-off games than in the World Series. The goal for every player is to get to the Series."

Kelly dealt with the media obligations, then in an act that demonstrated his constant consideration for his players, he stayed in the dressing area of the clubhouse to answer further questions. By doing that, he kept the television cameras out of the back room and left the players to celebrate in some privacy.

Almost an island unto themselves, the coaches sat in their room with champagne and savored the championship. The hours of hard work, often thankless and occasionally menial, had been rewarded, and this group of six celebrated quietly, marveling at the player's feats and Kelly's managing.

The admiration was mutual, as Kelly respected the work of his staff. No coach could likely match the pride felt by Dick Such in this celebration. A franchise whose identity for 30 years had been wrapped in the cloak of hitting, and whose 1987 World Championship was proclaimed to have been achieved despite a thin pitching staff, had advanced to the World Series largely on the strength of its arms. The Twins beat Toronto because their pitchers won almost every key battle with the Blue Jays' hitters.

Such is an analytical pitching coach who uses a portable computer to log performances and thoroughly studies pitching patterns. Although he is quiet, Such's opinions carry great weight with Kelly. He is always seated near Kelly in the dugout to give advice on pitching matters, and he was instrumental in the "mix and match" method employed by the Twins for the fourth and fifth starters in August and September.

Such's most important contribution may have been altering Morris's pitching motion. He convinced Morris to shorten his stride by three or four inches, a distance that helped the break of his forkball. Morris began to hold his hands closer to his body during his windup to better disguise the ball. Such also eliminated a bounce from Morris's glove during his delivery that was tipping batters to his pitches.

Such's patience is the virtue that Kelly most treasures. The fruits of that patience were seen in David West's performance during the play-offs. The two years of work on West's mechanics had been occasionally frustrating, but had paid off with a trip to the World Series. Such had toiled for years trying to formulate a major league staff for the Twins out of pretenders and imposters. The Twins now had developed pitching that commanded respect, and Such deserved much of the credit.

This team had defied virtually all of the prognostications. Toronto's bullpen was spotlighted entering the series, yet the Twins' bullpen "won the series for us," claimed Kelly. The five Twins' relievers did not allow an earned run in the five games.

Toronto's speed was supposed to be a difference, yet the Twins opened and closed the series with rallies fueled by stolen bases. What Kelly was most proud of was winning all three games in Toronto. This team did not have to fight the stigma that followed the 1987 Twins.

The clubhouse celebration lasted for two hours, most of which was restrained somewhat by the media presence. Before it ended, the party spread into a special room set aside for the wives of the uniformed personnel. For the players and wives of the "Gang of Seven," there was a special pride in lasting long enough to repeat the joy of 1987. Puckett had been named the Most Valuable Player of the play-off series, and an array of reporters besieged him. The happiest faces belonged to the first-timers, from veteran Chili Davis to rookies Knoblauch, Brown, Leius, and Sorrento. Then there was Morris, who knew he was five days away from the ultimate ending to his season, a start in Game 1 of the World Series at the Metrodome.

# THE BIG DANCE

*"I agree with the theory that just getting to the World Series is the big thing. Getting through the play-offs is the hard thing. That's the most pressure. The World Series is ice cream on the cake. Once you realize you're there, it takes a lot of pressure off."*
***Tom Kelly***

The World Series is baseball's "Big Dance," an October formal affair that concludes the season, and the Twins had received their invitation. The event prompts a reversion by professional athletes to their youth, for at the core of every major leaguer is the kid who spent hours on rocky, dusty fields, or schoolyards, or backyards, playing catch with his father. The stakes are high, but even the World Series can be reduced to a sequence of games played by supremely gifted adults with the joy and enthusiasm of children. Only in sports do we see adults lose their inhibitions and abandon their self-control to celebrate, rejoice, pout, or whine like children.

"The Big Dance" is baseball's annual opportunity to apply spit and polish to a sport that wears a rough look for the regular season of 162 games. There are no black ties and there are some beards of stubble, but everyone and everything seems fresher and cleaner. Uniforms are whiter, caps are straightened, fields (or artificial turf) are well-manicured, and stadiums look as if they received a spring cleaning in the fall. Like teenagers on prom night, baseball strives to impress and "style" at "The Big Dance."

The beauty of the World Series is that substance always wins out over style. The multiple-game format, central to baseball's attraction over six months, allows more often than not (Cincinnati's 1990 sweep of Oakland being an exception) for stories to be weaved, and emotions and tensions to grow, until after a week a marvelous mosaic has been created that separates this event from any other in sports.

The World Series is played in the homes of the competitors, not the sterile environs of a neutral site. Tickets are available to the fans who support their teams, and World Series crowds are knowledgeable and passionate. Celebrities are part of a World Series crowd, but they are only a sideshow. A World Series is not measured by who is there, but by the excellence of the games. Unlike the Super Bowl, the main event is on the field.

To reach the World Series twice in five years is an achievement truly appreciated given the following perspective. Most fans are unaware that six franchises (California, Seattle, Texas, Toronto, Houston, and Montreal) have never played in the Series. The Chicago Cubs last played a World Series game in 1945, and the Cleveland Indians' last try was in 1954. Even the New York Mets, for all their high-priced talent and accompanying publicity, have reached the Series just once in the last 15 years.

"The Big Dance" would introduce these Twins to a baseball public largely unaware of the team's accomplishments. A steady diet of national telecasts and superstation games rarely highlighted the Twins, so this October would be a coming-out party. Tom Kelly needed no headlines to have great pride in this team, and he knew that winning in Toronto made the season a complete success.

"I agree with the theory that just getting to the World Series is the big thing," Kelly explained. "Getting through the play-offs is the hard thing. That's the most pressure. The World Series is ice cream on the cake. Once you realize you're there, it takes a lot of pressure off."

After winning their division in Toronto, the only thing lacking for the Twins was a partner for "the Big Dance." Atlanta and Pittsburgh were contesting the National League Championship Series down to the wire, and no matter how long it took to decide the pennant, the Twins had five days to fill before the World Series opener. By clinching in Toronto on Sunday, the Twins had actually won too early. Major League Baseball issued a concrete schedule for the World Series, and it would not begin until the following Saturday. For major leaguers whose longest respite from play is the three days of the All-Star Break, five days seemed like an entire off-season. "If I had to set up the perfect world, I'd like two days off before the Series, maybe three," Kelly admitted. "Five days is just too long."

Kelly tried to keep his team sharp yet rested through workouts at the Metrodome. Monday, the day after the clinching, was an off day, to be followed by four days at work. The sessions were characterized by a looseness underscoring Kelly's theory about pressure in October. Players wore shorts and t-shirts as they went through their workouts, which were a typical Twins combination of determination and frivolity. As the week wore on, the determination waned and "boredom set in," according to Kelly. "I was bored too. It was just a rag-tag workout. It was just too long without line pitching, and as much as we tried to simulate that situation, it just wasn't the same as playing somewhere."

"I knew we wouldn't be tight or wound up, because we hadn't played enough baseball to build up emotions after the 162-game season ended," maintained Kelly. "But by Friday, the boys had enough of practice. If I had to do it again, I would suggest going to Arizona or Florida and playing a team of players in the instructional league, just as Oakland did in 1989 during the earthquake."

Conventional wisdom said the Twins would use these days to

sharpen their pitchers' hitting, bunting, and base running skills, because during Games 3, 4, and 5 in Atlanta the National League rules would be used, eliminating Chili Davis's bat and forcing the Twins' pitchers into unfamiliar roles. "It is embarrassing to a professional to have to try and do something that he hasn't done for years," admitted Kelly. "You put those pitchers in front of 40 or 50 million people watching these games and ask them to hit. That's not right, not fair. There has to be a better way."

The sentiments were classic Kelly. Instead of worrying about how his pitchers' inexperience at hitting might hurt the team, he thought of his players' feelings. Nothing served to better exemplify why Kelly was a manager for whom players performed. Kelly had played, and even though he was not their boss, he often thought like a player.

Kelly's anger over the World Series rules notwithstanding, the pitchers did get a week-long clinic on bunting and hitting. "We thought it was a waste of time," said Kelly. "But we had to try. We did it more for them to use those muscles, so they would not hurt themselves swinging in the games. We gave them a little bit more each day, but by Friday, we were all kind of tired of watching them swing and bunt." Of the Twins' pitchers, only Rick Aguilera had a recent history of any success as a batter.

As the Twins waited with growing impatience for Saturday, Atlanta and Pittsburgh stretched their series to a Thursday night seventh game. Steve Avery, a remarkably poised 21-year-old left-hander, pitched a shutout in Game 6 at Pittsburgh to keep the Braves alive. Kelly watched only parts of Games 6 and 7, getting some idea of the Twins' potential opponent. "Our scouts felt it would be better to play Atlanta. They felt we could pitch more effectively to the Braves' lineup. Pittsburgh had more firepower with the bats. We knew Atlanta would have better pitching, but we'll always take our chances trying to score a run or two."

The Twins had assigned Bob Gebhard and Terry Ryan to

follow Pittsburgh during the end of the regular season, while scouts Jeff Schugel and Kevin Malone followed Atlanta. The foursome met in the play-offs, giving the Twins a thorough read on their potential opponents.

"That's why I only watched parts of Games 6 and 7," explained Kelly. "We have scouts who did a great job, so I believed that whatever they presented would be right. They watched 17 to 22 games, so for me to zero in on one or two games and inject another opinion would be wrong. For me to watch Ron Gant in four at-bats and decide something after the scouts have seen 60 at-bats would not be right. So I just watched the first time around each lineup to see what pitches were thrown."

Kelly did not need to watch any more to have his fears about Atlanta's pitching confirmed. John Smoltz put the finishing touch on a remarkable 48 hours in Pittsburgh by blanking the Pirates in Game 7. Atlanta was in "the Big Dance" for the first time, matching the Twins' rise from last place in 1990 to a World Series the following year, thereby injecting a spark of hope into a game whose business side was becoming increasingly disheartening to many franchises. Being a first-time participant in October baseball enabled the Braves to pose as the underdogs, the very same position that seemed to fuel the Twins' drive in 1987. Secretly, the Twins preferred to be doubted by the media. Although many predicted an Atlanta victory in the Series, the Twins would not have to contest with the same forecast of gloom that accompanied them to their first "Big Dance."

In fact Kelly had few worries about his team in the days preceding the World Series. Other than the loss of the designated hitter in Atlanta, Kelly's sole concern was likely Erickson, whose outing in the play-offs, the manager hoped, was an aberration. The top of the batting order was healthier with Gladden's rebound against Toronto and Knoblauch's excellence in his first postseason series. Most importantly, Kelly was able to properly arrange his pitching. Morris would be able to start three games if needed, while Tapani would have seven days and Erickson 10 days of rest between starts.

Kelly changed virtually nothing at the ballpark in preparing for his second World Series. However, his own life away from the ballpark had changed dramatically. In 1987 Kelly was alone and dealing with the pain of a dissolving marriage. Four years later he was happily remarried, living in a new home with his 12-year-old son. "In 1987 I spent a lot of time at the park, because I was by myself," remembered Kelly. "Everybody I knew, all my close friends, were at the ballpark. When I was here, I didn't think about my other problems. As soon as I got to the Dome, my mind focused in on baseball. As soon as I drove away from the Dome, my mind would flip back to the other things. When you wake up in the morning and the first thing you think of is that you're getting divorced, you run to where your mind is clear. So being at the park was like a relief or therapy for me.

"My parents stayed with friends during the 1987 Series because I had a small apartment. This year, with a house and my family, my parents stayed with me and I spent more time at home. I didn't rush to the park for the Series games," recalled Kelly.

He may not have hurried there, but still the manager was at the Metrodome seven hours before the first pitch of the final Series game. Kelly was seasoned at handling the distractions inherent in the World Series, and he often spoke to his players during the season about the right way to say "I have to go now" to reporters, or to know when to let the telephone go unanswered when ticket requests became unwieldy. Kelly had learned in 1987 how important it is to have someone to share October with, and he knew the families who had supported the team through their formative years would descend upon Minnesota. Yet he knew the players could not be constantly distracted during every waking moment.

By Saturday the Twins needed to play, and finally their dance partner arrived. Atlanta flew to the Twin Cities on Friday, just after their victory over Pittsburgh. The Braves had one chance to familiarize themselves with the Metrodome during a Friday night workout, but their Game 1 starting pitcher had already lived one nightmare under the Teflon roof. Charlie Leibrandt was the surprise choice by Braves' manager Bobby Cox to begin the World Series. The 35-year-old left-hander had resurrected his career by winning 15 games and pitching 229 innings. If Atlanta's starters were to be ranked, Leibrandt would fill the fourth spot. But Cox had decided to use the people who were responsible for their season. It was a decision that was a combination of loyalty and consistency, traits that Kelly too would display in time during the series.

For Game 1, Kelly explained, "I felt if there was any advantage it was that we had seen Charlie for years with Kansas City. Now, Bobby knows his personnel better than anyone, and for him that must have been the right choice. But it helped the guys who had been here to hit off a pitcher they had faced before. Of course to people like Knoblauch and Leius, it didn't matter."

Leibrandt had been a successful pitcher in Kansas City, winning 17 games for the 1985 World Series Champions. There was one night in the Metrodome, however, that could never be forgotten. It was September 27, 1987, and a crowd of 53,106, the largest regular season crowd in Twins' history, turned out for the home finale, hoping for a Twins' win that would clinch a tie for the division championship. Knowing they could not see an actual clinching, they were out for blood on this night, and the team that played so well responded with an assault that left Leibrandt dazed. Consecutive home runs were hit in the first inning by Puckett, Gaetti, and Brunansky. Five runs scored before the inning ended, and Leibrandt was left with the memory of a disastrous outing before a roaring, hanky-waving crowd.

Leibrandt was matched with Morris, only one year his senior.

Yet there seemed to be a wealth of difference in the stature of the opposing pitchers. Morris was the Twins' horse, and they were preparing to ride him to the end. Atlanta had no such expectations of Leibrandt, only hoping for a solid start that would allow them to shift their focus from an emotional comeback against Pittsburgh to the World Series.

## GAME 1

As Game 1 began with a Morris pitch to Lonnie Smith, the Twins had supreme confidence in their horse. He was 5–1 in career postseason starts, and 13–3 at the Metrodome. The alignment by Kelly had Morris starting Games 1, 4, and 7, as Frank Viola had in 1987. What Kelly could not foresee was the equally important contributions to come from his middle infielders.

The game's first run was scored in the third. With two out, Gladden walked and stole second. Kelly approached the first game of the Series as he had the play-off opener, by running, stealing three bases in four attempts. It became quickly apparent to Cox, catcher Greg Olson, the Atlanta pitchers, and anyone else who cared, that the Twins would not alter their approach in the World Series.

Knoblauch then served a Leibrandt pitch on a line drive to right field. Dave Justice charged the ball and came up firing to home. In a sequence showcasing some of baseball's subtleties, Gladden was waved home by Gardenhire, Knoblauch rounded first base with the intention of going to second, and first baseman Sid Bream cut off the throw, electing to catch Knoblauch between the bases for an easy third out. Atlanta sacrificed the run, but Kelly felt "it was the right play for both teams. We want our runners to take that turn because we want the throw cut off to score the run. The out doesn't matter to us if the run scores. If I'm in Atlanta's position, I want to cut the ball, make the out and get off the field. Down 1–0 in the third inning isn't a big problem."

The extensive scouting reports on Atlanta certainly played a factor in Gardenhire's initial decision. Justice had a tendency to throw the ball high and occasionally overthrow his cutoff man. "If we wanted to try and take an extra base on anyone, it was him," explained Kelly. "So our end of the play was right."

A two-out stolen base had helped produce the first run of the World Series, and the perpetrators of this deed were the top two hitters. Gladden continued to provide a prototypical leadoff hitter's presence in the postseason, while Knoblauch's hits in his first two series at-bats firmly erased the word "rookie" from his biography.

Greg Gagne came to the plate in the fifth inning with his second-inning at-bat still on his mind. He had chased a high fastball to strike out, and he was determined to wait for Leibrandt to throw a pitch lower in the strike zone. Gagne's challenge was to prevent his first at-bat from affecting those to follow. The fifth inning presented the Twins with a chance to blow open Game 1. Hrbek had opened with a double to the right-center field gap, a hopeful sign that he would rebound from his three-hit play-off performance. Leius followed with a single to left, advancing Hrbek to third.

With no one out, the first obligation of the batter is to put the ball in play, and Gagne would later confess that his goal was to take a pitch to right field. He showed patience, however, in working the count to 3–1 before Leibrandt threw a fastball down the middle of the plate, just low enough to suit Gagne's swing. Gagne lifted a high fly ball into the left-center-field bleachers for a three-run home run, a real World Series home run.

For a moment it was 1987 again. Wayne Terwilliger jumped and delivered a high-five to Gagne at first base. Hrbek watched the ball's flight from third base and repeatedly pumped his right arm at his side (the residual effects of his June shoulder injury prevented him from lifting the arm over his shoulder, and made throwing a painful task). The Metrodome was awash in a blizzard of white hankies, and there was a momentary belief that the magic of four autumns past might live again.

A week earlier, a Toronto newspaper had quoted Gagne as saying he felt underappreciated for his contributions to the Twins. Now he bathed in the appreciation of a thundering Metrodome. "It seems that in every World Series, an unlikely hero or two emerges," Kelly recalled. "You see it time and time again, where a guy who's not supposed to get a big hit comes through. With Gags, he's so strong that if you throw him a low pitch, he can hit it out." Part of the euphoria created by Gagne's homer was the sense that a four-run lead was impregnable with Morris on the mound. For Game 1 that held true, and the performance highlighted Morris' resolve to excel at the very moments that cry for excellence. This was a night Morris fantasized about in his childhood in St. Paul. When it finally came true, Morris was a craftsman with only half of his tools. His best "stuff" was missing in action, but what he had was good enough to plow through the Braves' order three times.

"I was going to take him out to start the eighth inning," Kelly remembered. "But he hadn't thrown that many pitches [90 after seven innings]." However, Morris walked Lonnie Smith and Jeff Treadway to start the inning, and Kelly quickly summoned Mark Guthrie. "The emotions of the game can drain you more quickly than normal, and Jack just ran out of gas." The steady round of applause grew louder with each step Morris took towards the Twins' dugout, and as he crossed the third base line, he raised his cap in his left hand to thank the fans for their support on this night of his dreams.

It was a rare occasion when Kelly had second thoughts about a pitching move. He changed his mind by allowing Morris to start the eighth, thereby creating a tough task for the bullpen. "When I change pitchers, I'm always thinking about what the change will do to the next pitcher," Kelly said. "You want the new man to start fresh, or at the worst, inherit a small burden. If you leave one pitcher in too long, he leaves on a bad note mentally, and that could ruin his next start. That pertains more to younger pitchers. But you don't want a reliever coming in thinking he has to make perfect pitches right away. If you give him some room for error, then he can make a mistake or two and your team will still survive."

Kelly claimed his father, a minor league pitcher, had always "dictated to me that when you see the ball hit hard, it's time to make a change. If you've seen some warning signs and you wait too long, then you're not doing your job."

There were no warning signs in the seventh as Morris had retired the Braves in order. The consecutive walks to open the eighth, however, gave Atlanta a chance to reverse the fortunes of Game 1. The Braves' three most potent run producers, Terry Pendleton, Dave Justice, and Ron Gant, were scheduled to bat, and one more runner would bring the tying run to the plate.

Kelly chose Mark Guthrie to face the switch-hitting Pendleton. "We thought Pendleton had more power left-handed," Kelly said. "Also, I generally like to turn a switch hitter around later in the game." Pendleton hit .299 as a right-handed batter during the regular season with just four of his career-high 22 home runs coming from this side of the plate. After signing with Atlanta as a free agent, the third baseman had the best offensive year of his career. Now he was healthy, and able to try for a World Series win at the Metrodome, unlike 1987 when an injury limited Pendleton to seven at-bats for the Cardinals.

Atlanta's rally seemed to build as Pendleton laced a low line drive just to the right field side of second base. Knoblauch, however, bent to his backhand side, smothered the ball after its first hop, then flipped it to Gagne for the beginning of a double play. "It wasn't an easy play, but it's one we've seen Knobby make," Kelly explained. "I'd have been disappointed if he hadn't made the play."

Guthrie then walked the left-handed-hitting Justice, and Aguilera was called in to face Gant, who singled to produce the Braves' second run. Sid Bream, a left-handed-hitting first baseman with decent power, came to bat as the tying run. In the sixth inning, Bream had looked at a called third strike with two runners on base and two outs. Now in a similar situation, Aguilera induced a fly ball to center that ended the inning, and effectively, the game. "Bream had a tough time with men on base," Kelly said in a classic understatement.

After the Braves went out in order in the ninth to complete the 5–2 Twins victory, Kelly walked to the commissioner's box outside the Twins' dugout and handed his lineup card to Steve Palermo, the American League umpire who had been partially paralyzed in a July shooting incident. In a moving scene, Palermo had thrown out the first pitch of the World Series, walking to the mound with the aid of braces and crutches. Each of the six umpires embraced Palermo in a show of support for their comrade who was fighting long and difficult odds to return to umpiring.

Kelly had seen Palermo in the Twins dugout before the game. "You're never quite sure what to say, and I didn't want to say something stupid," recalled Kelly. "So, I think I made a couple of smart remarks like, 'How long are you going to milk this vacation?' I was glad he was invited, and he seems like such a strong-willed guy that I hope he can recover."

The Game 1 victory again featured the very thing that separated the Twins from Toronto in the play-offs. The Twins pitchers continually got the necessary out to retain control of the game. In this game the two Bream at-bats and Pendleton's double-play smash were situations where a hit could have changed the game's complexion. Instead, the Twins walked away with the outs and the game.

Knoblauch had excelled with three hits, two stolen bases, a hard slide that broke up a double play in the seventh, and a nice play to start the key eighth-inning double play. Hrbek had added a home run off reliever Jim Clancy to his earlier double, and Gagne, the ninth-place hitter, had delivered the game's decisive blow.

One unfortunate play was widely discussed after Game 1. After Gagne's home run in the Twins' half of the fifth inning, Gladden reached base on an error, and eventually found himself on third base as the Twins loaded the bases. With one out, Brian Harper hit a line drive down the left field line that immediately had the appearance of a hit. Gladden broke towards home, then had to shift into reverse as he saw left fielder Brian Hunter race towards the line and make the catch. Gladden raced back to the base, tagged it as Hunter caught the ball, and then sped to home.

"I never saw Danny do that before," Kelly remembered. "You learn from day one that if the ball goes in the air to the outfield, you go back to the base. He thought the ball was a hit, and went the wrong way. Then, he compounded the error by tagging up. Instead of staying at third, he made two mistakes."

Greg Olson received the throw well in advance of Gladden, who arrived in a hard slide that upended the catcher and sent him into a flip that stood him on his head for an instant. Despite his somersault, Olson held the ball and Gladden was out.

A slide that was criticized by former catcher Tim McCarver on national television did not surprise Kelly. "I wouldn't have expected anything else from Danny. Others may have tried fadeaway slides, but Danny goes straight into the plate. He's done it for years, so no one should have been surprised. Now, if I'm Olson, I'd probably be a little mad, but Danny didn't have his spikes up in Olson's face. It was a hard, aggressive slide. We're not here to play tiddlywinks." To Olson's credit, he never questioned Gladden's play, only saying that he understood the way Gladden played the game.

## GAME 2

Sunday night was pitchers' night as the starters dominated Game 2. Atlanta's Tom Glavine was one of only two 20-game winners in the National League, and ranked near the top of the league's qualitative pitching statistics. Kevin Tapani, two years older than Glavine but with two fewer years of major league experience, rebounded well from a beating in Game 5 of the play-offs.

There was only one lineup change in Game 2, and it drew scant attention. Bobby Cox inserted Mark Lemke at second base replacing Jeff Treadway. A .320 hitter had been replaced by a .234 hitter, but Kelly understood Cox's motives. "Lemke has much better range. I think Lemke would have reached Knoblauch's ball in the third inning [of Game 1] that scored our first run."

Lemke's debut was inauspicious. Gladden started the Twins' half of the first inning with a pop into short right field. Lemke and Justice, so intent on watching the ball against the unfamiliar Metrodome roof, bumped as the ball hit Lemke's glove. The slight jostling caused the ball to drop to the carpet and sent Gladden into second base. "They just ran into each other," Kelly recalled. "You see it happen a handful of times each year."

Knoblauch walked, and with Puckett at the plate, Kelly decided it was time to continue the aggressive play displayed in Game 1. A hit and run with Puckett at the plate was not a frequent occurrence, but "Puck had been great on the hit and run this year," explained Kelly. Here, with the runners moving from second and first, Puckett chopped a ground ball directly at third base, a ball that the Braves could not have placed more perfectly by hand. Running to cover the base, Pendleton simply had to wait for the ball to hit his glove, step on third in the same motion to force Gladden, and fire to first for an easy double play. "If Puck had hit the ball a foot to the left of Pendleton, it's a hit. He just hit it right to where Pendleton was running."

Chili Davis had completed his 10th major league season, and

was in the World Series for the first time. Davis was intensely proud of the effort he put forth to rehabilitate his career in 1991, and equally proud of the important role he played in the Twins' success. His opportunities in this Series, however, would be limited largely to the games in the Metrodome because the Twins could not use the designated hitter in Atlanta.

He had not hit safely in Game 1, and now he was the Twins' last hope to provide a first-inning lead in Game 2. On 0–1, Glavine threw a change-up that stayed up in the strike zone and Davis drove it into the left-field stands. The first World Series hit of his career sent Davis on a memorable trip around the bases, and sent the Twins into a 2–0 lead.

Atlanta scored once in the second inning, and in the third inning a play occurred that altered this series much the way that Carter's injury had affected the play-offs.

With two outs and a runner on first base, Gant singled to left field. Lonnie Smith tried to advance to third, and Gladden quickly threw there in hopes of nailing Smith. Smith arrived simultaneously with the throw, and his slide effectively blocked Leius from catching the ball. The throw skipped down the third base line towards home plate, where Tapani fielded it and fired a quick strike to Hrbek at first. Gant had taken a large turn around first, and Tapani's instinct was to try to pick him off the base.

Kelly viewed this as a mistake. "I was angry because I don't like seeing the ball thrown all over the field," he said. "If Tap makes a bad throw, we have a circus with people running all over the place. We try to stay away from circuses."

The throw was accurate to Hrbek, but Gant beat the throw as he lunged upright into the bag with his right leg. Gant was safe for a moment. Then, in one motion, Gant's upper body began to topple into foul territory, and he put his left hand to the ground for balance. Hrbek had placed a tag on Gant's right leg and kept the glove there as Gant's fall moved him into Hrbek's body. Finally,

Gant's right leg came off the base, and with Hrbek's glove still tagging the leg in full view of umpire Drew Coble, Gant was called out.

The argument that ensued from Gant and Cox was fully expected, but the repercussions over the next week were totally unexpected. "I've said this a lot, and I still feel the same way. I wish Gant would have been called safe," Kelly maintained. "There would have been runners at first and third with two outs, with no runs scored and who knows what the next guy would have done. But the umpire took a lot of heat, and Hrbek took more heat and nonsense than I ever would have expected. What happened sort of spoiled the Series for them. It's supposed to be the happiest time of your career, but I think for Hrbek it was ruined by what happened with some individuals."

"If Gant slides back into the base, he has no problem. But he doesn't slide, he gets off balance and you can see his leg start to buckle. It was no more of a tag than Herbie ever gives a guy, but when you're off balance like Gant was, you'll go."

As the game moved along, the play was temporarily forgotten in a string of fine pitching and outstanding defense. A leadoff double by Olson in the fifth led to a tying run for the Braves. Meanwhile, Glavine did not allow a hit after Davis's home run, until Harper singled with two outs in the seventh. Lemke and shortstop Rafael Belliard took several hits away with strong defensive plays, while Glavine kept throwing strikes.

Careful observers of this World Series noted that the eighth innings seemed to contain the most crucial moments. Atlanta's best chance in Game 1 had been in the eighth. Game 2 followed the same pattern.

Belliard was the first batter in the eighth, and he capitalized on a rare lapse by the Twins in positioning. "We should have played in closer and made him swing the bat," Kelly admitted. "We played back and let him bunt." Belliard's two-strike bunt was a bold maneuver, and it paid off with a leadoff single. Lonnie Smith sacrificed Belliard to second, and Pendleton then squibbed a bouncer wide of first base that he ran out for an infield single.

The unfolding scene was one the Twins were used to seeing in the postseason. The opposition had a scoring threat with their best hitters at the plate. Fans were also accustomed to seeing Kelly use his bullpen in these spots, but on this night Kelly sat still in the dugout. "Tap had given up two crap hits. They hadn't hit the ball at all," maintained Kelly. "He didn't deserve to come out."

Gant was the batter, and he had a chance to completely negate the impact of the controversial third-inning play. Tapani fell behind at 2–0, and in a move hitters say is symbolic of baseball in the nineties, he threw a change-up for a strike. No longer could hitters automatically sit on a 2–0, or for that matter a 3–0, fastball. The next pitch was a fastball that Gant fouled behind home plate. Harper caught it for the second out.

Justice was up next, and Guthrie was ready in the bullpen. Again Kelly resisted the temptation and stayed with his starter. The count went to 3–2. Justice, a left-handed-hitter who according to Kelly "has a long swing and is a lowball hitter," saw a change-up on the full count pitch. Tapani had located the ball perfectly, high and on the outside part of the plate, away from Justice's power. The result was a harmless fly to left. The inning was over with no runs, another Twins' "October special" by their pitchers.

"The key here was what I saw on the tape of this game," Kelly remembered. "After Justice flied out, they showed the Braves dugout, and Glavine is sitting there with this look on his face that he couldn't believe that they didn't score. To me, this is an important part of baseball. Pitchers must be ready to get the first batter of an inning. If we score some runs, and our pitcher has been sitting for a long time, we have to get on him, and make sure he's ready to face the first batter. [Dick] Suchie is really good about making sure our pitchers bear down right away. To me, it was plain as day on the tape. Glavine's emotions took over after the disappointment of them not scoring."

Leius led off the bottom of the eighth, and saw a first pitch fastball that Kelly believed Glavine "wanted outside but came down the middle of the plate." Leius, not automatically taking the first pitch, drove a high fly ball that just cleared the left-field Plexiglas. No rookie had homered in a World Series since Willie McGee in 1982. Leius, who had appeared to have a ticket to Portland two weeks before the season opened, had sent the Metrodome into a state of frenzy on the first pitch after Tapani's superior pitching had kept the tie intact.

The leadoff home run gave Kelly enough time to prepare Aguilera, and the Twins' stopper was as impressive as anyone could remember. Bream led off and struck out swinging at a nasty forkball. Hunter dropped a single in front of Puckett, who was positioned by the warning track to prevent an extra base hit. Then Aguilera caught Olson looking at a slider, and pinch hitter Tommy Gregg looking at a fastball to end the game. "He struck out three guys on three different pitches," Kelly marveled. "That was awesome, but remember that after Aggie lost some wins for Tap during the season, he came back and threw real hard the next time. He was near unhittable in this game."

The Twins had established a 2–0 lead in the Series, and planted some seeds of doubt in the minds of the Braves. The Twins' pitchers were phenomenal while pitching to Atlanta's top hitters with men on base. For all the whining that followed about the Hrbek-Gant entanglement, most Braves and their supporters conveniently forgot the opportunity that Gant and Justice had in the eighth inning. That had been Atlanta's turn to hit, and Tapani had stopped them cold.

Heroes changed on a daily basis for the Twins. Pagliarulo had struck the single most damaging blow of the play-offs, and now Gagne and Leius had followed in the World Series. The revolving door of success that had started during The Streak in June had continued right into the heart of October. The Twins were now two wins away from a World Championship, but they were also heading into the heart of a firestorm in Atlanta.

## GAME 3

Tom Kelly knew something was wrong when he saw the FBI agents enter the clubhouse. It was hours before Game 3 in Atlanta, and a distraction of the most serious nature loomed right in the middle of the Twins' clubhouse. "When I saw the FBI come in, and say they wanted to talk with me and him [Hrbek], I knew things had gone too far," admitted Kelly.

From the moment early Monday morning when the Twins' charter touched down at Hartsfield International Airport, seemingly all of Atlanta's wrath had been directed toward Hrbek. The city had been overtaken by front-runners, the fans who show up to pull for a team when they win, but completely ignore the same team in lean times. The Braves had been ignored for most of their 25 years in Atlanta, but after reaching their first World Series, they had been discovered.

What Atlanta craved was a villain, someone to blame for the Braves' 0–2 start. In this highlight-oriented world, Hrbek became an easy target as news programs continued to replay the tag at first from many different angles. The more publicity the play received, the more wrath was directed at Hrbek. It probably never entered the minds of Atlanta fans that Gant and Justice had failed in the eighth inning, when Game 2 was waiting to be won. A much simpler course was to blame Hrbek.

As the Twins were flying to Atlanta, Hrbek's mother and sister each received threatening telephone calls at their Minnesota homes. During the off day, Hrbek received several additional calls in his Atlanta hotel. "When the FBI comes in, it's obvious that these were calls to be taken seriously," Kelly insisted. "When it involves family, we all get a little sensitive. I know he can take anything from fans, but he gets protective of his family. It was a shame that a few individuals interested in the Braves winning had to do something so bad.

"I could tell on Tuesday afternoon that he was being affected," continued Kelly. "When the FBI showed up, he wasn't at the park yet, which is uncharacteristic for him. He decided to stay at his hotel longer, which forced him out of his routine.

"When he arrived, we had a chance to talk," said Kelly. "I asked how things were going, and he told me that the phone calls to his family weren't pleasant. There wasn't anything I could say to ease his mind, because the game means nothing when you're dealing with family."

So Game 3, already expected to be difficult enough for the Twins without the bat of Davis, had another obstacle added with the cloud of uncertainty hanging over Hrbek.

Heading to Atlanta brought Kelly into direct contact with the World Series rules change he so passionately disliked. The Twins were hurt by the loss of Davis's bat from the starting lineup for the games in Atlanta, yet the Braves gained an advantage in Minnesota by taking Lonnie Smith, a defensive liability, out of left field and keeping him in as the designated hitter.

During the Monday workout, Kelly had Davis in the outfield, taking flies and playing caroms out of the right field corner. He could not start in his normal role, but Kelly knew that Davis would play in these games, at the least as a pinch hitter.

Not everyone else was quite as aware. During the mandatory press conference Monday, Kelly fielded a most incredible question. "Someone asked me who was going to be the DH here," Kelly recalled. "The first thing that hit me was that we didn't have the DH in Atlanta, so why would you ask me that? Then, I realized that Chili has been our only DH all year, so that made the question more foolish. It was embarrassing to everyone in the room."

The questions that Kelly had fully expected did come. He was asked how he would manage without the DH, a question bearing the implication that the American League manager lacks the intellectual capacity to execute the double switch (two players entering the game at the same time and exchanging spots in the batting order.) "That's just one of those questions that you get at the big events, because people need something to write about or talk about," Kelly explained. "You rarely get that question from the well-known, well-respected writers. Sure, there's something to the change in rules, but too much is made of it. It sure isn't rocket science."

The Twins' Monday workout confirmed why Atlanta Stadium was called the "Launching Pad." "The ball carried unbelievably well, and the infield was so hard that it was like playing on the freeway," Kelly confirmed. "It's a real credit to Atlanta's pitchers that they can have so much success in that park." Kelly respected the Braves' starters, but he never believed it could be so difficult to get one hit in this hitter's paradise. He would learn in Game 3.

Steve Avery, a 21-year-old left-hander who was the Braves' second-winningest pitcher, with 18 wins, was the Atlanta starter. Avery was doing to the National League in the second half what Scott Erickson had done to the American League in the season's first half. Avery was 10–3 after the All-Star break, then twirled consecutive 1–0 shutouts of Pittsburgh in the play-offs, winning MVP honors.

Erickson had 10 days of rest between postseason starts, and the Twins hoped his batteries would be recharged. While Avery was soaring, Erickson's play-off start had been a disappointment. The reasoning was that he suffered an emotional drain that sapped him of his strength. On top of the Hrbek scenario, the Twins had to deal with the aura of invincibility projected by Avery, the same aura Erickson had projected in May and June.

After one inning the Twins led 1–0, but the score was

completely deceiving. Gladden started the game with a fly ball into right center field that was misplayed by Gant and Justice, and rolled untouched to the wall for a triple. Knoblauch brought in the run with a sacrifice fly. Avery then retired Hrbek on a ground ball and struck out Puckett with a formidable display of his outstanding repertoire.

Erickson retired the Braves in order in the first inning, but not without setting off warning signals for Kelly. "Scott wasn't really throwing the ball," said Kelly. "If you watched closely, you could see the ball far too long. His body slowed down, and you would think that pitching in the World Series would generate some adrenaline. It wasn't pretty, but he held them for a while."

Erickson did hold Atlanta until the fifth inning, when the Twins played an atypical inning. Atlanta had scored single runs in the second on a Belliard single, and in the fourth on a Justice home run. Lonnie Smith then hit a high change-up for a home run with one out in the fifth, and Pendleton walked. Erickson recovered to induce a pop-up from Gant, and a grounder to second base from Justice. However, Knoblauch committed a rare error on the grounder, and the Braves stayed alive in the inning.

"The game wasn't running smooth for Scott, and when that happens, you can have problems in the field," admitted Kelly. It was one of Kelly's commandments of baseball: Throw strikes, make them hit the ball, and good things will usually happen. This game was laboring for the Twins, and the problems accumulated as West relieved Erickson.

Without David West, the Twins would not have made it to Atlanta. The unsung pitching hero of the play-offs, though, could not repeat that success in the World Series. Ten pitches produced two walks that forced in the fourth Atlanta run, and moved Kelly to call on Terry Leach. Leach ended the inning by striking out Lemke.

The inning unfolded against every grain of Kelly's baseball

philosophy. There were three walks, and a key error that prolonged Atlanta's turn at bat. If Justice was retired, the inning would have ended at 3–1, but more importantly Erickson would have walked off the mound to be pinch hit for in the sixth. Kelly was forced to use two more pitchers to end the inning, and had to bring in Bedrosian to start the sixth. The "domino effect" that Kelly dreaded had struck his bullpen, and the results were painful for a nine-man staff. "If one spoke is out of whack, it knocks the others off," Kelly believed.

Avery had breezed through five innings. With a 4–1 lead in the sixth, his armor appeared to crack. Ortiz led off with a single and Larkin, batting for the pitcher, followed with a line drive down the left field line for his first World Series hit. Smith, playing left field in Atlanta, raced towards the line and prevented the ball from reaching the corner. In an example of extreme base running caution, though, Ortiz stopped at second. Against Smith's weak throwing arm, even the slow-footed catcher was expected to take third and Larkin, despite a bad knee, would have had a double. Instead of second and third with no outs, the Twins had runners without great speed at first and second. Avery retired the next three batters, and the base running error in judgment had cost the Twins at least one run.

Puckett officially arrived at the World Series as he led off the seventh with a home run to left. Hitless in his first 10 at-bats, Puckett kindled hopes of a resurgence similar to his MVP performance in the play-offs.

Avery finished the seventh, but the last two innings "were not pretty" from Kelly's perspective. "He got a little tired from the World Series excitement, and in the eighth he was done," Kelly said. "The Braves said he didn't have his normal curve, which is hard for us to judge since we hadn't seen him before. But from our spot it looked awfully good."

Cox sent Avery out to start the eighth, while Alejandro Pena warmed up in the bullpen. Kelly was sitting on a powerful corps of pinch hitters, and he decided this was his time to move. "It was 4–2, and you pretty much have to make a run at it there. The bottom of our order was up, so there was no guarantee we'd get to use these hitter again."

Brian Harper was first off the bench, pinch hitting for Ortiz, and he hit a hard ground ball that handcuffed Gold Glove third baseman Pendleton for an error. Pena was brought in as Davis was announced as a pinch hitter for the pitcher. The veterans had faced each other many times in the National League, but Pena had not seen the improved, stronger Davis that had stroked 29 home runs for the Twins. "Chili's strong, and he got a hold of a pitch and got it up in the air, and we knew how well the ball flies there," Kelly said, remembering Davis's stunning two-run homer that tied the game.

The Atlanta crowd, whipped into a frenzy by two days of Hrbek-bashing in the media, had been jubilant until Davis's one swing. Fans were further silenced when with one out, Knoblauch and Hrbek hit consecutive singles. Runners were at first and third, with Puckett at the plate. It wasn't enough to say that Puckett only needed to put the ball in play, because he had grounded into a major league leading 27 double plays. Still, all the momentum belonged to the Twins, and one more hit with their best hitter at the plate would have left the Braves and their juiced-up crowd dazed and confused.

The ensuing events caused Kelly to admit that "humans play this game." Unbelievably to the Twins, Puckett struck out swinging at a high fastball. Shane Mack followed with the same result. Pena had somehow found the resolve to retire a pair of .300 hitters in another of the eighth-inning showdowns that highlighted this series.

After the forgettable fifth inning, Minnesota's bullpen regained its form of the play-offs. Bedrosian and Willis each worked a pair of scoreless innings, and when Pena stopped the Twins in the ninth, the game headed to extra innings.

The Twins had missed a chance to take the lead in the eighth, and they would have two more opportunities in the extra innings. However, the eighth inning had used the Twins' best bats off the bench. So in the 10th inning, Kelly was forced to make a difficult decision. With two outs and Gladden on second base, Atlanta left-hander Mike Stanton intentionally walked Puckett to bring up the fifth spot in the Twins' order, occupied at this time by Willis. Kelly had already used six position players in reserve roles, and his choice for a pinch hitter was between Al Newman and Paul Sorrento. Strictly on percentages, the switch-hitting Newman would get the nod, but Kelly opted for Sorrento. "I think he had a better shot there than Newman," claimed Kelly. "Plus, I had to save Newman to hit for Pags [the on-deck batter]. It may not have looked right, but we did it the right way." Sorrento's first World Series at-bat ended in a strikeout against Stanton, who would prove to be unhittable for the Twins' left-handed batters.

By the 12th inning, Kelly had "fired all the bullets trying to win the game." Newman had pinch hit in the 11th, so the only available players were pitchers Morris, Tapani, and Aguilera. Still the Twins were given an opportunity when, with one out, and Gladden, who had singled in his last two at-bats, on first base, Lemke missed Knoblauch's double-play grounder. The ball kicked off his glove into short right field with Gladden taking third base. Hrbek was the scheduled batter, and after seeing Stanton strike him out in the tenth, Cox went to the bullpen for another left-hander, Kent Mercker.

"The only thought I had was to squeeze," Kelly admitted. "I thought about it since he was struggling. But the guy's a hitter. He's paid to swing the bat, so asking him to bunt in the World Series would have been wrong."

No one in Atlanta Stadium was thinking about a squeeze

bunt, but Kelly was always thinking ahead. He knew that Hrbek was his only good chance to get this run home. Puckett was next, and Kelly realized the Braves would walk him with the pitcher's spot behind him and no pinch hitters available. As Hrbek walked to the plate, Aguilera was called in from the bullpen where he had been warming up. "We saw what was going to happen, so we called Aggie down to prepare him to hit," Kelly said. "The key was that Herbie had to put the ball in play." This was the third at-bat for the Twins with a runner on third and one out since they had tied the game in the eighth. And for the third time, the Braves' pitcher won the battle as Mercker threw a called third strike past Hrbek on the inside corner. To Kelly, it was inside. "I've looked at the pitch a hundred times, and it is still inside. In baseball, the old adage is you swing the bat at anything close with two strikes." The home plate umpire was Drew Coble.

Puckett was issued the anticipated intentional walk, and Aguilera strode from the dugout to bat for Mark Guthrie. It was well known that Aguilera was a capable hitter. An infielder when he went to Brigham Young University, he was converted to a pitcher in his sophomore year. His hitting skills were never lost, and Aguilera's career batting average was .203 in the National League.

Veteran right-hander Jim Clancy was the pitcher, and he threw ball one in the dirt. Aguilera took a strong swing at the next pitch, and hit a line drive to center fielder Gant for the third out. "If Aggie had been just a second quicker, he would have hit a better line drive that might have hit the gap," recalled Kelly. "He had a good swing, but it's still atrocious to have a pitcher batting in an extra-inning World Series game."

Kelly had managed consistent with his regular season style. He was rarely conservative and, particularly on the road, managed aggressively to win. The thought of saving people for later in a game when the opportunity to win was present never entered his mind. Thus he made his moves in the eighth through eleventh innings, in each frame trying to push one run across the plate.

When the Twins failed in the twelfth, the feeling in the stadium was that this was Atlanta's game to win. The Twins had been one hit away too many times, and now they were down to their last pitcher with an empty bench.

With one out in the last of the twelfth, Justice singled. Hunter popped out to second base, and with the count at 0–2 on Olson, Justice stole second. Aguilera's impeccable control vanished in the rest of the at-bat, and Olson walked. "We pitched to Olson like he was Babe Ruth," Kelly said.

To the plate came Lemke, who earlier in the inning looked as if he would be responsible for a Twins' win. Now he was one hit away from donning the hero's cloak. Aguilera threw a "decent pitch" that Lemke hit on a soft line into left field. Justice never broke stride, as he rounded third just as Gladden picked up the ball. It looked like a good throw would catch Justice, but Gladden's effort hit about 30 feet in front of Harper and died. Justice slid across home plate with the run that kept Atlanta alive in the Series. "It was a tough play, because Lemke didn't hit the ball very well," claimed Kelly. "And Danny had a good chance at the plate, but he just didn't throw it very well."

It was well past midnight, but Atlanta erupted in celebration as if they had just passed the exam for entrance into sports legitimacy, winning a World Series game. Atlanta was now in the big time. Kelly was disappointed to let this game slip away, when a 3–0 lead was so close, but he took satisfaction in a comeback against quality pitchers that forced extra innings. Lastly, there was the gratification of knowing that the Twins had just competed in a "hell of a game," one that would live as a World Series classic.

Writers from around the nation questioned Kelly's managing in Game 3, particularly when he admitted after the game that Aguilera would only pitch two innings, and that Gladden would have been the next pitcher. Kelly wanted to make a point. If he had to make his pitchers bat in the World Series, what could be so wrong about an outfielder pitching? Those who criticized Kelly were not familiar with his managerial style. Atlanta's lead backed Kelly into a corner, forcing him to use pitchers and pinch hitters more quickly than he would have liked. Then he went for the win, and was thankful that Atlanta ended the game before Aguilera threw many pitches. It was a wonderfully tense battle that had to be quickly erased from the minds of the participants as Game 4 loomed close at hand.

## GAME 4

Brian Harper didn't just catch in Game 4, he defended home plate like a zealot. The fifth inning saw Atlanta parlay a single, a stolen base, a double, a walk, and a near wild pitch into no runs, due to a remarkable display of defense by a man still relatively new to catching.

Harper, a player worthy of admiration, was someone who had persevered through 11 years of professional baseball, three of those major league years, before landing with the Twins in 1988. He came to Minnesota with the promise of becoming a catcher, a position he had played early in his baseball career. Harper could hit with power as a younger player, and with more contact as he matured. You could just pencil in a .300 batting average next to Harper's name at the beginning of the season.

Game 4 starters Morris and John Smoltz were deadlocked at 1–1 in the fifth inning. Both teams were hitting the ball in the early innings, so it was no surprise when Smith started Atlanta's half of the fifth with a single. He capitalized on Morris's slow delivery by stealing second. Pendleton then hit a blast to deep left-center field. As Puckett took off after the ball, it appeared to everyone that this ball would be for extra bases. Everyone, that is, except for Smith. Inexplicably, Smith froze at second as if he were going to tag up if Puckett caught the ball. A moment of horror followed for Smith, as the ball flew past Puckett to the wall. Third base coach Jimy Williams waved Smith home as Knoblauch fired a relay to Harper. The late start cost Smith, who clearly saw Harper catch the ball with the plate blocked. Smith opted to lower his shoulder and go straight into Harper. The play was every bit as aggressive as Gladden's slide into Olson in Game 1. Harper stood his ground, took the fierce shot from Smith, and held the ball. "Give Harp a lot of credit," Kelly said. "That's one of the best collisions I've ever seen. It's a gutsy play for a catcher, and remarkable that he held the ball."

Pendleton went to third on the play at the plate, and after Gant walked, Morris threw a forkball in the dirt to Justice. Harper blocked the ball, and it bounced in the air, but landed just a few feet away. The bounce tempted Pendleton, and he committed himself to attempting to score. Harper picked up the ball in his bare hand, and dove across the plate to tag out the sliding Pendleton. When Justice flied out, Harper's inning had ended. His refusal to allow runners to touch the plate kept the game tied.

Pagliarulo was making his first World Series start against right-hander Smoltz, and he had driven in the first Twins' run with a second-inning looping single. Facing Smoltz for the third time, Pagliarulo drove a pitch over the right field fence. His third hit had provided the Twins with a boost reminiscent of his game-winning home run in Toronto.

Kelly then made a decision that could be judged as his most unusual of the postseason. One out after the home run gave the Twins a 2–1 lead, Larkin pinch hit for Morris. "I thought Jack was at the end of his rope, and our bullpen was doing well," explained Kelly. Morris had thrown 89 pitches on three days' rest, and never even thought about being removed after six innings, but Kelly decided to piece together the final nine outs from his bullpen.

Willis was called on for the seventh, and he retired the first two batters. Kelly remembered watching with astonishment after Smith stepped up to the plate. "We threw Lonnie a first pitch fastball, which is exactly what our reports told us not to do," Kelly admitted. The pitch ended up flying over the center field fence for a game-tying home run. "Harp and I had a little discussion over that pitch. That was the only mistake of a great game. Willis's fastball had been sinking well, but this one didn't sink."

Neither team used their stopper, and the Braves' relief pitching was better on this night. Stanton arrived with one out in the eighth, and retired five consecutive batters with pitches in the 90-mile-per-hour range. The Twins' pitching was handled by Willis and then Guthrie, who faced Lemke with one out in the ninth. The Twins' outfield did not play with the belief that Lemke could drive the ball while batting right-handed. "Give our scouts credit," said Kelly. "They told us Lemke could hit the ball deep from that side. We thought our outfield was all right at the time. But I'm not sure that we could have caught that ball even if we had played back."

Guthrie's fastball over the plate was lifted in the Atlanta air to deep left-center field. The Twins' outfielders, Gladden and Puckett, drifted back thinking the ball was catchable, but the ball kept carrying. It finally hit on the warning track, and before the Twins could relay the ball to the infield, Lemke was on third.

Jeff Blauser received an intentional walk, and Francisco Cabrera, a right-handed batter, was announced as a pinch hitter. Kelly brought Bedrosian in from the bullpen, and Cox countered with a lefty, veteran catcher Jerry Willard. "Bedrock had a little more experience for this situation, and I thought he had a better chance for a strikeout," Kelly explained. The Twins' manager also passed on walking Willard to load the bases, choosing instead to attack a pinch hitter.

Willard hit a high fly ball to right field that Mack camped under in anticipation of a play at the plate. As the ball towered in the air above the playing field, there was a rare opportunity for fans to enjoy the several seconds, and savor the decisive play that was about to unfold. Again it would unfold at Harper's feet.

Mack caught the ball and made a strong throw, slightly to the third-base side of home plate. Lemke, standing 5 foot 9 inches tall and weighing 167 pounds, was not a candidate for a collision, so he approached Harper and tried to evade him by running around the catcher perched up the third base line. Harper made a fine short-hop catch of Mack's throw, and swept his arms towards Lemke who flashed by his left shoulder. There was contact, and an instant hope that perhaps Harper had made another spectacular play. A safe sign from umpire Terry Tata deflated that hope, and sent Harper into a rage.

"It was a good play for us," maintained Kelly. "Rock [Bedrosian] popped up Willard pretty well. Shane made a good throw, and Harp made a good play to handle it. He just couldn't get the tag on Lemke. It was clear from the dugout that the umpire made the right call, and I never argue if I think they're right."

Kelly never moved from the dugout as Harper screamed at Tata in vain. Harper had hit Lemke with his shoulder, but not with his glove. There had been no tag.

The Series was suddenly tied, and Atlanta had a new hero. Mark Lemke, a career .225 hitter, had five hits in the last two games, and been involved in the game-winning play on consecutive nights. He didn't even start in Game 1, and his error in Game 3 had come perilously close to sending the Braves into an inescapable hole. Now the Series was tied, as the Twins had lost twice in 24 hours on games decided at home plate. Brian Harper had owned that plate for most of this night, but Atlanta finally snuck one man past him at the most opportune time.

## GAME 5

The Twins' baseball season was in its eighth month, and Tom Kelly still was looking ahead. Hours before Game 5 of the World Series, the topic discussed in the manager's office of the visiting clubhouse in Atlanta Stadium was Game 6.

Kelly, Andy MacPhail, and the coaches met early in the afternoon to discuss Scott Erickson. He was slated to start Game 6, but Kelly had reservations after watching Erickson's performance in Game 3. "We had to find out if Scott was hurting, because he couldn't pitch Game 6 the way he pitched Game 3," claimed Kelly. "I couldn't let our team lose that way."

Erickson was called in to Kelly's office. MacPhail and Dick Such were also present. "Scott convinced us he was all right, and that he was going to throw the ball and compete in Game 6. We had to know, because it would affect our pitching plans for Game 5 if he couldn't go on Saturday."

After four exhausting games, Game 5 restored the central nervous systems of the teams to a more normal state. Tapani was victimized by the only glaring fault of his otherwise sterling season, when six consecutive Braves reached base in a four-run fourth inning. Kelly and Such were consistently perplexed by Tapani's tendency to surrender hits in bunches. Kelly also felt that "Tap had a tough time with back-to-back starts against the same team."

For five innings Glavine stymied the Twins as he had in Game 2. In the sixth, with a 5–0 lead, Glavine lost his control, a problem he rarely, if ever, encountered. Four walks in the inning was a charitable means of allowing the Twins one chance at the lead. With two outs, two runners on base, and three runs having scored, Greg Gagne faced reliever Kent Mercker and sent a bulletlike line drive directly at Lemke on one hop. The inning and the Twins' best chance were over.

The final three innings were the most painful and embarrassing of the Series for the Twins. Atlanta's bats exploded in their last game before the home fans, and the game turned into an hour-long party for the long-suffering Braves' fans. A tired Twins' bullpen, with Bedrosian and Willis each pitching for the third consecutive night, was pounded into submission. The final was 14–5, and it was difficult not to confuse the atmosphere in Atlanta with a championship celebration. Long into the morning, the sound of drums pounded incessantly with the belief that the Braves' momentum was unstoppable. This team had clearly fed off the emotions generated by their city. Just as the Twins had prospered all year with a slew of different heroes, the Braves had unleashed Lemke, Willard, and Stanton on the Twins. They had won two games in Pittsburgh's ballpark to win the play-offs, so the Braves had to believe that one win at the Metrodome was feasible.

After spending all season proving this team was different from their 1987 edition, the Twins were now thrust into the position of having to claim they could repeat that team's most important achievement. The 1991 Twins, like the team of four years before, did not win a Series game on the road, and had to rely on the security of their perfect Metrodome record for hope.

The Twins fled Atlanta quickly. From the ugliness of the treatment received by Hrbek to the tomahawks, chops, drums, and Jane Fonda and Ted Turner, home seemed very appealing to the Twins. As they filed onto their plane an hour after Game 5, Kelly recalled a somber mood. "The seats weren't down for our card games. Usually the plane is ready, with some seat backs down so we can sneak a couple of hands in before takeoff. Now we had a ruckus, because our games were delayed. After losing three straight, the least we could do was get our card games right." Kelly's joke about the importance of the card games bore a touch of seriousness. His roller coaster analogy in spring training was critical now. The Twins could not fall into an emotional pit. Kelly had set the example by conducting himself in an unflappable manner following each loss. A longtime public relations executive who has worked at many World Series remarked that he had never seen a manager handle losing Series games better than Kelly did in Atlanta.

## GAME 6

Jack Morris went up to Kelly and Such during batting practice prior to Game 6, and said he was ready to pitch on two days' rest. Morris was still unhappy over leaving Game 4, and he wanted desperately to pitch again when his team needed a win.

Kelly had settled on Erickson, saving Morris for the Game 7 he hoped would be necessary. There were other lineup decisions to be made for the matchup with Avery. Chili Davis had started in right field in Game 5, as Mack was held out after an 0–15 start. "Shane just needed a break. He was really pressing," explained Kelly. "He can be a little insecure about himself as a player. A big leaguer has to shrug off an 0–4 game and say I'll come back strong tomorrow. That's not a slump. Now if you go 0–18, that's a slump, and maybe you look at films. But with experience and more self-confidence, Shane will conquer that problem.

"That move in Game 5 was not to get Chili's bat in the game," said Kelly. "Shane just had to have a break. If we had been at home, I still would have done it, and just put Larkin or Bush in the outfield and keep Chili as the DH."

For Game 6, Mack was back in the lineup. Brian Harper, though, did not start. Kelly would start Ortiz, though it meant keeping a .300 hitter on the bench when there was no guarantee of a game tomorrow. This was "the Big Dance," and Kelly believed you danced with the people who brought you there. Ortiz had caught Erickson all year, and "to change now would be wrong. If I had done that, the players look at me and wonder what I'm doing. Plus it's not fair to ask Harper to go into the Series and catch a guy he hasn't worked with all year."

A serious dose of reality was handed the Twins when they looked at having to beat Avery and Smoltz to win the Series. In the twisted logic that sometimes makes so much sense in baseball, the Twins may have benefited from the negative air that surrounded their homecoming. For the first time they were the underdogs.

Even in the Twin Cities, very few gave the hometown nine much of a chance to win two games against Atlanta's pitchers.

Kelly knew that any hope of survival rested on Erickson's approach to this start. Falling behind Avery could be fatal, so Kelly had Mark Guthrie ready if a quick "hook" was needed. "I stopped asking about Erickson's warmup," Kelly recalled. "It was really a moot point, because if he wasn't throwing the ball, I had to get him out in the first or second inning."

Even though the Braves put two runners on base in the first inning, Kelly was pleased with his starter. "Scott went out there to compete. He really threw the ball and went after hitters. Some of his pitches hung up high, but he also threw some good inside pitches." A decision had been made to reestablish the inside corner against the Braves' batters, something Kelly felt his pitchers abandoned in Atlanta.

Kirby Puckett came to bat in the bottom of the first with a bat that was darker in color than his normal bat. Knoblauch had singled with one out, and Puckett followed with a hard grounder just inside third base. In the first inning of Game 2, a ball hit in the same spot had been speared for a double play. Here, there was no runner in motion, and Pendleton was stationed at the normal third base position where he watched helplessly as the ball headed for the left field corner. Puckett chugged into third while Knoblauch scored. "Kirby has a light bat and a heavy bat," Kelly said. "With Avery pitching, he's smart enough to know when he needs the lighter bat, and he wound up pulling the ball."

Two batters later, Mack escaped from the shackles of his tormenting slide with a single, scoring Puckett for a 2–0 lead. "Shane's hit made everybody feel better. They were all pulling for him," said Kelly.

By the third inning viewers knew this night would belong to one of the game's premier players. Ron Gant batted with one out, one runner on, and drove an Erickson breaking pitch to the deepest part of the Metrodome. Kelly didn't think the ball had enough to get out of the park in left-center field, but he knew it would be close to the fence. As the ball soared towards the seats, all eyes focused on Puckett, whose choppy strides carried him to the base of the wall. Watching the play repeatedly over time, it is remarkable to note that Puckett's eyes never left the flight of the ball, yet he knew exactly when he ran out of room to run. Reaching out with his bare right hand to the padded fence, Puckett lifted his stocky body as high into the air as possible, and an instant before the ball caromed off the Plexiglas, snatched it with his glove. "It was a beautiful, outstanding catch," marveled Kelly. "Puck got a good jump, saw the ball all the way, and he's always been better going back on the ball. We've seen him make that catch before, but in these kinds of games, you need plays like that." In fact, Puckett had made more spectacular catches, but never one that could match the circumstances of Game 6 in the World Series.

It took Pendleton to hit a ball that Puckett could not reach. After the Twins had failed to turn a double play on a Smith ground ball in the fifth inning, Pendleton hit a mammoth home run to center field, tying the game. "If we played Atlanta again, I think we would finally have a better idea of pitching to Pendleton," admitted Kelly. "Batting left-handed, he likes the ball down, and that's where Scott's pitch was. When we threw the ball up to him, he didn't hit it."

Justice followed Pendleton's lead later in the inning with a monstrous drive into the right field upper deck that was barely foul. Somehow Erickson, who appeared on the verge of being finished, survived and worked into the seventh. The Twins had regained the lead in the last of the fifth with an atypical Twins' run. Gladden walked, stole second, and scored on fly balls by Knoblauch and Puckett.

Lemke continued his dreamlike World Series, as he started the seventh inning with his ninth hit in five games. That single finished Erickson's night. "He gave us a real solid effort and took the game into our late-inning relief," Kelly recalled.

Guthrie was the reliever, and he started well by striking out pinch-hitter Blauser. Smith walked, and Pendleton cued a breaking ball off the end of his bat to the right side on which the Twins could not make a play. "That's when you knew things weren't going good," Kelly said. "Guthrie is a lefty falling off the other side of the mound. If you were going to throw the ball to the perfect spot, that would be it."

With the bases loaded and Gant batting, Willis relieved. The Metrodome scenario of Game 2 was revisited as the Braves' big hitters were up, with a chance to deliver the big blows that could win the World Series. Again a Twins' pitcher delivered, as neither man could get the ball out of the infield. Gant hit a ground ball to Gagne that could not be turned quickly enough for a double play. On the force play, Lemke scored the tying run. "Gagne and Knobby made a great play to even get it close," Kelly stated. "Gant didn't hit the ball that hard. Then Train [Willis] made some nasty pitches to Justice." The Braves' clean-up hitter never hurt the Twins with runners on base in the Series, and Willis struck him out on a forkball that dove down and inside. Two days after being brutalized for an inning in Game 5, Willis had stopped the Braves' biggest bats. "What really bothered me about the whole Hrbek situation was that the Braves had chances in the games here," mused Kelly. "They had their big hitters up with runners in scoring position and they didn't score. We really made the pitches when we had to. Our pitchers dominated the Series."

Unlike Game 3, once this game was tied neither team could mount a serious threat. This classic game turned on subtleties. In the Twins' half of the seventh, Gagne singled with one out. Facing reliever Stanton, Gladden went ahead in the count at 3–0. "I gave Danny the green light here," recalled Kelly. "Crow said something to me about Knobby being next, and he was hot. But I took a chance to win the game, because I figured Danny would get a good swing. Sure enough, Stanton laid the pitch in there, Danny took a good rip at it, and hit the ball right at the shortstop [for a 6–4–3 double play]. You just shake your head and go on from there."

Willis again pitched masterfully, and turned the game over to Aguilera in the 10th. In extra innings, Kelly could not hold back his closer with the season at stake. "He was out there until the fat lady was ready to sing," chuckled Kelly. Atlanta had Pena pitching and their big batters due, so there was apprehension in the Metrodome when Pendleton led off with a single. Now the Braves tried to be aggressive and take advantage of Aguilera's weakness in holding runners close. Pendleton took off on the first pitch to Gant, but Aguilera's pitch forced Gant to reach for the ball and pull a soft liner that Gagne caught. He easily tagged Pendleton at second for a double play.

In the 11th, Bream led off with a base hit down the right field line. As the ball headed to the corner, Mack sped to cut it off, and Bream, whose speed has been curtailed by bad knees, had to hold at first. "Shane made a good play on that hit, and Bream made the right decision," Kelly admitted. "What we were unsure of was the bunt from Hunter. We didn't really have a handle on how good a bunter he was." Keith Mitchell was the pinch runner at first, and he broke for second on the first pitch to Hunter. Harper, who entered the game as a pinch hitter in the seventh, threw a strike to Knoblauch to nail Mitchell. Like Puckett's catch, Harper may have made similar throws before, but never one in these circumstances. Relieved of the leadoff runner, Aguilera easily disposed of the next two batters.

In the bottom of the 11th Leibrandt surprised everyone by taking the mound. Pena had blown the Twins away for two innings, but Kelly reasoned that "if he keeps pitching and we win, then he's gone for Game 7. It was the same situation I was in with Aggie in Game 3. They had the lead in the Series, so it was a very tough decision. All I know is we were happy Pena was out."

Cox had younger pitchers more accustomed to relief available in Mercker and Mark Wohlers, but he entrusted the game to the veteran who had started Game 1. Puckett was the first batter, and Kelly had a good feeling as he watched his star dig in to the batter's box. "He had his lighter bat again, and he looked like he was ready to hit. He took the first pitch which was a good sign. By not chasing Charlie's first pitch, he gave us an air of confidence that he had a good handle on the at-bat. He was waiting for a pitch that stayed up a little bit." That pitch came on a 2–1 change-up, and Puckett drove it to deep left center field. As the ball sailed over the retired numbers of Harmon Killebrew, Rod Carew, and Tony Oliva, the thoughts of Twins' fans were voiced by radio announcer John Gordon who said, "The Twins are going to the seventh game!"

There was bedlam in the Metrodome. Puckett circled the bases with his usual warm smile replaced by a crazed look that signaled the importance of the classic game just played. Leibrandt walked off the mound trying to bury his face in the crook of his right arm. The Twins greeted Puckett as if his hit had won the World Series. Such were the incredible emotions generated by these memorable games. Kelly even shared in the moment, and he hugged Puckett in front of the dugout before he regained his more stoic managerial posture. There was one remaining game for Kelly to prepare for.

"We were all excited, but the only player I was concerned about was Knobby," recalled Kelly. "He was a little out of whack, and I had Stelly [Rick Stelmaszek] get him under control. You can't blame him for being excited, but we still had to play another game." It was hard to blame the Twins for their excitement. One star had just pulled them back from the brink of extinction, and another was ready to pitch the game of his life.

## GAME 7

Tom Kelly does a very popular local radio talk show every Sunday morning during the baseball season, and the morning of Game 7 was no different. He can't remember a single question asked, but it is indicative of the way Kelly approached the second Game 7 of his career. Kelly fooled around in his yard at home, did the radio show that "at the time, seemed very trivial," and worried more about his fantasy football team than the upcoming game.

Football was tuned in on the clubhouse televisions when the players arrived before Game 7, and there was keen interest in the scoring summaries of games in progress. The team's fantasy league, which kept many of the players and coaches in touch during the off-season, dominated the conversations.

It was time for the last dance, something like the last day of school. The finality of this day was uncommon in baseball. No game tomorrow, no planes, no workouts. For the manager there was no lineup card to fill out after today. A group that virtually lived together for more than 200 games would begin to scatter, some never to return. One game would determine whether they could leave with their heads held the highest.

When Morris had watched Puckett's home run sail out the previous night, he thought of the words from the late singer Marvin Gaye, "Let's get it on." Kelly's move in Game 4 now appeared brilliant, for "the horse" would be well prepared for this final game.

Smoltz, a Detroit native who grew up with Morris as his baseball hero, was Atlanta's starter. His shutout of Pittsburgh in Game 7 of the National League play-offs silenced any doubts as to his ability to handle pressure. "Tommy Lasorda said it best, he was the best pitcher in the National League over the second half of the season," stated Kelly. "He had a nasty slider, a good fastball that he moved in and out, and a good change-up." No one expected runs to be easily scored in this seventh game.

The signature moment of this Series for many came not with

a play, but with a gesture made by Lonnie Smith just before the first pitch. As Harper walked behind the plate after catching Morris's warmups with his mask perched atop his head, Smith offered his right hand to his onetime St. Louis teammate. Harper grabbed it in a handshake that said more about this World Series than anyone's words. "That was very impressive by Lonnie," admitted Kelly. "He played hard, had a good series, and then this. I admired him. It was the icing on the cake for the World Series."

Morris and Smoltz took matters into their hands, and matched zeroes into the fifth inning. Lemke continued to defy every Twins attempt to stop him as he lined a single to center. Belliard sacrificed him, and Smith came to the plate.

"Pags looked in at me and I said he'll swing," Kelly said. "So Pags played back, and I about died when Lonnie bunted." Smith dropped down a bunt single, moving Lemke to third. "If I was the manager, I'd be mad. Lonnie has hit well, and I'd want him to swing the bat, and drive in the run."

Morris faced his first test, as Pendleton and Gant were coming up with runners at the corner. The Twins had learned their lesson with Pendleton. "Jack threw him a high pitch, and he popped it up," Kelly recalled. Gant was next, and after Harper saved a run by blocking a forkball in the ball, Morris froze the batter with a nasty 3–2 fastball on the outside corner. The crowd erupted as Morris pumped his right arm in a manner similar to the style first brought to Minnesota by Juan Berenguer.

Through seven innings, the Twins managed four hits off Smoltz and only once moved a runner to third base. Morris had allowed only five hits and had stopped Atlanta's only chance in the fifth. This deciding game was scoreless as it moved to the eighth, perhaps the most tense inning in World Series history.

Smith started the Braves' eighth inning with a half-swing single to right field. With two strikes on Pendleton, he swung at a forkball and slightly tipped the ball that skipped off the dirt just in front of Harper's glove. By a fractional measurement, Pendleton had stayed alive. On the next pitch he rocketed a line drive towards the left-center-field gap. As the ball left his bat, a sickening feeling overwhelmed the Twins as there was no doubt that Smith would score on this hit.

In a play eerily reminiscent of his blunder in Game 4, Smith, who was running on the pitch, eased up as he approached second, and then stopped completely as he rounded the base. "I don't know if he got deked by Knobby. Only Lonnie can answer that," observed Kelly. "I just don't think he knew where the ball was." Replays clearly show that Smith slowed when he saw the deke, but stopped well after that as he looked in vain for the ball in the outfield. By the time Smith saw Pendleton's ball at the left-center field fence, he could only advance to third. The Twins had received a reprieve, but it appeared it could be only temporary.

Gant batted next, and swung at a breaking pitch on the outside corner, sending a squib down to Hrbek for an easy out. For Atlanta, that was a relatively pressure-free at-bat and Gant could not produce. His failure took the bat away from Justice, who was intentionally walked. "We wanted to pitch to Bream and try for the double play," remembered Kelly. "We also knew he was having trouble with runners on base." Kelly visited the mound with Guthrie and Bedrosian warming up in the bullpen, but there was no thought of changing pitchers. Morris could rest in November; the outcome of this October was his to decide.

Bream had three hits in 23 at-bats for the Series, and his fortunes did not change. Morris threw a forkball that ran up and away from the left-handed batter. Bream pulled the ball on the ground to Hrbek, who despite a sore shoulder made a short-arm throw to Harper to force Smith at the plate. Harper calmly stepped out from the plate and returned the throw to Hrbek for a 3–2–3 double play that ended the inning.

It was an incredulous moment in the Metrodome as the

emotionally strung-out fans could not grasp the failure of the Braves to score. Morris jumped in the air, windmilling his right arm as the double play was completed. He had survived with a Houdini-like escape. Meanwhile, Kelly again noticed something subtle on the telecast of the game. "They showed Smoltz on camera, and the look on his face was just like Glavine's in Game 2," claimed Kelly. "He couldn't believe his team didn't score."

A terrible base running mistake and some phenomenal pitching by Morris had kept the game scoreless. Now the Twins took aim at Smoltz's dejection. Bush led off with a pinch-hit single. Gladden flied to center after failing to bunt pinch runner Newman ahead. "After we couldn't bunt, I thought I'd put the hit and run on for Knobby," Kelly explained. The rookie, who by Game 7 was the steady foundation of the Twins' lineup, used his patented inside-out swing for a single to right that sent Newman to third. "After that hit, I was sure we'd score a run," Kelly believed. The run would have to come from Hrbek as Puckett received his third intentional walk of the Series from reliever Stanton.

Hrbek had been struck out three times by Stanton in the Series, but here he had an at-bat that reminded Kelly of the hit he had off David Wells in Game 5 of the play-offs. "He had a real good swing, but got jammed just a little bit," said Kelly. "The ball hit down on the label and he just couldn't get the good part of the bat on the ball." A soft liner floated towards second base which Lemke caught. Lemke then stepped on the base to double off Knoblauch.

Just as stunning as the 3–2–3 double play turned by the Twins, Hrbek's line drive double play brought elation to the Braves. Kelly remembers Stanton jumping in the air as Lemke made the catch. The Twins were as deflated as the Braves had been a half inning earlier, and Kelly was faced with what he considered his sternest test of the entire World Series. "It was hard to keep jumping the players after we didn't score runs when we should have," remarked Kelly. "You're always keeping on the players with a 'Come on, let's go, we'll find a way to win.' But it's hard because you're disappointed yourself. And we couldn't let what happened to Glavine in Game 2 or Smoltz in this game happen to us."

Morris personally guaranteed that, as he easily retired the Braves in the ninth. He returned to the dugout and was met by Kelly. "I told Jack, 'That's enough for today. You did a great job and it's time for somebody else to pick you up.' He was sitting there, very matter of fact, saying, 'I'm fine. I can pitch. Save Aggie.' We were talking nine innings while pitching on three days rest for the second time. That's such a remarkable effort. Finally, Suchie came by and said, 'He seems fine.' So I said something like 'What the heck, go ahead.' I added the now-famous 'It's only a game' line later."

Morris's refusal to leave the game looked to be academic as the Twins mounted a ninth-inning rally. Davis singled to right-center, a ball that Kelly felt "might be a double, but Chili made the right play." Harper then bunted a ball to the right side that eluded Stanton, who injured his back in a reach. Pena relieved, and Mack was sent up to bunt the runners ahead. "But he didn't have a good effort on the bunt, so I let him swing," Kelly remembered as he watched Mack hit a ground ball that Lemke and Belliard turned slickly into a double play. The Twins now needed a hit, and Pagliarulo was intentionally walked to bring up Newman. Kelly had little confidence in Newman's hitting, so he went to Sorrento. "I had waited all week to put Sorrento in against Pena," claimed Kelly. "He's our best fastball hitter. The emotions of the game turned out to be too much. The first pitch was the one for him to hit, and he just swung too hard." Sorrento fouled off three pitches before missing a fastball for strike three.

This became only the second Game 7 to reach extra innings in World Series history. Morris, who had been christened "the horse" by Kelly in the spring, was living up to every bit of the role. Like a champion thoroughbred, Morris had always pitched with more strength as he closed in on the finish. As he set the Braves away easily in the 10th, there was a growing feeling that this game was the Twins' to win, if only they could produce the one hit that had eluded them in Game 3.

Gladden led off the last of the 10th and had a "great swing. He hit a tough pitch that came running in on him," Kelly remembered. His hit dropped in left center and took a high hop off the glove of onrushing left fielder Hunter. Gladden never hesitated as he slid into second base with a double. "That's the play we want," said Kelly. "Once the ball bounced past Hunter, he was going into second."

"We couldn't fool around here. Gladden had to be bunted over. During the season, Knobby was trying to bunt for hits in sacrifice situations, and we had to have a discussion about that. But when he puts his mind to it, he can bunt and he moved Danny over nicely."

Knoblauch had one sacrifice bunt all season, and his second one moved the Twins just those agonizing 90 feet from third to home away from a World Championship.

"I knew they would walk Puckett, but I wasn't sure about Hrbek," Kelly admitted. "I know he had a lefty [Mercker] ready in the bullpen, but it was a sound baseball decision for Bobby to walk Herbie. That way, you face a pinch hitter who has been sitting for six or seven hours since he took batting practice.

"Geno [Larkin] knew he going to hit here," said Kelly. "He ran out of the dugout quickly. He had been waiting for his chance."

Larkin had feared this chance might not happen. The tendinitis in his knee had flared badly in Toronto and the situation, according to Kelly, was "touchy." Trainers Dick Martin and Doug Nelson worked extremely hard with Larkin to keep him available for pinch hitting. He now stood at home plate in the at-bat that every player dreams about. With one swing a World Series can be won. Anyone with the self-confidence of a major leaguer wants this chance, and

Larkin had been disappointed when he was bypassed earlier in the ninth inning.

The quietest and the hardest-working Twin was at the plate, and Kelly "did not expect this run to score easily. The way the games had been going, a quick finish was unexpected."

Atlanta pulled its outfield in to shallow positions, so Larkin, a good contact hitter, needed only to hit a fly ball. Pena's first pitch was a fastball down the middle and Larkin lifted a fly into deep left-center field. Two strides after swinging the bat, Larkin shot his left arm into the air knowing he had hit the ball well enough. As the outfielders watched helplessly, the ball landed shy of the warning track, and Gladden ran the final 90 feet. Total chaos followed, as the dugout emptied. Morris, who had pitched one of the greatest games in baseball history, was the first to grab Gladden as he stomped on home plate. Two piles of leaping players, one on Gladden and one on Larkin at first base, eventually merged in the middle of the diamond. For a few moments, in full view of millions, grown men became boys. There was unabashed joy as the players unleashed the most intense emotions most of them had ever experienced. It was a celebration that we never expect from professional athletes. Within moments, the players were joined by their families on the field, and in one of the Series' most poignant scenes, Morris's two sons embraced their father.

In the midst of this spectacle, Kelly came on the field. Part of Kelly's legend in 1987 was born in his refusal to join in the on-field celebration. "My close friends then were the guys in the dugout like [clubhouse attendant] Chico [McGinn], who couldn't go on the field, so I thought I belonged there with them. This time I got drawn to the field. These things aren't preplanned."

As he ran on the field, Kelly added his own touch of class to this unforgettable week. He walked over to the Braves' players who were filing off the field. "It just seemed like the right thing, to say something to them," Kelly felt. "I think a couple of guys talked to some of the players. But it was just a reaction. I talked to Gant. He seemed somewhat despondent, but it turned out that he was fine. I shook some hands in passing, but after that Series, I just felt it was right."

Whisked away for television and media demands, Kelly did not know about the victory lap the players ran around the field in the ensuing celebration. The manager was unaware of that spontaneous lap until he watched the World Series highlight film one month after Game 7.

Sitting in his office long after the game ended, Kelly had a chance to share with friends and associates the enormity of what had transpired. His team had won 103 games in anger, and had clearly proven to be the best in baseball. He had fought shingles, and had fought for Pagliarulo, Leius, and Knoblauch. Hrbek responded to his early-season jolt, and Mack produced handsomely after an early-season break. A pitching staff that he had only dreamed of had excelled. It would take time before all of the accomplishments attained hit home.

Managing a second World Championship team in five years was a mind-boggling feat, given that the Chicago Cubs have not won a single World Series since 1908 or the Red Sox since 1918. Two Series was one more than had been won by Kelly's friend and a respected manager, Tony LaRussa.

The gratification of having participated in an event that truly was defined as a classic was immediate. As someone who has lived the game of baseball, Kelly cherished his presence at such a glorious Series. "A lot of big-time, national writers came in to the office during the night," recalled Kelly. "They said it was an honor to be here and witness that Series. That means a lot from guys who know what they're talking about."

Players filtered in to Kelly's office to share a toast and a good cigar. In fact, Kelly lost two boxes of "good cigars," a clear sign that this was a meaningful night. As morning crept towards sunrise, the party broke up for Kelly, who had to take his son Tom home.

## THE AFTERMATH

Kelly found little rest during the following week. There was a Monday morning appearance on the television show "Good Morning America," followed by the Tuesday victory parade, a trip to Florida for the organizational meetings, then on to Washington, D.C., for the traditional White House visit, and finally back to Minnesota in time for a 30-inch Halloween snowstorm.

"After I got through the weekend of shoveling snow, things turned strange. For a couple of days, I woke up thinking we had a game. I was worried about a lineup, and who was pitching that day. By Wednesday, I told the story in the clubhouse to Jim Wiesner, and he told me that Stelly had just told him the same story. It turned out that I felt real sick for the next week, and the doctors told me it was just my body trying to wind down from all the tension. I wound up pounding the vitamins and I gradually felt better. But it was another week before I calmed down."

An enduring memory of the 1987 victory parade for many Minnesotans was the sight of Kelly riding alone in the victory parade. In 1991, his wife Sharon rode alongside. "If you reach the ultimate in your profession, you want to share it with somebody. I didn't have that opportunity in 1987, and it wasn't pleasant. Having Sharon with me this year was so much better."

# Epilogue

Tom Kelly does not remember when he said it, or even understand why, but he knows he made the statement. Jack Morris was pitching at the Metrodome in the second half of the season when Kelly suddenly turned in the dugout and said to no one in particular, "I think Jack might be better off somewhere else next year." Kelly later reflected, "There was so much going on for him, with family, worrying about who was sitting in his private suite when he pitched, and then his divorce. There were times he just seemed worn out. It was a spur of the moment statement, and I wonder why I said it. But I know I did, and I remember Suchie not responding. I said nothing more."

The day after he ruled the baseball world in Game 7, Morris officially filed for free agency, a technicality demanded by his contract, or so it seemed. Andy MacPhail publicly stated his first off-season priority was to resign Morris, but the price escalated as other free agent pitchers of lesser accomplishments signed exorbitant contracts.

"I used to think it was important for a player to succeed in a city, because he could then do anything he wanted in the city after he finished playing. But a friend told me something this winter that made sense," recalled Kelly. "He said that the star player doesn't need the town, the town needs the player. The player makes so much money, he can do anything he wants when he retires."

After hearing all through November that Morris was sure to stay, the Minnesota fans were stunned in early December when Morris made noises about Toronto and Boston. When Morris accepted an offer from the Blue Jays that far surpassed the money he had been offered by the Twins, there was outrage in Minnesota. The public remembered the tears shed by Morris the previous February when he signed with the Twins, the emotional cheers before the first games of the play-offs and World Series, and the happiness that Morris professed to have found in Minnesota. This wasn't supposed to be about money, but in the end, everything really is fueled by dollars.

The Twins and Morris had a rare relationship in modern baseball, one that was mutually beneficial. Morris performed beyond all hope and expectation, and his Game 7 will forever live in baseball's lore. His open-ended contract allowed him to reap, for perhaps the last time, the benefits of free agency. Morris took Toronto's money, and will soon learn if it can compensate for the happiness he left behind in Minnesota.

Days after Morris's departure, a second body blow was delivered to Twins' fans as Dan Gladden signed with Detroit. This was the age-old sporting case of the young (Pedro Munoz) replacing the old, with an economic twist added. Gladden is a member of an endangered species, baseball's middle class. There are fewer openings for a veteran who is not a star but can contribute. Those players are being squeezed out of the major leagues by the burgeoning superstar salaries, and the eternal presence of minimum-salaried rookies.

The Twins have not only groomed a replacement for Gladden, but Junior Ortiz, Steve Bedrosian, and Terry Leach, all free agents, fell victim to the same syndrome. Lenny Webster will get his chance to be the backup catcher, while Carl Willis, Paul Abbott, and others will fill bullpen spots.

The most puzzling off-season development for the Twins was the Al Newman affair. Newman left the Twins by refusing their arbitration offer with no negotiating in early December. Newman wanted an offer in November, while the Twins' priorities were

Jack Morris and Brian Harper. Taking pride in his five years of playing and working in the community, Newman felt slighted and decided to play elsewhere. He was not as fortunate as Gladden; he misread the market and was forced to sign a minor league contract with Cincinnati.

Two free agents stayed in Minnesota, Harper and Mike Pagliarulo. Circumstances affect the off-season game, so that if Munoz was a catcher or third baseman, one of these two may have been allowed to leave, while Gladden would have stayed.

The bottom line meant a large number of goodbyes for a World Championship team. Seven of the players who comprised the 25-man roster for most of the season are gone (Morris, Gladden, Newman, Leach, Ortiz, Bedrosian, and Allan Anderson). The 1991 Twins will not have a chance to defend their title, for the changes have included impact players. In the spring of 1992, more young faces gathered in Fort Myers hoping to impress Kelly (who was rewarded by Carl Pohlad with a new three-year contract), and wedge their way onto a major league roster. The Twins hope they can find a Knoblauch and a Leius from their farm system, and a Willis from their six-year free agents. If their system is ready to graduate products to the major leagues, especially pitchers, then another trip to "The Big Dance" may not be far off.

# The 1991 Minnesota Twins

| | | | | 1991 STATS | | | |
|---|---|---|---|---|---|---|---|
| PLAYER | POS | AGE | GAMES | AT-BATS | HR | RBI | AVG |
| Jarvis Brown | OF | 24 | 38 | 37 | 0 | 0 | .216 |
| Randy Bush | OF | 32 | 93 | 165 | 6 | 23 | .303 |
| Carmen Castillo | OF | 33 | 9 | 12 | 0 | 0 | .167 |
| Charles Davis | DH | 31 | 153 | 534 | 29 | 93 | .277 |
| Greg Gagne | SS | 29 | 139 | 408 | 8 | 42 | .265 |
| Dan Gladden | OF | 34 | 126 | 461 | 6 | 52 | .247 |
| Brian Harper | C | 31 | 123 | 441 | 10 | 69 | .311 |
| Kent Hrbek | 1B | 31 | 132 | 462 | 20 | 89 | .284 |
| Chuck Knoblauch | 2B | 23 | 151 | 565 | 1 | 50 | .281 |
| Gene Larkin | OF-1B | 28 | 98 | 255 | 2 | 19 | .286 |
| Scott Leius | 3B | 25 | 109 | 199 | 5 | 20 | .286 |
| Shane Mack | OF | 27 | 143 | 442 | 18 | 74 | .310 |
| Pedro Munoz | OF | 22 | 51 | 138 | 7 | 26 | .283 |
| Al Newman | IF-OF | 31 | 118 | 246 | 0 | 19 | .191 |
| Junior Ortiz | C | 31 | 61 | 134 | 0 | 11 | .209 |
| Mike Pagliarulo | 3B | 31 | 121 | 365 | 6 | 36 | .279 |
| Kirby Puckett | OF | 30 | 152 | 611 | 15 | 89 | .319 |
| Paul Sorrento | 1B | 25 | 26 | 47 | 4 | 13 | .255 |
| Lenny Webster | C | 26 | 18 | 34 | 3 | 8 | .294 |

| PLAYER | POS | AGE | GAMES | INNINGS | W | L | SV | ERA |
|---|---|---|---|---|---|---|---|---|
| Paul Abbott | P | 23 | 15 | 47 | 3 | 1 | 0 | 4.75 |
| Rick Aguilera | P | 29 | 63 | 69 | 4 | 5 | 42 | 2.35 |
| Allan Anderson | P | 27 | 29 | 134 | 5 | 11 | 0 | 4.96 |
| Willie Banks | P | 22 | 5 | 17 | 1 | 1 | 0 | 5.71 |
| Steve Bedrosian | P | 33 | 56 | 77 | 5 | 3 | 6 | 4.42 |
| Larry Casian | P | 25 | 15 | 18 | 0 | 0 | 0 | 7.36 |
| Tom Edens | P | 30 | 8 | 33 | 2 | 2 | 0 | 4.09 |
| Scott Erickson | P | 23 | 32 | 204 | 20 | 8 | 0 | 3.18 |
| Mark Guthrie | P | 25 | 41 | 98 | 7 | 5 | 2 | 4.32 |
| Terry Leach | P | 37 | 50 | 67 | 1 | 2 | 0 | 3.61 |
| Jack Morris | P | 36 | 35 | 246 | 18 | 12 | 0 | 3.43 |
| Denny Neagle | P | 22 | 7 | 20 | 0 | 1 | 0 | 4.05 |
| Kevin Tapani | P | 27 | 34 | 244 | 16 | 9 | 0 | 2.99 |
| Gary Wayne | P | 28 | 8 | 12 | 1 | 0 | 1 | 5.11 |
| David West | P | 26 | 15 | 71 | 4 | 4 | 0 | 4.54 |
| Carl Willis | P | 30 | 40 | 89 | 8 | 3 | 2 | 2.63 |

# The 1991 American League Championship Series

**GAME 1, October 8 at Metrodome**

| | | | | | | | |
|---|---|---|---|---|---|---|---|
| Toronto | 000 | 103 | 000 | - | 4 | 9 | 3 |
| Minnesota | 221 | 000 | 00 | - | 5 | 11 | 0 |

Tom Candiotti (L), David Wells (3), Mike Timlin (6)
Jack Morris (W), Carl Willis (6), Rick Aguilera (8-SV)

**GAME 2, October 9 at Metrodome**

| | | | | | | | |
|---|---|---|---|---|---|---|---|
| Toronto | 102 | 000 | 200 | - | 5 | 9 | 0 |
| Minnesota | 001 | 001 | 000 | - | 2 | 5 | 1 |

Juan Guzman (W), Tom Henke (6), Duane Ward (8-SV)
Kevin Tapani (L), Steve Bedrosian (7), Mark Guthrie (7)

**GAME 3, October 11 at SkyDome**

| | | | | | | | | |
|---|---|---|---|---|---|---|---|---|
| Minnesota | 000 | 011 | 000 | 1 | - | 3 | 7 | 0 |
| Toronto | 200 | 000 | 000 | 0 | - | 2 | 5 | 1 |

Scott Erickson, David West (5), Carl Willis (7),
Mark Guthrie (9-W), Rick Aguilera (10-SV)
Jimmy Key, David Wells (7), Tom Henke (8), Mike Timlin (10-L)

**GAME 4, October 12 at SkyDome**

| | | | | | | | |
|---|---|---|---|---|---|---|---|
| Minnesota | 000 | 402 | 111 | - | 9 | 13 | 1 |
| Toronto | 010 | 001 | 001 | - | 3 | 11 | 2 |

Jack Morris (W), Steve Bedrosian (9)
Todd Stottlemyre (L), David Wells (4), Jim Acker (6),
Mike Timlin (7), Bob MacDonald (9)

**GAME 5, October 13 at SkyDome**

| | | | | | | | |
|---|---|---|---|---|---|---|---|
| Minnesota | 110 | 003 | 030 | - | 8 | 14 | 2 |
| Toronto | 003 | 200 | 000 | - | 5 | 9 | 1 |

Kevin Tapani, David West (5-W), Carl Willis (8),
Rick Aguilera (9-SV)
Tom Candiotti, Mike Timlin (6), Duane Ward (6-L),
David Wells (8)

## The 1991 World Series

**GAME 1, October 19 at Metrodome**

| | | | | | | | |
|---|---|---|---|---|---|---|---|
| Atlanta | 000 | 001 | 010 | - | 2 | 6 | 1 |
| Minnesota | 001 | 031 | 00 | - | 5 | 9 | 1 |

Charlie Leibrandt (L), Jim Clancy (5), Mark Wohlers (7), Mike Stanton (8)
Jack Morris (W), Mark Guthrie (8), Rick Aguilera (8-SV)

**GAME 2, October 20 at Metrodome**

| | | | | | | | |
|---|---|---|---|---|---|---|---|
| Atlanta | 010 | 010 | 000 | - | 2 | 8 | 1 |
| Minnesota | 200 | 000 | 01 | - | 3 | 4 | 1 |

Tom Glavine (L)
Kevin Tapani (W), Rick Aguilera (9-SV)

**GAME 3, October 22 at Atlanta**

| | | | | | | | | |
|---|---|---|---|---|---|---|---|---|
| Minnesota | 100 | 000 | 120 | 000 | - | 4 | 10 | 1 |
| Atlanta | 010 | 120 | 000 | 001 | - | 5 | 8 | 2 |

Scott Erickson, David West (5), Terry Leach (5), Steve Bedrosian (6), Carl Willis (8), Mark Guthrie (10), Rick Aguilera (12-L)
Steve Avery, Alejandro Pena (8), Mike Stanton (10), Mark Wohlers (12), Kent Mercker (12) and Jim Clancy (12-W)

**GAME 4, October 23 at Atlanta**

| | | | | | | | |
|---|---|---|---|---|---|---|---|
| Minnesota | 010 | 000 | 100 | - | 2 | 7 | 0 |
| Atlanta | 001 | 000 | 101 | - | 3 | 8 | 0 |

Jack Morris, Carl Willis (7), Mark Guthrie (8-L), Steve Bedrosian (9)
John Smoltz, Mark Wohlers (8), Mike Stanton (8-W)

**GAME 5, October 24 at Atlanta**

| | | | | | | | |
|---|---|---|---|---|---|---|---|
| Minnesota | 000 | 003 | 011 | - | 5 | 7 | 1 |
| Atlanta | 000 | 410 | 63 | - | 14 | 17 | 1 |

Kevin Tapani (L), Terry Leach (6), David West (7), Steve Bedrosian (7), Carl Willis (8)
Tom Glavine (W), Kent Mercker (6), Jim Clancy (7), Randy St. Claire (9)

(The 1991 World Series, continued)

GAME 6, October 26 at Metrodome

| | | | | | |
|---|---|---|---|---|---|
| Atlanta | 000 | 020 | 100 | 00 | - 3 9 1 |
| Minnesota | 200 | 010 | 000 | 01 | - 4 9 0 |

Steve Avery, Mike Stanton (7), Alejandro Pena (9), Charlie Leibrandt (11-L)
Scott Erickson, Mark Guthrie (7), Carl Willis (7), Rick Aguilera (10-W)

GAME 7, October 27 at Metrodome

| | | | | | |
|---|---|---|---|---|---|
| Atlanta | 000 | 000 | 000 | 0 | - 0 7 0 |
| Minnesota | 000 | 000 | 000 | 1 | - 1 10 0 |

John Smoltz, Mike Stanton (8), Alejandro Pena (9-L)
Jack Morris (W)